SHIP MASTER

THE LIFE AND LETTERS OF
CAPT. ROBERT THOMAS
OF LLANDWROG AND LIVERPOOL
1843 – 1903

This book tells the story, mostly in his own words, of one of that generation of superb seamen who contributed so much to Victorian Britain. The master of a sailing ship was a man apart. Robert Thomas is one of the few to have left a record of his life and times. He sailed in slate schooners, in the Mediterranean and South American trade, in the emigrant and timber ships of North America, in the salt fish trade of Newfoundland, and finally established himself as master of large full-rigged ships in the Cape Horn and Far East trades. Robert Thomas's 'diary' also movingly reflects his passion for education, his loathing of poverty and injustice, his concern for people. This is truly a human, and humane, document.

Aled Eames is the author of a number of outstanding studies in the maritime history of Wales, including *Ships and Seamen of Anglesey, Porthmadog Ships, Meistri'r Moroedd, Letters from America: Captain David Evans of Talsarnau 1817-1895, Ships and Seamen of Gwynedd/ Llongau a Llongwyr Gwynedd*, and is one of the editors of *Maritime Wales/Cymru a'r Môr*.

This book is dedicated to the memory of Miss Catherine Bruce Thomas
(1878-1957) who carefully preserved the 'diary' of her father, Capt.
Robert Thomas, and his letters, according to his wishes, 'as a treasure
in memory of your affectionate father'.

SHIP MASTER

THE LIFE AND LETTERS OF
CAPT. ROBERT THOMAS
OF LLANDWROG AND LIVERPOOL
1843 – 1903

ALED EAMES

GWYNEDD ARCHIVES SERVICE

ISBN 0 901337 25 0

PRINTED AND BOUND BY
GEE & SON (DENBIGH) LTD.

CONTENTS

LIST OF ILLUSTRATIONS

ACKNOWLEDGEMENTS

Had it not been for the interest in maritime history of Mr. Reginald Froom of Liverpool this book would not have appeared. Some years ago, when *Ships and Seamen of Anglesey* was published, Mr. Froom wrote to me expressing his regret that I had not known of the 'diary' of his grandfather, Captain Robert Thomas, which would have added to the section on the Davies family, as Captain Thomas had served many years in Anglesey owned vessels. Thanks to the infectious enthusiasm of Mr. Bryn Parry, County Archivist of Gwynedd, it has now been possible to publish this quite remarkable document, and some of the accompanying letters and photographs so carefully preserved with loving care first by Miss Catherine Bruce Thomas and then by her nephew, Mr. Reginald Froom. We are grateful to the descendants of Captain Robert Thomas for their ready permission to present his letters and papers to a wider public. For my own part, I am much indebted to Mr. and Mrs. Froom for much kindness and hospitality.

This book has been prepared for publication, alongside other work on Welsh shipping, during the first weeks of my tenure of a Caird Research Fellowship at the National Maritime Museum. It is with much pleasure that I acknowledge my gratitude to the Trustees of the Caird Fund for their generosity which has enabled me to check the relevant details relating to Captain Thomas's career in the very favourable atmosphere of the Caird Library at the Museum. To Dr. Basil Greenhill, Director of the National Maritime Museum, whose own wide-ranging and masterly work in maritime histoy is a constant inspiration, and to his colleagues, I am grateful for much kindness and encouragement. In consequence of my presence in London, all the work of seeing the book through the press has been undertaken by Mr. Bryn Parry, who has already been so closely associated in recent works with studies in the maritime history of Gwynedd. His

7

colleagues in the Gwynedd Archives Service, Mrs. Christine Owen, Mrs. Pearl Jones and Miss Wendy Roberts, have not only been responsible for typing all of Captain Thomas's diary and letters but also my own rather less legible script. I am pleased to record my sincere gratitude to them for all that they have done.

Bryn Parry himself will know how much I value his unfailing interest and support. Gwynedd is indeed fortunate in its Archivist, as all who have had reason to work with the Gwynedd Archives Service will know.

A NOTE ON EDITORIAL METHOD

The text of the 'diary' and letters (Gwynedd Archives Service XM/4338) has been transcribed as written by Capt. Thomas, although his punctuation has been rationalised, where possible, and obvious spelling errors have been corrected.

ROBERT THOMAS

Captain Robert Thomas put down his pen, looked thoughtfully around his cabin, listened to the gentle movement of the ship he had come to know so well, and sighed. It was a sigh of contentment mingled with sadness. He had completed the task he had set himself some months previously when the *Merioneth* had sailed out of Penarth Roads for San Francisco on 5 February, 1883. Each day when wind and weather permitted he had painstakingly set down in the thick brown Letts Diary the main events in his life as he now recalled them for his eldest daughter, Catherine Bruce. Very much aware that his life at sea had deprived him of the company of his young family, and that he had had little opportunity to talk to them, Robert Thomas had decided it was time to record his activities, the impressions that far-distant ports and peoples had made upon him, his feelings and, above all, the utter loneliness of his life. Already many of his contemporaries had met untimely deaths, and, although he was barely forty years of age, he was only too conscious that his daughter might never read his diary. On this quiet October day in the Pacific Ocean, fifteen days out from San Francisco, the *Merioneth* was heading south for Cape Horn and home. Their outward passage had been a long one, one hundred and twelve days, and as he had just written on the last page of his diary they had had 'fearful weather, losing all my sail and ship springing a leak, and the loss of one pump, but we got out all right, but had to go to dry dock to stop leak.' Now, however, as he stepped out on to the deck of the *Merioneth,* a stocky bearded figure, Captain Thomas's longing was for strong fresh winds which would speed his vessel homeward so that he could present his beloved daughter with this account which he had so carefully written.

Captain Thomas had been in command of the *Merioneth* for

the past three years. She was the first iron ship he had sailed in, but he reckoned her 'a fine strong ship and a good seaboat.' Her owners, the Davies family of Menai Bridge in North Wales, had successfully managed over fifty wooden North American built ships and barques since the 1840s and Robert Thomas had graduated from serving before the mast in some of these ships. From the emigrant ships to North America, the Davies vessels had moved in mid-century to the Far East and the Pacific trades, and, in particular, to the guano trade of the West coast of South America. By the eighteen seventies, like so many British ship-owners, the Davies family saw that the comparatively cheap American wooden vessels would best be replaced by British built iron ships which could stand the strain of heavy cargoes such as railway irons, coal, nitrates and phosphate rock which often badly strained wooden hulls. Robert Davies bought a new wooden ship, built at New Brunswick in 1866, the *Conway Castle*, but in the same year he also acquired the *Dolbadarn Castle*, an iron ship, built by T. R. Oswald at Sunderland three years previously. The *Malleny*, built at Liverpool in 1868 and bought by Davies in 1871, must have impressed the Menai Bridge owners for they decided to go to the same builders for a fleet of iron sister ships. Between 1875 and 1877 seven iron vessels left the Baffin Street yards of Roydens, the Liverpool builders, all of them additions to the Davies fleet. The *Anglesey* and *Merioneth* were completed in 1875, the *Caernarvonshire, Denbighshire* and *Flintshire* in 1876, the *Cardiganshire* and *Montgomeryshire* in 1877, all obviously built to similar specifications, between 1,200 and 1,400 tons. The *Caernarvonshire* and *Flintshire* were almost identical, as were the slightly larger *Merioneth* and *Denbighshire*, whilst the last two vessels built, the *Cardiganshire* and *Montgomeryshire*, were the largest. The *Anglesey*, the first to be completed, was shorter and proportionately beamier than the other vessels, but in appearance there was little difference between these sister ships. To command the new ships, which obviously represented a major investment following the sale of many of their wooden vessels, Richard and Robert Davies and their nephew, Charles Pierce, who was gradually taking over the management of the firm, chose only the most efficient of their master mariners.

10

Thus, as he looked aloft with an experienced eye, taking in at a glance the trim of the yards and the set of the sails, Captain Thomas had reason to be proud both of his fine ship and his own achievement in obtaining such a good command. Many of his crew had sailed with him before and had known of his reputation as a sail carrier, whilst those shipped willingly or unwillingly a couple of weeks ago at San Francisco had come to respect and recognize his quiet authority. But, as the North East Trades carried the *Merioneth* inexorably towards the wet and squally weather of the Doldrums no one aboard, least of all Captain Thomas, could have envisaged that within a few years the little *Merioneth* was to become the toast of San Francisco and Captain Robert Thomas the talk of seamen from Hong Kong to Valparaiso. It was not the future that occupied Captain Thomas's mind as he paced the *Merioneth*'s deck on this October day in 1883, but rather the portrait of the past, his past, which he had recalled in his diary so that his daughter should have the story of his life. It was a story worth the telling.

*   *   *   *

Robert Thomas, fifth of nine children born at a humble cottage, Tanlan, in the village of Llandwrog, near Caernarfon, was destined to become one of the outstanding master mariners of a generation of superb seamen in the age of sail. The vast majority of these fine seamen left little in the way of records relating to their lives and, for the most part, their names are just names alongside their ships, in faded registers and yellowing crew agreement lists. On those long, weary troublesome passages round Cape Horn or to the Indian Ocean and the Far East, the master of a sailing ship was a man apart. Some took to the bottle, many became utterly depressed and behaved eccentrically; some whiled away the hours between gales indulging their hobbies, fishing, shooting, compiling scrap books, others slept or bullied their crews. Robert Thomas is one of the few to have left a record of his life and times, and if for no other reason, we should therefore treasure the remarkable document which is reproduced

11

in this book. It is, however, doubly valuable for Thomas's own career represents and reflects so many aspects of the world of nineteenth century merchant seamen in sail. He sailed in the slate schooners which played such a significant part in the development of the maritime tradition of North Wales, he sailed in the Mediterranean and South American trades in the appallingly leaky and ill-equipped ships of miserly shipowners of the pre-Plimsoll era, in the emigrant and timber ships of North America, in the salt fish trade of Newfoundland which was to attract so many Porthmadog ships in later years, and he finally established himself as master of large full rigged ships in the Cape Horn and Far East trades. Most of all, however, there is the evocative way in which Robert Thomas, who on the first page of his 'diary' modestly draws attention to the limitations of his own schooling, has written an account which movingly reflects his passion for education, his loathing of poverty and injustice, his concern for people. This is truly a human, and humane, document.

In concluding his 'diary', Robert Thomas assures his daughter that his account is 'a short sketch of life up to now which had I not wrote it down you would never learn it. I have had to trust to memory entirely but all of it is the faithful truth but the dates are wanting.' I have attempted, by tracing the movement of the ships in which he sailed in *Lloyd's Lists* and *Lloyd's Weekly Shipping Index*, occasionally supplemented by contemporary newspapers, to provide the missing dates whenever possible so that the reader may judge for himself the remarkable accuracy of Thomas's account, written as he himself states in his cabin at sea, without access to the papers and documents which I have had at my disposal in the quiet of the Caird Library of the National Maritime Museum almost a hundred years since Robert Thomas made his first entry in his Letts Diary of 1882.

*　　*　　*　　*

The village of Llandwrog today still retains some of the traces of its long association with the family whose presence dominated

12

the lives of almost all the inhabitants in Robert Thomas's day. The Glyns of Glynllifon traced back their ancestry to the ninth century and by the fifteenth century they were related through marriage to the ruling families of the area such as the Bulkeleys of Beaumaris. Under the Tudors the family gained much authority in Gwynedd, and Thomas Glyn, who sided with Parliament in the Civil War, and his brother, John Glyn, who later became Recorder of London and Lord Chief Justice, extended this influence. Thomas Glyn's daughter Frances, who inherited the Glynllifon estate, married Thomas Wynn of Bodfean, and the Wynn family had long established themselves at Glynllifon by the time Robert Thomas was a small boy. According to the 1851 Census there resided at Glynllifon, in addition to Lord and Lady Newborough (the first Lord Newborough was created an Irish peer in 1776), their nine children, two visitors, eighteen female staff, including housekeeper, ladies maids, nurses, a cook, kitchen maids, scullery, laundry and dairy maids, two governesses (and a young woman from Altona, Germany) and seven male members of staff, including the butler, footmen, a coachman, stableman and a hall boy. Robert Thomas was destined to come to know Glynllifon well for it was among the female staff of Glynllifon that he was to meet his future wife. But in 1851 Robert Thomas is recorded in the Census Return as a boy of eight, son of William Thomas, joiner, aged forty, and Ruth, his wife, aged thirty-nine; the family of six living children and their parents resided at Tanlan. The neighbouring families living at Tŷ Bach, Gwernyfalau, Lleiniau, Brynglas, Tai Gwynion, Cae'r Eglwys, Tŷ Isaf and Tŷ Canol Llan had children who must have been Robert Thomas's schoolmates, children of small farms, agricultural labourers, a boot and shoe maker, two blacksmiths. Only one mariner is recorded as having been at home on Census night, 1851, Frederick Jones, aged fourteen, son of William Jones, 1 Llandwrog Cottages.

A few years previously, when Robert Thomas was a child of four, Henry Vaughan Johnson, writing from Lincoln's Inn in October 1847, sent his report to the Committee of Council on Education as one of the Commissioners appointed to enquire into the state of education in Wales, 'especially into the means afforded

13

to the labouring classes of acquiring a knowledge of the English language.' Although Johnson and his fellow Commissioners were themselves much criticised for unduly maligning the Welsh people, and assuming that ignorance of the English language was, in all respects, synonymous with illiteracy, his report on the school which young Robert Thomas was soon to enter corroborates in a vivid way the account which he himself was to write in his diary aboard the *Merioneth* nearly forty years later, and goes some way to explain his zeal for self-education. Recognizing that the Church of England school at Llandwrog was 'situate in an important district abounding with slate quarries', Johnson reported that the 'master appears to have had very few opportunities of receiving instruction. He speaks broken English. He asked question such as these: 'How many Gospels are? How many Apostles are? Although grammar and geography are professed, nothing was known of either subject. In geography I was told that Wales is to the East of England, and Ireland to the East of Wales.' Llandwrog's school was no exception and it was this that both infuriated and aroused the consciences of both Anglicans and Nonconformists in Wales. In fairness to Johnson it has to be said he was reporting what he saw. Moreover, he recognized the linguistic problem: 'owing to the prevalence of Sunday Schools in Wales, adults among the poorer classes are far better acquainted with the Bible than persons of the same class in England, consequently the teachers who frequent such schools possess a better knowledge of Scripture than would be inferred from their deficiency in other qualifications; but being accustomed to read and explain the Bible in Welsh they are at a loss when confined, as in all day-schools, to the English version and the English language.' It has always to be remembered that Robert Thomas's 'diary' was written by a man who, as he himself states on the first page, had had little schooling and whose first language was Welsh not English.

There is ample evidence in the 'diary' of the impact the dire poverty of his early life made upon the future master mariner. He remembered the humiliation of not having clothes to wear, 'scarcely having clothes decent enough to go to chapel on

14

Sunday', the hard earned but welcome sixpences from visitors, for cleaning their shoes, taking and fetching their letters to and from the post, 'and the everlasting bow whenever I passed them within several hundred of yards', the back breaking work in Lord Newborough's fields, but also all the fun and horseplay associated with communal work with boys of his own age. Despite what appeared to him the princely wage of £8 a year for working with Dr. Hamilton Roberts, the quarry doctor and an important figure in the slate quarrying community of Bethesda, Robert Thomas soon recognized that life ashore had little to offer a poor widow's son. Writing some thirty years later, he recalled with some bitterness the degrading hiring fairs where farm servants were hired twice a year at Bontnewydd, a village near his home, where hundreds of people from Pwllheli, Clynnog, Nefyn and the surrounding districts congregated . . . 'it was a disgrace to a Christian country to see a parcel of men and women in a row on each side of the road and farmers, etc., surveying and engaging them as he would buy cattle . . . what a life a servant girl on a farm had of it, more like slaves than free people.' Little wonder that many thousands sought to escape from this rural drudgery in the very emigrant ships in which Thomas was later to serve. Something of the poverty and bitterness of those early days is evoked in the letter which he wrote many years later from aboard the *Merioneth* on 11 November, 1883 as she sailed for Cape Horn: 'I have gone with mother many a time to Carnarvon with a pig with a string fast its legs, and if suitable price was not got we had to bring it home again . . . I look back with wonder and pain at those days, for now I suppose it would be out of all reason for a woman and children from Llandwrog to drive a little pig to Carnarvon and then stand all day with it in the wet and cold and perhaps after all no one asking what it was for.'

On these often hearbreaking visits to Caernarfon there were occasional compensations. It is likely that Robert and his brothers eagerly made their way to the slate quay where the hobblers were busily loading the small sloops and schooners alongside, two and three abreast. Through the nineteenth century scores of small slate ships sailed out of Caernarfon for Liverpool,

15

London, the ports of the North East and Scotland, the Irish ports, Hamburg and the Elbe ports, the Baltic and some indeed for America. In the 1850s, when the young Robert Thomas was going from Llandwrog to Caernarfon with his mother, the dramatic expansion of London, Liverpool, Manchester, Newcastle and their suburbs, the rapid growth of newer towns like Middlesborough, led to an unheard of demand for building materials, and this in turn led to the extraordinary increase in the ships built for, and sailing in, the slate trade from Caernarfon, Port Dinorwic, Bangor and Porthmadog. No doubt the eyes of the young Thomas brothers would have been attracted to the slate/emigrant barque *Hindoo* and the ship-rigged *Higginson,* owned by Humphrey Owen and his sons, which sailed regularly for such seemingly far off places as New York, New Orleans and Quebec. When Robert Thomas was a boy of five the Davies brothers of Menai Bridge, in whose service he was to spend most of his life, had three large new North American built ships sailing from the Straits within days of each other, laden with slates and hopeful emigrants, many from Thomas's own district. As he grew older he would no doubt have joined the groups of young lads who gathered eagerly around some old shellback, sitting on a bollard on the quayside at Caernarfon, beneath the imposing castle walls, who spun yarns, which lost nothing in the telling, of the exploits of some of the boys who had once played on the very quay but were now masters and mates in the fine Liverpool clipper ships. Many of these lads did in fact become well known master mariners, men like the three friends born within a stone's throw of each other at Porth y Foel, Caernarfon, Captain Henry Jones, master of perhaps the best known of all Mackay's great ships, the *Lightning*; Captain H. Hughes, who made some remarkable passages between North America and London in the *City of Sydney,* and Captain Richard Hughes, master of the *Royal Oak* and *Whirlwind* in which he gained a reputation for his swift passages from the China Seas. When Captain Henry Jones's *Lightning* was finally destroyed by fire, his mate was Captain Richard Jones, born in Caernarfon in 1822, who had previously been master of the Owen's *Hindoo* and *Higginson* and the

Mrs. Ruth Thomas, Tan Lan, Llandwrog, mother of
Captain Robert Thomas.

The daughters of Captain and Mrs. Robert Thomas: (from left to right) Cecilia Ruth, born Caernarfon 1882, Catherine Bruce, born Glasgow 1878, and Roberta Isabel, born Caernarfon 1888.

Davies's *Highland Mary* and *William Wright*. The late 1850s and early 60s were exciting years for any boys who gazed at the ships, however small, which nestled under the walls of Caernarfon Castle for they represented a tradition which reached out to much wider horizons, to the fine clipper ships of Liverpool and the Thames, to the far-off ports of Australia and India. Inevitably this romanticism played an important part in attracting boys to a seafaring career, but it was not the only reason, and should not be over-stated.

It has been rightly asserted by the maritime historians Basil Greenhill and Robin Craig that the sea was a last resort occupation, that seafaring was a way of life followed by the inhabitants of the coastal villages of South West England, the West of Scotland, North East England and Wales because they had but little choice. As already indicated, Robert Thomas knew full well the harshness and the unpleasant reality of life ashore. He was soon to experience the reality and harshness of life at sea. But as he himself states many years later, that first decision to go to sea was not only the dire need and economic necessity of supporting his widowed mother but also a certain romantic optimism that life at sea could not possibly be as bad as the drudgery and misery of life in an agricultural community in mid-nineteenth century Wales. 'Of course I thought like others of my age and experience that I had done just the grand thing and would never require to work again but see foreign parts and foreign people, always in my best clothes, for I had never seen a sailor in his old dirty clothes as at sea.'

In shipping aboard a coastal vessel, the schooner *May,* for 8/- a month, Robert Thomas was following the well worn route of so many able young men from Wales who started their sea-going careers as boys or cooks. He appears to have been offered the standard wage paid to boys sailing from the Menai Straits ports at this time – John Parry, an Anglesey boy who joined the *Catherine Williams* at Port Dinorwic a few months earlier, was paid the same rate, 8/- per month, by her master, Captain Thomas Hudson, one of the best known of the local schooner captains of the period. Whatever he may have thought at the time, Robert Thomas, in retrospect, noted in his 'diary'

17

years later that this mere pittance was no fitting recompense for the duties expected of a boy aboard a schooner, particularly in the days before the railways had come to cut the profits of masters and owners of the slate schooners. And, in typical Thomas fashion, he does not mince his words: 'Oh, my Lord God, father of the fatherless, forgive this man for offering a poor orphan such a sum of money for nothing better than be everyone's slave on board, for a boy in those days, and in a small vessel, was nothing better. I sometime wonder if God will hold such men guiltless that lived on men's and boys' labour at the expense of their body and soul, for a boy at sixteen years of age to work at $3\frac{1}{2}$d a day and such work as a boy in a schooner. I maintain he would not have much heart to look to his soul. This, my dear Brusey, was when owners of schooners were making their fortunes in a short time because there were not so many railroads then as there are now and consequently all the goods in England was carried from one place to the other by schooners, and steamers were very scarce then, which made it better for sailing ships.'

Thomas did not sail in the *May*, but his conditions of work were no better when he signed his apprentice's indentures which bound him to sail in any ship which Mr. Thomas Hobley of Caernarvon wished him to serve, a three-year engagement at an agreed sum of £30 for the three years. Thomas Hobley was not untypical of the shipowners of the area in the mid-nineteenth century. A member of a prominent Methodist family, he had much in common with his co-religionists, men like Edward Ellis, ship-builder of Bangor, John Phillips, the energetic Calvinistic Methodist preacher and fund raiser for Nonconformist schools and the Normal College at Bangor, who still had time to invest in many ships, Mesach Roberts, druggist of Bangor, prominent member of the Bangor Board of Guardians (it was rumoured that the ragged schools were a good source of cheap labour for his ships), and, of course, best known and most successful of all, the Davies brothers of Menai Bridge. The Methodists certainly had a reputation for zeal for their religion and a shrewd business interest in shipping, but the latter was often associated, certainly in the eyes of their seamen, with incredible meanness, not to say harsh self-interest. Robert Thomas's experiences in the *Pioneer* and the *Oberon,* told simply and honestly, provide a telling indictment of Thomas Hobley. They are probably typical of the conditions at sea in the ships of these gentlemen who sat piously and comfortably in their chapels and shook their heads sadly when they heard, as they surely must have done, the complaints and tragedies relating to their ships and the men whose toil brought them the handsome profits which enabled them to build their fine houses and their many chapels.

In fairness it has to be remembered that the contrast between the 'two nations', the rich and the new rising merchant classes on the one hand and the labouring poor on the other, was not confined to conditions at sea, for life ashore also had its stark contrasts. And dreadful conditions at sea were, of course, not confined to ships owned by Welsh Methodists! Robert Thomas looked back to his voyage to Newfoundland in the *Heidee* from Liverpool: 'her forecastle where we lived was a small dark hole and not even decked over, the coal locker being underneath, and a few planks here and there to stand . . . she was a regular wet dirty little brute.' He was not guilty of overembellishing the situation; a few years earlier a Scottish merchant, John Mitchell, in evidence to the Select Committee appointed 'to inquire into the Shipwreck of British Vessels', drew attention to the conditions in which seamen lived in words which are reminiscent of Thomas's comments about the *Heidee.* 'In British ships the men are not treated as they ought to be. I have taken particular notice of their place of abode, which is in almost every ship of small size, a small dark cave, without light or warmth, . . . it is sometimes six or seven feet square for six or seven men, stowed half-full of ropes and sails, damp and wet . . . ' The Report on Shipwreck and the subsequent Parliamentary Papers which carefully catalogued the statistics of wrecks and loss of life at sea around the British coasts and elsewhere indicate the validity of Thomas's 'diary' regarding those nightmarish early years which he spent not only in Hobley's ships but also in the South American and Newfoundland trades.

The 'diary' for these youthful years, however, contains much that is of general interest apart from life at sea. With his young

19

daughter's education ever in mind, Robert Thomas gives a brief account of the South American cattle hide industry as it appeared to him in the sixties, before canned meat and corned beef : 'In these slaughter houses they in the killing season killed some thousands a day of cattle, both horses and horned cattle, for the sake of their hides, tallow and bones, and they were then really just learning how to dry the beef, but before this the meat and bones were spread on a plain. The vultures and the sun would soon put the meat out of sight. The bones would then with the hides and tallow [be] shipped away on board some ship. I believe now nothing goes to waste; the beef is all cured now in some way or another.' Conscious that the account was for his daughter's eyes, Thomas discreetly describes his work ashore as pot-boy in what must have been a somewhat dubious house, but there was no doubt about the adaptability of the young Welsh country boy at work in a 'hotel' in a South American port. 'It's seldom they employ any women servants in such houses . . . great many people slept at the house and my principal work was what they call Chamber maid's work, such as making beds, emptying slops, scouring the floors and for which I was to get my victuals and 15 dollars per month, about £3 of our money, and when the ship went away I had to carry water on my head in a pail from the beach and help at cooking and sometimes act as waiter etc. – and as in all foreign houses . . . coffee was always kept hot, and when anyone called for coffee Bob might have been seen napkin on his shoulder and coffee pot in one hand and hot milk pot in the other.'

This was a far cry from quiet Llandwrog and the quay at Caernarfon where Robert and his brother Edward spent their hours at home yarning about the famous *Donald Mackay*, the superb clipper in which Edward had sailed in the fleet of James Baines of the *Black Ball Line*. Had he managed to get a berth with his brother aboard another of the emigrant ships, the *Ocean Chief*, Robert might have never returned to Caernarfon, for Edward Thomas quit the sea when he reached Australia. It is fortunate that Robert Thomas remained for some years in humbler ships, content to return from coastal or Newfoundland voyages to strut along the quayside at Caernarfon

20

as any young seaman until his money ran out. 'I stayed home for a while as sailors before the mast generally do till all the money is gone' — it was as far as the ambitions of hundreds of his contemporaries in the ports of Wales reached. When his money ran out, Thomas acted in what must have been the typical way for seamen from these small Welsh slate ports so close to each other — no ship available at Caernarfon and therefore a walk to Port Dinorwic or Bangor to look for a ship. The *Dart,* which he joined at Port Dinorwic, was engaged in the trade in which hundreds of Welsh schooners of her type busied themselves in mid-century — north about to Montrose, ballast for Newcastle, coals for Dublin. Again describing his voyages in 1863 in the barque *Queen* of Liverpool to Quebec Thomas gives a vividly authentic account of what must have been an experience common to many thousands of seamen engaged in the North American timber trade, loading the timber in icy conditions and then the hard and dangerous passage home in ships which were frequently overloaded.

It was the Welsh slate and North American timber trades which established the fortunes of the Davies family in whose ships Robert Thomas was to spend the remainder of his life, sailing in their service from 1864 to his death in 1903. This in itself is interesting for of all the shipowners of North Wales, many of whom were regarded as harsh employers, it is the ships of the Davies family which seamen recalled as the ones which most ruthlessly exposed sailors to hazards in the pursuit of high profits. An account of the Hughes and Company Ships of Menai Bridge (as the Davies ships were registered) has been published in *Ships and Seamen of Anglesey,* and therefore their activities must be stated very briefly here. John, Robert and Richard Davies, sons of Richard Davies, a Llangefni shopkeeper, had come a long way by the time Robert Thomas entered their service in the 1860s. Some thirty years previously they had invested in local coastal vessels bringing goods from Liverpool to Menai Bridge and Red Wharf, little vessels like the *Eliza and Catherine,* the *Mona* and the *Lady Bulkeley.* In the year of Robert Thomas's birth, 1843, John Davies, the eldest and reputedly the ablest of the brothers,

21

had persuaded his family to buy the first of their large North American built ships, the *Chieftain,* no doubt inspired by the success of their neighbours, the Owen family of Rhuddgaer, who already had several North American built ships profitably engaged in the export of slate and emigrants to America, returning heavily laden with timber. By the fifties the Davies family had a rapidly increasing fleet sailing not only to North and South America, but also to Australia and India, sharing in the dramatic expansion of the British merchant service and the very considerable profits that came the way of thrifty shipowners. Almost invariably the commanders of their ships and the officers and tradesmen, the sailmakers, the ship's carpenters and the like, were Welshmen, the majority of them from Gwynedd, and often enough, by accident or design, particularly in the early years, members of the Calvinistic Methodist chapels which the owners did much to support.

John Davies died young, in 1848, but his brother Richard became sufficiently wealthy to break the Tory-Anglican monopoly of political power in North Wales, become Member of Parliament for Anglesey in 1868, and the first Nonconformist J.P., High Sheriff and Lord Lieutenant of the County. Known as the 'silent member', Richard Davies was not a popular man, but the wealth derived from his ships assured his political success. When he died in his mansion at Treborth, near Bangor, in 1896 his estate was valued at £294,446, 11s. and 6d, a considerable fortune in those days. He had married Anne, the daughter of Henry Rees, the most famous of the Welsh preachers of his day, leader of the Calvinistic Methodists in Wales and Liverpool, and in the final years of the firm's existence it was their son, Henry Rees Davies, who managed the ships. Robert Davies, an eccentric bachelor, spent much time in the early years with curious schemes for the management of the ships, but later became something of a recluse, and easing his conscience (so the seamen said) by donating very large sums of money to various causes connected with the Calvinistic Methodists, £170,000 to the Welsh Missionary Society in India, £10,000 to the orphanage at Bontnewydd (near Robert Thomas's home), £10,000 to the British and Foreign Bible Society, and thousands of pounds to erect chapels

22

both in Wales and England. Contemporaries estimated that he gave up to half a million pounds to charities, but even then his estate, when he died in 1905, was valued at £446,383, 14s. and 7d. His nephew, Charles Pierce, who appears to have managed the ships ably during the seventies and eighties, as well as being a leading figure in the development of Bangor, also died a wealthy man. This then is the background to the ships in which Robert Thomas served, where an Able Seaman was paid £2 10s. a month and where a master gratefully accepted between £12 and £15 a month.

Robert Thomas's 'diary' of the years he spent in the Davies ships, from his days as a young steward aboard the *John Davies* to the long homeward passage in the *Merioneth,* speak for themselves. The reader should remember that his experiences, aboard the fever-ridden emigrant ship *Superior,* losing the rudder of the *Northumberland* in a gale off the River Plate, the vivid description of conditions loading guano, the crimps of Callao, leaking ships, recalcitrant crews, drunken and depressed masters and the remarkably well written account of the loss of the *Minnehaha* – all these experiences were shared by hundreds and, indeed, thousands of British seamen in the second half of the nineteenth century. The chapter of misfortunes with which Thomas was confronted in his first command, the *Glentilt,* are enough to make one wonder why men ever went to sea, but when reading Thomas's graphic account of his vessel on fire it is useful to realise that disasters to coal-laden ships were commonplace – in the twelve months ending in June 1874, for example, 42 British sailing ships and seven steamers were destroyed by fire, and a further 26 sailing vessels and three steamers severely damaged. Reading through *Lloyd's Lists,* one comes across the familiar words 'abandoned on fire'; 'left with cargo of coal – not since heard of'; 'ten feet of water was pumped into the hold of *Staffordshire* at Stanley, Falkland Islands, before the fire was extinguished. Surveys on vessel report ceiling and upper deck badly burnt.' A few months after the *Staffordshire* had put into the Falklands, Robert Thomas brought the *Glentilt* there, 'leaking, on fire, a rudder gone . . . charred timber coming up in pieces through the

23

pumps. The very ship we stood on was burning away under our feet · . .' Captain William Thomas Germain, marine superintendent for the Menai Bridge shipping company, had reason to be satisfied with Robert Thomas's actions in his first command; others of the Davies family ships were not so fortunate. *Lloyd's List* for February 7, 1883, contains an account of the burning of the *British Empire,* from Sheerness for Bombay, which had to be abandoned by her crew who took to the boats and had to watch her burn 'almost to the water's edge' before they were rescued by an American ship some fifty miles from the Indian coast.

When he arrived back and discharged his cargo in Hamburg in June 1876 after a voyage of over two years in the *Glentilt,* Robert Thomas was informed at the Menai Bridge office that he could only have three days at home before he joined his next ship, the *British Princess.* No doubt he would also have heard at the office the details of the loss a few weeks previously of another Davies vessel, the *Victory,* which foundered off the Humber shortly after she had left the Tyne with a cargo of coal for San Francisco in April 1876. The Spurn lifeboat had been launched, but the *Victory* had gone to pieces, with the loss of all hands, on the banks before the lifeboat could get anywhere near her in the gale. The body of Captain David Jones (whom Robert Thomas probably knew well) was found floating in a lifebuoy off Spurn, picked up by No. 6 Hull pilot boat and landed at Grimsby. *Lloyd's List,* 18 April, 1876, contains the melancholy details: 'Last night the body of a middle-aged man was landed here . . . In his pocket was £10.4.6 in gold and silver, also a silver watch with Williams marked in the inner case. He had no whiskers, but dark hair under the chin, partly turning grey.' A few days later it was confirmed that the body was that of Captain David Jones of the *Victory* 'which left the Tyne at 4 on Tuesday afternoon with a cargo of coal, bound to San Francisco; 25 hands aboard, also Tyne pilot. Ship totally uninsured.' Hardly encouraging news for Captain Robert Thomas whose sister died within a few hours of his arrival at home, and who was only able to have one day in the company of the delightful young woman whom he had met over two years previously, Catherine Jameson, a servant in the home of Lord Newborough at Glynllifon. Within a few days he was at sea again, with a cargo of coal bound for Callao in the *British Princess*; such was the lot of a shipmaster in the 1870s in the service of Hughes and Company, Menai Bridge.

After a voyage of a little over a year, Robert Thomas was home again, and this time he married his fair Kate. Daughter of Captain James Jameson who died of yellow fever aboard the sailing vessel *Larne* at Tobago in 1853, Catherine Bruce Jameson was born at North Camperdown Farm, Sandwich Parish near Lerwick, Shetland Isles, in the year of her father's death. As a young woman she came to serve as maid in Lord Newborough's household and eventually was ladies maid to the Misses Wynn· She had first seen Captain Thomas on a Sunday when she was attending Llandwrog Church with the New-borough family and Captain Thomas was home on leave. In view of her father's death of yellow fever, it is not surprising that she was apprehensive when, after a brief honeymoon, Robert Thomas sailed again for fever-ridden Rio de Janeiro in the *British Princess,* but in this matter again Thomas had little option : 'What could I do? I could not afford to leave my ship' – it was the typical situation for master mariners who knew the ship-owners had the whip-hand. There are indications in the correspondence during the next couple of years that Thomas was getting increasingly restless regarding the poor wages offered by his Menai Bridge employers. Charles Pierce was probably chiefly responsible for the policy change in the mid-seventies when the new 'County' class of iron ships were bought from Roydens, the Liverpool ship-builders, to gradually replace the wooden North American built ships. These were the boom years for the building of British iron sailing ships and Pierce was setting a pattern which was soon to be followed by a large number of North Wales shipowners, men like William Thomas, Liverpool; Thomas Williams, formerly marine superintendent to James Baines; W. E. Jones, Port Dinorwic; John Owen, Tŷ Coch, Caernarfon, and the newly-formed *Gwynedd, Arvon, Eryri* and *North Wales Shipping Companies* in which many

25

hundreds of quarrymen and shopkeepers invested their savings. Robert Thomas's letter in which he mentions the concert held aboard one of the many Welsh ships together off the guano islands indicates the extent of this North Wales investment in deep-sea ships in the seventies and early eighties, and it is likely that had he not been offered the command of one of the new Davies ships, the *Merioneth*, he would have found employment with one or other of the Welsh shipping companies. It is clearly impossible to predict what would have happened had he done so, for many of them were lost within a few years of building, but one thing is certain – Robert Thomas established an outstanding reputation for his service in the *Merioneth* and the *Afon Alaw* which became by far the best known of all the Davies ships. In 1883, when Robert Thomas wrote his 'diary', that was, as already indicated, in the future. It is time, without further preamble, to look over Captain Thomas's shoulder at his 'diary' in the cabin of the *Merioneth*.

THE 'DIARY'

My own darling child, Catherine Bruce,

It has often come to my mind to give you a short history of my life, for as I am so little with you you will know but little of my past life – and your good mother knows but little before our engagement on acquaintance which began about the latter end of 1873, and as I have in my past life nothing at least in public that I need be ashamed of nor you to blush for any mean act of your father. I dictate this to you for real fatherly love, and you being our eldest child and have been your mother and mine companion a little more than is general the lot of children of your age, and my own child whenever you do read this and find errors both in grammar and in spelling throughout you will not laugh or jest about it as the schooling I had was a penny a week school and no one to care or indeed know how my learning was progressing. My parents like many more being themselves unlearned thought that as long as I attended school daily and regularly I was bound to learn and their obligation and duty performed, & the schoolmaster as all schoolmasters in those days calculated that their duty also was justly done as long as I had a lesson from some other boy or teacher and a good hand-flogging in due seasons for there were no Government school inspectors in those days. And so as my parents thought they had done their duty, the schoolmaster his and I was confident I was doing even more than common duty. The consequence was that I left school at 13 just capable of writing a Welsh letter pretty fair but a very ungrammarian English one. The reason I had to leave school so early was the death of my dear father who had been ill & off work for over a 12 month.

My dear Brusey, I was born at Tanlan, Llandwrog, in 1843. I was one out of nine children, but one, Catherine, died when

27

only one year old. She was the twin sister of your Aunt Ann. Our names were as follows, 'Gainey', 'Thomas', 'Ellin', 'Edward', 'Robert', 'Jane', 'Catherine', 'Ann'· The other was a little boy who only lived few days or indeed few hours. My life till I was 13 years was like any other poor boy's, scarcely having clothes decent enough to go to chapel on Sunday, and that was in a time when farm servants went to chapel in fustian trowsers and a slieve waistcoat. Times are changed now as only few are to be seen in such dresses now even on a working day. Clogs we generally wore. Only the children of well to do farmers could afford shoes for every day. Women also went to chapel in peticote & a short shawl or a cotton jacket & clogs on their feet, and some & indeed all well to do women had cloth shoes buttoning on fore part. After this the elastic sides came &c. I also when very young belonged to the church choir. Mr. R. Thomas, butler of Glynn,[1] was the leader on a *Bass veiol* & sometimes, but always on practice night, with the violin. Mr. Williams the clergyman would give us a dinner at Tynllan about once per annum. And I can never forget how my brother Edward and me were so grieved when on one occasion Edward and me were told our names were not down for a dinner. Oh what a disappointment this was for us poor boys who never saw a bit of fresh meat but once or twice in a twelve month, and what a mean action on the part of Mr. W. But still he was not a hard man, nor an unkind one. Indeed he was quite the reverse and his motto for this action was because he thought it would be better to give the money to my father who was home sick and out of work, but still it was meanness to the core for the dinner only cost him 1/6 per man and my poor father would far sooner see his poor boys getting a good dinner & enjoyment than having the price of it himself. But the poor must stoop & so had we, for we were all greatly indebted to Mr. Williams for a great deal of the necessaries of life (Oh poverty what a loathsome article thou art)·

[1] Glynllifon, the home of the Lords Newborough, dominated the area. For an account of the development of the estate, see Professor Glyn Roberts's article in *Transactions of Caernarvonshire Historical Society,* Vol. 9, 1948.

When my poor father died I had to look for some thing to live on & soon gave up the school, and one morning Mr. Williams, Rectory, send for me & afterwards my mother, and I was offered to go there to service to clean boots, shoes &c. & my only wages was to be plenty to eat and clothes found, which was perhaps as much as I was worth. But we generally had visitors who almost all gave me a sixpence or a shilling for cleaning their shoes, take & fetch their letters to & from post, and the everlasting bow whenever I passed them within several hundred of yards, so my six pence & shilling were well earned.

In this manner I in about 12 month had from 10/- to 15/- saved in the keeping of my old friend and fellow servant Margaret Williams, but I believe most of this money I got from Mr. Williams himself who very often gave me a sixpence for being a good boy & keeping clean straw under the pigs & calf, but more often for finding a hen's nest full of eggs, and it would be a curious wilderness where I would not penetrate for a nest. Another sixpence came very often from Mr. W. for telling the truth, for whatever I had done wrong I would always be forgiven and a sixpence if I would confess the truth, which of course I always did. But I am sorry to say this old habit of Mr. Williams did not answer with the next boy after me who took advantage of the old gentleman's kindness & did all kind of mischief to boot (& got his /6d). I stayed here for two years and I suppose I will not be exaggerating if I say this was the happiest time of my life, for though I look to the two years with horror very often, I was now getting too old for Mr. Williams' service and work for my clothes & victuals. So he got me a situation with Mr. Hamilton Roberts of Bethesda, by Bangor. The place was called Brynmeirig and Mr. Roberts was the quarry doctor & very seldom practised outside of that. My wages here was £8 per year. What a large sum it seemed then to me 160/- per year or 13/4 per month and buy clothes out of this. My work was to look after two cows, a pony & 2 pigs, clean knives & shoes, run to the post & all errands, beside milking the cows & churn, and when this & mangling was done I had to go to help the gardener to finish a fair day's work. But there was plenty to eat here and very good and on the whole a good place

29

for a boy of my age in those days. I stayed here 6 month only &
gave a month warning. I believe I had about £3 pound coming
to me then. I then went home & for the first time in my life
felt an inclination to go to sea. This was in Nov. 1858. My sister
Gainey got married in May or April this year. I really do not
know what or how I was to live when I came home this time.
My brother Tom worked at Glynn as sawyer & joiner, my
father's old berth, & he paid my mother for his food only. My
brother Edward was pupil teacher at Llandwrog and his little
salary was entirely dependant on his passing his examination.
My sisters Jane and Ann were small girls at home, so it's obvious
we were very poor. My sister Ellin was now in service at Chester
and I ought to mention that she was in service at the Rectory
as dairymaid &c part of the time I stayed there, but she left
on account of ill health.

I had now determined to go to sea and my mother found it
useless to try to prevent me. I went to Carnarvon and partly
engaged (or shipped) to the Schooner *May*[2] and at the extrava-
gant wages of 8/- per month.

Oh my Lord God, father of the fatherless, forgive this man
for offering a poor orphan such a sum of money for nothing
better than be every one's slave on board, for a boy in those
days & in a small vessel, was nothing better. I sometime wonder
if God will hold such men guiltless that lived on men's & boys'
labour at the expense of their body & soul, for a boy at 16 years
of age to work at /3½ a day, & such work as a boy in a
schooner. I maintain he would not have much heart to look
to his soul. This, my dear Brusey, was when owners of Schooners
were making their fortunes in a short time because there were
not so many railroads then as there are now & consequently
all the goods in England was carried from one place to the other

[2] The schooner *May*, 84 tons, built in Prince Edward Island in 1855, was
owned by Jones and Company, Caernarvon, H. Jones, master, and was
listed in *Lloyd's Register* as a Bangor coaster, i.e. a slate schooner.

by Schooners, & steamers were very scarce then, which made it better for sailing ships.[3]

I did not join the *May* but got my self apprenticed to Mr. Thomas Hobley of Carnarvon as a ship apprentice and I bound myself to sail in any ship that Mr. H. wished to send me to. The engagement was for 3 years and wages £30 for the 3 years. I signed my indentures in the custom house at Carnarvon. So that now indeed I was bound to try my fortune at sea. And of course I thought like others in my age & experience that I had done just the grand thing and would never require to work again but see foreign parts & foreign people, always in my best clothes, for I had never seen a sailor in his old dirty clothes as at sea.

My dear Brusey, before I commence on my sea life I will just note a few narratives in my life before I went to Mr. Williams. One of my numerous occupations were to go coursing with Mr. Thomas of Glynn. If he intended to course in a neighbourhood away from home I had to go a day before hand to muster the scattered greyhounds which were generally billeted on tenant farmers and bring them to the place of meeting next morning. All I had for this was perhaps a new pair of shoes & perhaps some old clothes. I also, at different seasons, worked at Glynn, @ 6d per day, gathering stones, picking potatoes, transplanting turnips or swedes, also drying turf or at least spread them to dry. At these times there often worked with me about 30 other boys and it took all of my Lord Newborough's labourers to keep us in order. On one occasion we had filled the cart and then ran into the wood close by to pull crows' nests, but we forgot to watch for the empty cart till we heard my Lord's voice in the field, so you may be sure there was some scrambling down and a run to the field where My Lord was waiting and watching us. So he told the steward to pay us all off that night, but we found afterwards that he was only joking to frighten us, but it made us very good but very grave during

---

[3] During the period 1786-1850 a very large number of small vessels was built in Gwynedd for the slate and copper trades, particularly at Pwllheli, Porthmadog, Caernarfon, Amlwch, and Bangor. cf. A. Eames, *Ships and Seamen of Anglesey* (1973), *Porthmadog Ships* (1975), *Ships and Seamen of Gwynedd* (1976), L. Lloyd, *The Unity of Barmouth* (1977).

the day, and as we had a fellow with us (Shion Tybach) who would either pray, curse & swear or any other occupation as long as he was told he was a hero & a good fellow, so when the next cart was filled we were close to a hedge & here we got Shion to pray for L. Newborough to be moved by the spirit to forgive us. So Shion turned his face to the hedge by which there were some rubbish and as he got warm in his prayer he got to talk loud, & on which a hare got up from the rubbish & close to Shion's face. It frightened him and with a yell and a curse he jumped up. This was too much for the grave & religious men with us, who swore they would never work with such a lot of scamps. So we were again in peril of being dismissed, but we got over this again and had another gaffer, a quiet man who let us have our own way. With him we worked well.

Another job I had then in hand was to look after the Bwlan Chapel preachers' horses, for at that time people used to go about any distances on horseback. So if a preacher was due at Bwlan to preach on Sunday I had to watch for him on Saturday night & take his horse, if he had one, to one of the farms in the neighbourhood. For this the average pay was 5/- a year, but in my term they promised me a pair of shoes which was couple of shillings more. And they had the impudence to pronounce in the chapel one night that a collection would be made next Sunday to get me a pair of shoes, but we put a stop to this & I believe I got 5/- some time after.

The vessel I joined was the Barque *Telegraph*,[4] then lying at Liverpool where I joined her about January 1859. This was a strange life for me which had hardly ever put my foot on board of a ship of any size in my life. Indeed I do believe that the only times I was on the deck of a vessel was Lord Newborough's Yacht at Belan and on trip across from Carnarvon to Anglesey in the little steamer. The first day I joined I fell down fore hatch but providentially there was a layer of salt in bags on the bottom so I was none the worse. I worked in this vessel till she was

---

[4] *Telegraph*, barque, 357 t., built Quebec 1855, owned by Hobley and Co., Caernarfon. She had probably been bought by Hobley in 1859 from Thomson and Co., Belfast. Her master in 1859 was E. Jones.

Robert Thomas in his early days at sea, apprentice to Thomas Hobley, Caernarfon. Captain Thomas had the original of this photograph reprinted by Elite Photographic Studio, 838 Market Street, opp. Fourth, San Francisco, on one of his visits; the studio at the time was owned by Jones and Lotz, and managed by C. E. Dunn.

838 Market Street,
San Francisco, Cal.

Captain Robert Thomas, master of the *Merioneth,* at San Francisco,
probably about the time of the record breaking passage 1887/8.

nearly ready for sea (she was bound to Australia), then I was not allowed to go in her but had to go to Hull to join the Brig *Pioneer,* the captain of which I knew (but unfortunately not much). The *Pioneer* was a brig carrying about 300 tons and was then discharging grain from the Mediterranean and after which we loaded salt for Newcastle.[5] So you will see that I first went to sea from Hull.

When leaving Liverpool the owner Mr. Hobley gave me 12/- to pay my fare, which I believe was 10/6 or 11/-, but by the time I started from Tithebarnstreet Station I do not think I had a copper left, although Mr. H. said very proudly & with his patronising looking face that he was giving me 12/- so that after paying the train I would have the rest to pay for victuals on the way. I left Liverpool some time soon after dinner and all went on well till I came to a place called Milford Junction where the train stopped, and the Guard calling out 'all change' out I jumps and into another train, but unfortunately a wrong one. Nor did I find my mistake till I heard the guard & porter calling out 'York' all change. So instead of being in Hull I found myself in quite another direction in York and it was then just getting dark. I had not a cent in my pocket and my English was very backward & Welshy, but some sailorman, quite a stranger to me, happened to start with me from Liverpool for Hull and with whom I became acquainted in the train, happened to make the same mistake as myself. In fact it was more his fault than mine as he was an older man and on this account I followed him.

The stationmaster at York, after having satisfied himself that it was a mistake, told us to be there at a certain time – he would send us back with that train. So my friend the sailor took me to a place & paid for refreshment for both. We arrived at Hull about Midnight a bitter cold windy night and my sailor friend again took me to a lodging house where he payed for my lodging and a good supper. And may God bless him if on this side of the dark river. In the morning I went to look for the *Pioneer*

[5] *Pioneer,* brig, 191 tons, built 1856 in Nova Scotia, owned by Hobley & Co., master Williams in *Lloyd's Register,* 1859.

33

and when I found her the captain told me he had gone to meet the train the previous evening and had seen my box had come but of course not the owner. Nothing particular occurred while here, but I commenced to know a little of a ship. On the passage from here to Newcastle I was very ill (Sea Sick). What a dreadful sickness it is, and worse than all no one to pity one. We got to Newcastle all right and after discharging cargo took a cargo of coal for Limerick, Ireland. We made a fair passage, discharged cargo and took ballast for Cardiff, where all left the Ship except Captain & myself. I do not think I ought to have followed the sea after this, as I was seasick for several days every time I went to sea, inded I was this way for many years after, even when getting a man's wages. After discharging ballast we loaded for Malta. This was what I greatly wanted was to go on a foreign voyage. We shipped crew, about 9 we were all told. It was here in Cardiff that I first had my hair cut by a barber, the captain giving me /3 to pay. When I had my hair cut the man said my head was dirty & asked if he might shampoo it and I said yes, not thinking that I would have to pay more and when I told the man I had only /3d he told me to bring another /6d there again.

We sailed in due time from Cardiff and proceeded on our voyage and the cook losing his passage I had to take that berth, which was a pity, but an apprentice on board a ship is nothing better than a slave, especially in this class of ship. That was a hard time for me on account of seasickness and ignorance of the work.

We passed C. St. Vincent very close with a stiff breeze of fair wind and the next land of course was about the Straits of Gibraltar. I had even then read about Nelson's battle of C. Trafalgar and I took great interest in these places which were shown me. We passed Gibraltar on an evening and hoisted our name up by means of flags. In due time we arrived in Malta but I am sorry I cannot give any dates, but it was in the summer. A whole host of small boats came out to meet us & a pilot, and as it was calm the boats were put ahead to tow us to the harbour. This was the first port out of G. Britain I had been in, Limerick excepted, so I took the greatest interest in all, & more than all in the Bay they told me St. Paul was shipwrecked. Also it was a sight to see the crafts coming in from Sicily loaded with the choicest fruits which were afterwards piled up on shore in every hole & corner.

There are two harbours here. Only vessels discharging general cargo &c are in this one and vessels discharging coal & steamers coaling are in the other where we had to go & discharge it at the back of the town.

In the first harbour are the Man of Wars, all on the East side of it as near as I can remember, although it [is] a good bit over 20 years since I was there. I also remember there were forts all round & all the guns facing the harbour, but my dear child you must find all this out from history which will learn you better than this.

After discharging we took in ballast and sailed for the Black Sea, being bound to Galatz in the river Danube and the first land we made was one of the Greek islands where we encountered head wind and I think we passed not far from Patmos Island where our St. John saw the Heavenly visions & wrote the Revelations.

After tacking about a long time we got as far as the Dardanelles, a narrow straits between Mediterranean & the Sea of Marmora, on one side of which we must send for a pass to proceed and if not a large fort on the other side and a little higher up will soon know the reasons why. After leaving the Dardanelles we enter the Sea of Marmora which is an oblong sea, both sides being visible, and as we went along we soon observed the towers of Constantinople looming in the distance and as we aproach it some business people came out to meet us. We cast anchor opposite the town and the Captain goes ashore to enter & clear the ship. This took couple of days & when we again sailed we had a river Danube pilot with us. We now sailed through the Bosphorus, a narrow straits and very deep water indeed too deep except in some few creeks. Constantinople is beautiful to look at and splendid villas all along the water's edge. Every gentleman's house front door is open to the sea and they pay their visits &c in smart looking boats for the streets, although looking so grand from the ship, are yet too narrow, filthy & dirty for carriages. The ladies seldom go out & when

35

they do their faces are hidden except the eyes. This is [on] account of their religion, for the Mahomet religion doth not allow the women to show the face only to her husband and very nearest relative, but are kept as house furniture to look at. The same religion also allows its members to have more than one wife so that most of the noblemen have several women who they keep with great jealousy for I suppose the poor things would run away from such bondage if not carefully watched. But we will now leave them and their many slavewifes and thank our Maker for sending His dear Son to save us from such things & show us the way to live, and to return to my story, for you will learn all about Constantinople, the Turk & the Mussleman in modern books at school. Before leaving the Bosphorus we again have to send our pass on shore before we are allowed to proceed and after which we commence to open the Black Sea which I fully expected to find black or at least darker than other seas, but not a particle of difference did I see, but it was very hot. In few days we anchored off the mouth of the river by the small town or village of Sulina on the left hand. In the morning we took a Russian or Mongolian pilot to take the ship in over the Bar where our own pilot above mentioned took charge. He was a Greek and a very smart man in handling a ship. Galatz is I believe nearly a hundred miles up the river, the current of the river runs down at the rate of 2 or 3 miles an hour, the land is very low & all the houses built on piles on that account as the river frequently overflows its banks. There were I believe but one tug boat on the river then and of course too dear for a small Brig to have anything to do with. So when there was calm or light head wind all hands had to go on shore to track, or pull the ship by means of a rope from the mast head, for it had to be high so as not to get entangled in the wilderness of briars, bamboos & all kind of rubbish, which in some places were very high, so high indeed that we could only see the ship's masthead. In the meantime we had to find our way best we could across muddy brooks & swamps, very often to our middle in mud and water and scratched in the legs by the briars & scratches in the face by the foremost man letting the branches back with a spring in one's face. All hands would

36

be ashore except Captain, pilot and cook & unfortunately for me this time the captain had shipped a cook at Constantinople.

At meal times the ship's bow was turned in against the bank for the ground was all soft & steep too. We then drove a pile into the earth & made fast to it and at night passed an extra line. 6 A.M. after coffee on shore again till breakfast but the greatest annoyance of all were the mosquitos. There were millions of them & oh what hungry monsters. In the mornings we could hardly see after their bites and our poor legs were in a worse condition. Very often in tracking a huge snake would crawl across our path. At last after nearly three weeks of this toiling we reached Galatz.

Galatz is on the right hand of the river and ships lay alongside the wharf. While the clearing between the ships & the houses opposite is covered by grain in great heaps and of every kind; the town is very dirty and the least wind raises such dust enough to choke anyone. One evening in particular it came on such a gust of wind that many would have died if it had lasted any length of time, but as it was I remember well that I lay flat on the decks trying to breathe some pure air. Happily it lasted but a short time.

We loaded barley, and the way they load is a double gangway for the natives to carry the cargo on board which they do in bags on their shoulders but the bags are not sewn, so they walk on board on one gangway, empty their bags in the hatch as they pass & return on shore by the other gangway, and in this manner they go like a string of human beings all day & with a kind of a marching regularity they will load a ship in a very short time. The crew meanwhile are stamping down & trimming the cargo in the hold, a very hard work on account of the dust which makes the blood flow from the noses. After loading we sailed down the river, no tracking being required in going down the river.

When we got to Sulina we had to anchor and so as to lighten the ship to go over the bar there being not water enough to cross the bar loaded. The lighter was a good size Schooner, which took half the cargo. I believe a steamer towed us out, the Schooner included. After anchoring outside the bar we of course

commenced to reload, although it was very rough, the wind
being right in on the land so that we had no shelter. And before
we had even finished it came on a gale of wind which obliged
us to let the Schooner go, who ran in to shallow water.
Moderating the next day we resumed our voyage and in two or
three days got to Constantinople. It was about this time that
the S.S. *Royal Charter*[6] was lost on the coast of Anglesey. She
was from Australia with I believe about 500 passengers, most
of whom were men that had made a fortune in the golddiggings.
There was a fearful loss of lives. Indeed very few were saved.
She had merely anchored here for the night to be ready for
Liverpool next day, but coming to blow hard before they could
get out they cut away the mast, the rigging of which getting
foul of her propeller caused her to go on shore. I have no dates
my dear child but events like the above will correct my state-
ments, & when you read in History of the loss of the *R. Charter*
you will know when I was in the Black Sea first time. After the
necessary delay at Constantinople we again sailed for home and
went through the Dardenelles much faster than in going up, on
account of the current always running from the Black Sea to the
Mediterranean, for you will find in your atlas at school that
several large rivers runs to the Black Sea and the Sea being only
small it stands to reason the extra flow of water must find an
outlet, which it does as stated. But this again makes the Mediterranean Sea the reverse because the Atlantic Ocean sends a
strong current to the Mediterranean through the Straits of
Gibraltar and again the Black Sea pours all its waters into it &
several very large rivers such as the Nile &c. Some people
maintain that it evaporates & others that an under current takes
it out by the S. of Gibraltar, and I have not read what is the
real cause but I suppose it must be one or the other. Your
geography will tell you and you must enlighten me on this
subject when I come home again.

---

[6] October 25/26, 1859. On the night of the *Royal Charter* wreck between
sixty and seventy vessels were lost on the coasts of Britain, many of
them small vessels with crews of two to four men. *Parl. Papers 1860,
LX,* 529-30. Evidence relating to the loss of the *Royal Charter,* 560.

We had very bad weather this time and off Malta lost our Jiboom and several geese we had on deck from Galatz where they must have been cheap else not one of them would have been there. We also called at Gibraltar for orders this time. I cannot go & give you the history of Gibraltar but leave that to you. It now belongs to England and considered one of the strongest places in the world as a Fort, being honey-combed and a cannon wherever one could be put to be of service. It once belonged to the Moors and afterwards to the Spaniards and taken from them by Admiral Rooke & Sir Cloudesley Shovel of the English navy, and England has kept it ever since. It was taken by the English in May 1704. After staying there couple of days we again set sail for Falmouth for orders where we arrived few days before Christmas 1859, because it was here I spend my first Christmas on board a ship. And a fearful day it was, blowing a hard gale right in & raising a heavy sea. We had our orders to go to Antwerp to discharge and where we arrived all right. The voyage being now over the crew were discharged, all except Captain & me & (second mate) now Capt. Evans, Barque *Mona* and of Dinorwic Street, Carnarvon.[7] It was very cold & the dock frozen up. The owner Mr. T. Hobley came here and with the captain asked me, which was as well as being ordered, to keep watch over night. And he the owner would give me 2/- per week pocket money. A man from shore would charge him 3/- or 4/- per night. But this was not the real hardship, but the fires had to be put out at 5 p.m. and not again lighted till 7 a.m. Was this not a cruelty to a poor ill clad boy to have to be on that cold deck all that long frosty winter night without a spark of fire, and this to save the pocket of such a hard hearted scamp? (God hath already visited the wretch) . . .[8] if they would work he would take her to Falmouth but they would not agree to this.

The wind coming fair the Captain, Mate, Cook and one A.B· hove up the anchor and carrying me aft to a chair by the wheel,

---

[7] In 1883 when this was written, the master of the barque *Mona* is listed in *Lloyd's Register* as M. Evans. The barque *Mona* built in Sunderland in 1878 by Osbourne and Graham, was of 1,645 tons, 205/24.5/21.2 and managed by John Owen of Tŷ Coch, Caernarfon.

[8] There are two pages missing in the original document here.

while they got the ship under weigh, which was done and in a day or two we got to Falmouth, the crew meantime keeping at the pumps. In Falmouth we ran her aground on a beach where she was again caulked and lightened by 30 tons and in the meantime all the crew left, leaving only the captain & me on board. The owner also agreed to let me leave her but the captain again stood against it. My mother had sent me money which she had borrowed and which I returned when I found I could not go. So disgusted and sick I was this time of the sea and ships that had I got away I do not think I would ever have gone to sea again.

We shipped another crew and again proceeded on the voyage and it turned out one of the finest passages I ever made and we made a very quick passage. Trieste, as you can see by your Geography, the principal seaport in these parts and is in the Adriatic Sea or as some people call it the Gulf of Venice, and as I said before it is in Austria. On the other side is that old famous state or town of Venice, once a republic of itself and built on the water on small Islands & piles, the streets being so many canals & people going visiting or shopping did so in boats called Gondolas of which you will often read. In ancient history it was a very wealthy place but it was a very wicked place. A man's life was not safe there one hour, and 1797 Napoleon took it by treachery & deceit and that was the end of this small republic.

My dear child you must learn all these things in your book. Who Napoleon was and the difference between a government governed by a crowned head and a Republican government.

Now you see I have got myself away from the subject I intended to write.

We got to Trieste all right. The harbour is protected by a breakwater, and we layed stern on to the Quay, two anchors ahead & a piece of the cable chain astern round a (dolphin), that is several large piles drove down close together & bolted together above water, and after discharging cargo we went to the old harbour and hove the ship down and caulked her bottom again beside puting on some poisonous stuff to keep the worms from eating the timber.

When this was done we again took in ballast and again proceeded to the River Danube but to Ibraila this time a little higher than Galatz and went through all the hardships of tracking the ship up and this time I was nearly gone with a fever, but a doctor gave me medicine which checked the fever but left me the ague or intermittent fever and which clung to me for month till I was very weak.

Almost everybody got this ague and our Cook, an old man from Falmouth, died at Sulina on the way down, and when we left Sulina there were only the captain, carpenter & myself beside a shoreman working his passage to Constantinople to work the ship, and although I had the fever lightly every day from there home I still did my work as cook & steward, but two or three men layed up all the passage home. We went to Queenstown this time for orders and payed the sick men off and after getting some good fresh provision here I got clear of the ague. We got our orders here for London and I ought to have told you that our cargo this time were Rapeseed, a very small seed fine as powder nearly. I believe they make oil with it. It was on this passage that we killed my old friend a black pig which we had first voyage at Galatz· We were great friends for we had spend much hard times together but he was a fearful thief. Would go to the galley, open all the saucepans and contents. On one occasion I had a piece of meat roasting in the oven & being done I left the oven door open while I took the soup aft, but when I went for the roast meat found old Jack coming out with it, but being too hot he had to toss it along and I just caught it when Jack was just sure of it. And you must not blame me my dear child if I did take the meat, clean it and take it to the cabin. But I did not eat it. But there was much coolness after this between Jack & me, but I was very sorry to see my old friend getting killed. We had our usual gale of wind after this for sailors are very superstitious and maintain that it will always blow after killing a pig or a shark.

We arrived in London in due time and went to the Victoria dock to discharge and again pay off men. How downhearted it used to make me to see the men going home after a voyage while I had always to be on board. It's the wrong thing to do with a boy, because a boy's greatest ambition is to [go] home off a voyage.

After discharging here we took in ballast for Newcastle to load coals for Cork, and it was on this passage that I passed my second Christmas at sea. We made a fair passage from N. Castle to Cork, where we discharged cargo and again took in ballast, but this time for Carnarvon. What a treat to me, and who should come on board when we came to anchor but my brother Edward who himself had been for a short voyage to the Black Sea in a steamer as under steward. That night I went home with him. Oh what joy to be home again. First time for over two years.

My dear child I have now closed my time with the *Pioneer*. It's a long time since I wrote the name before commencing this. She was to be repaired at Carnarvon and I was glad to get clear of her although I ought and do try to thank God for his mercies towards me in her. But the marks or consequences arising out of the bad usages & hardships I endured on board of her will stick to me as long as life lasts.

I may as well now tell you of the end of her. The next voyage she got on a lee shore & all hands except the boy left her in a boat. The boat capsized and all were lost. The boy was taken off the rigging afterwards but I believe died from the exposure. The ship was saved and but little worse. The next voyage or second she was lost altogether and I believe with all hands. I will say or write nothing more about her, but I have as you see left two blank pages in case I may think of anything interesting that happened on this my first voyage to sea & my first vessel.

And now my dear Brusey I must introduce you to my next ship. The Barque *Oberon*[9] was at Carnarvon bought by my owner and others when on shore an abandoned wreck on Sarn Badrig reef, Cardigan Bay.

[9] The *Oberon*, a barque built at Bridport in 1852, 347 tons, 112.5/24.2/14.7, had probably been bought cheaply after grounding on Sarn Badrig, and no doubt repaired cheaply, hence the problems encountered on the subsequent voyage. Her master's name in 1861, under Hobley's ownership, is given as W. Evans. *Lloyd's Register* 1861. She had originally belonged to Bowring of Liverpool.

They got her off the reef & brought [to] Carnarvon for repairs and was when we came there launched off the slip, having apparently been thoroughly repaired. Also new masts, rigging &c. She was an English built vessel and to carry I believe from 400 to 500 tons. I thought then that she was very large but when I went on board to work it damped my spirits a bit when I found she was making a great deal of water. We left Carnarvon on a Saturday evening for Swansea to load coals for Coquimbo, Chile. This was a long voyage for me to go round the Horn.

We were towed from Carnarvon by the steamer *Fairy* and we fired off some blank charges off Belan which was answered from the fort by Lord Newborough's employees. We had very bad weather from here to Swansea but got there in due time and also in due time sailed on our long voyage. Every thing went on well, but when we got to hot weather the allowance of water came on very hard on me. 3 quarts is the allowance and you must remember this is for tea & coffee, dinner and drinking for 24 hours. My old complaint, the ague, coming on me now made it very hard, for a man with a fever ague wants a great deal of water and I could have drank 3 quarts in an hour if I had it. I do not think I ever suffered more in my life than I did then for the want of drink. I would lay in my bed and fall into a stupor and would imagine I could see fine crystal streams of water close by & would jump up with a start duly to be mocked by the absence of water and a parching thirst. What a torment!

I even crawled along the coal in the hold to where a cask of water was and with a small wooden needle case I had in my pocket I would fasten a string to it and dip few thimbles full of water up. What cruelty it was to keep me in that state. I shall never forget it. Well we crossed the Equator and by & bye got down south and after passing the River Plate we had fearful gales & fearful sea which continually kept us well drenched at the pumps and as the gale increased so did the water increase and it soon became apparent to all that the vessel was not equal to what she was supposed to stand and when it moderated the crew informed the captain that the ship was not seaworthy and that they would not proceed in her or with their [voyage?]

43

till she was made at some port seaworthy. He refused for some time to comply but seeing they were determined he bore up for the next port which was Montevideo on the Plate and where [we] arrived in few days. After arrival at Montevideo a survey was held on the ship, and they recommended that 150 tons of coal should be discharged and the ship caulked over again above water. A few days after all the men ran away and finally myself and the other boy, whose name was Fred, ran away.

A boarding master took us in and kept us in one night but next morning gave us each a dollar and showed us out of the town & bid us get out to the country where we would get employment from farmers till our ship was gone, when we could come back to town. We walked that day about 15 miles to a village, where we bought something to eat. We had previously fallen in with a foreign sailor who could talk a little Spanish, and before we got to the village a nigger overtook us and walked with us, but did not enter the village with us.

We had left the village about a mile behind when we saw some mounted police coming after us in full gallop who with but little ceremony drove us sword in hand back to the village and into the lockup. We knew there was something wrong but could [not] understand what they said, but as near as I could understand from our foreign sailor they had seen us in Co. with the nigger who was a notorious thief. They of course took us for accomplices, but I suppose our innocent looking faces and youth convinced them there was not much harm in us. So after a good night's rest on a cold earth in a lockup inside the stocks and covered with a bullock's hide we were allowed to leave in the morning, but our bellies were empty, and when we went near any house the door was locked or the man would meet us well armed outside and we found it was vain to go farther, but the wisest course was to walk back, while we yet had the strength do so. There is nothing that will cow [a] a person down more than make him go without food. Our foreign friend left us, so Fred and me turned back but before coming to town we went to a large stable house to look for work, but the killing season was over and so was the work. In these slaughter houses they in the killing season killed some thousands

44

a day of cattle, both horses & horned cattle, for the sake of their hides, tallow & bones, and they were then really just learning how to dry the beef, but before this the meat & bones were spread on a plain. The vultures & the sun would soon put the meat out of sight. The bones would then with the hides and tallow [be] shipped away on board some ship. I believe now nothing goes to waste; the beef is all cured now in some way or other. But as I have already wrote the season was over and there was no work for us and indeed who would have employed poor forlorn wearied lads like us unless they were very hardly pressed for time.

We got back to Montevìdeo late one evening both hungry and tired and cared but little whether taken to prison or not as long as we had rest & something to eat. On the main street we saw an English man of war's man and we at once went to him & said we were hungry. An English sailor can never see another hungry if he can help him and so it was in this case. Jack at once asked us to the nearest store although it was late and gave us a *bountiful repast* of bread, sardines & claret wine after which we got more cautious about being taken, for well we knew that we were looked for high & low. So we very cautiously wended our way to the boarding house where our clothes was. They did not half like to see us back again, for if we were taken they would have lost by us as our clothes would have to be got & perhaps a heavy fine for harbouring deserted sailors.

However we were kept out of sight and in a few days an Austrian captain came and took Fred who signed articles before the A. consul. The captain only wanted one so I was left all alone again. After this commenced to work in the house but always keeping out of sight. It's seldom they employ any women servants in such houses. This one was called the 'London Hotel,' what we would rate about the 4th rate, but great many people slept at the house and my principal work was what they call Chamber maid's work, such as making beds, emptying slops, scouring the floors and for which I was to get my victuals and 15 dollars per month, about £3 of our money, and when the ship went away I had to carry water on my head in a pail from the beach and help at cooking and sometimes act as waiter &c.

45

– and as in all foreign houses this coffee was always kept hot, and when anyone called for coffee Bob might have been seen napkin on his shoulder & a coffee pot in one hand & hot milk pot in the other. So things came to look brighter. Also the carpenter of the ship, a man from Carnarvon, had left the ship and had come to the house where he did a lot of jobs in the joiner line & we slept in the one room, also the sailors that had run away day before Fred & me came back from the country with few dollars in their pocket but looking none the better for the country life they had led.

Two of these men joined the American man of war here, but the captain would not have me as he did not require lads, and what a blessing it was I did not go for it was just on the beginning of the American war, a war as you will find in history between the North & South.[10] You will read more of this as you read this.

I stayed at the L. Hotel for about two month I suppose, the carpenter working where he could but still sleeping with me. We used to get on well together and as they never eat but twice a day in these countries, I as chief cook &c. &c. &c. generally got a bit supper for us two in our bedroom, and one night after eating a box full of sardines we hove the box to the streets and unfortunately hit a night watchman who made a great noise and came to the house to demand the person that had hit him, but of course he could not be found, and from this time forth we did not have any more suppers.

One Sunday forenoon an American captain came on shore and wanted a crew to join his ship at once. She was a full rigged ship and called the *Lancashire* of New York from Hamburgh bound to Buenos Ayres with general cargo, but in coming up the river had got aground & through which the old crew would go no further. Well my dear child before noon I had shipped as A.B. on board the *Lancashire* to go to Buenos Ayres, which

---

[10] A number of Welsh seamen found themselves involved in the American Civil War. For the experiences of one of the more successful cf. A. Eames, L. Lloyd and B. Parry, *Letters from America: Captain David Evans of Talsarnau* (1975).

is a little higher up the river and on the other side, a Republic of its own like Montevideo. It goes now by the name of the Argentine Republic.

We were also to stay by the ship at B. Ayres till cargo was discharged. My old friend the carpenter was on board with me as A.B. In fact all were ABs although most of us were not entitled to that name. We got to our destination & discharged cargo.

I must here inform you that no large ship can go nearer than 8 miles to the town of B. Ayres on account of shallow water so we discharged the cargo into lighters. I was paid off with about £4 when cargo was discharged and I refused to go further in the ship. I went to board to a German house, a private boarding home & very respectable. I shall not try to describe this town, as you will find all that in the books. I stayed here I suppose for three or four weeks. The carpenter had shipped in a barque for home & where he was very shortly afterwards drowned in a smack. I think her name was *May Flower*.

My money being all gone I had to look for another ship and got one, viz. the ship *Sportsman* of Boston U.S., Capt. Thompson, and if you overhaul the books at home you will find a Bible I got from him and in this you will find the dates.

I shipped as ordinary seaman 2 dollars under the wages of A.B.s at Buenos Ayres at the time, but still I was getting 2 dollars more than the A.B. on board who had shipped in her at Boston, but the captain told me not to mention this in the ship as it would make the men jealous of me. I was sent on board in a large boat – what they call whale boat, but I was not on board long before I wished myself on shore again for I could see she was what we sailors call a wild packet, or in other words where discipline is kept and carried on by kicks & cuffs which was quite common in those days, especially American Ships. Of course I had never seen it before. However I was allowed to stay in the forecastle for the day.

The next morning we were roused out and before I was aware of it all the men were on deck, for a call to turn out in this ship meant a call to work as well. Before this I had been used to see men called at 5.30 to get their coffe and turn to to work at 6.

47

Not so here. Turn out meant turn to as well, then a bare $\frac{1}{2}$ hour to breakfast and an hour to dinner and knock off work when too dark to see, and with this wage I could see the men were cowed down and had no life in them after work as we used to have in English ships, skylarking &c. But in the *Sportsman* there was none. We sailed from Buenos Ayres in ballast for Boston where we arrived in due time and may here add that I was never better treated as I was here. Indeed I may say that I was better treated here than ever I had been at sea for I was the only lad on board and the Americans are noted for good treatment to lads, but we had a bad disagreeable set of sailors who [were] all jealous of me being well treated.

While they were knocked about constantly the captain had on board his wife and little girl and many a happy hour I had with her playing about the deck. I believe I was the only Protestant in the forecastle & Mrs. Thompson often lent me books to read. We had a nigger cook & his wife as stewardess with both of which I was very friendly. When we got to Boston everyone left her, myself included, but on coming on board next day the captain told me to stay by the ship on daily pay & board on shore and all I had to do was to keep the decks clean. There was a night watchman. Both mates had left so that I was the only one left of the old crew. The ship was chartered by the government to carry provisions to the troops down South, and I intended to go with her, till one day I went for my dinner my boarding master asked me if I wanted a Ship for Liverpool and the love of home conquered my better conscience and I said yes, and this without telling Capt. Thompson, and leaving some money behind and after signing articles &c. I went on board with five sovereigns in my pocket from the month advance drawn in the vessel. I found the vessel all ready to sail. She was a large Barque called the *Kate Waters* and under British colours on account of the war.

I found on board of this one some of the greatest rascals that ever went on board of a ship. This will be in December 1860 for we spent my third Christmas at sea on the passage. I had two pounds in gold left of my advance which my boarding master told the rascals on board, who tried all they could to get at them, not knowing that in going to the wheel that night I had given them to the captain to keep for me. I got on well with the captain and officers as every one in the forecastle were Irish except me and I am sure, young as I was, that I was a better sailor than one half of these.

We got to Liverpool all right and before our advance was out. Consquently we had nothing to take & I had only the £2 to go home with for I was determined to go home as I had not heard a word from them since I left Swansea nearly 12 month ago. So I took a cab to carry my clothes and self from ship to landing stage where I knew the Menai Bridge steamer would be on Saturday morning. My old shipmates looked hard at me going away in a cab while they had to shoulder their clothes and they did not know what money I had nor where I had them kept on the passage as they had overhauled all my clothes and my body had also been carefully searched.

The *Prince of Wales* steamer[11] left the landing stage & I on board but judge my feelings when we had just left, I found my old master or owner T. Hobley talking on the Bridge to the Captain, the very man I was afraid to meet. But had I even spoken to him I doubt I had a guilty conscience & so I thought every one knew it and all I could do now was to get out of sight to the fore cabin and at Menai Bridge I had to wait till Mr. H. had left before I would venture out. At the station I had to wait till all had tickets & the train in before I could be served. At Carnarvon I had to wait till Mr. H. had booked his luggage before I would venture to the cloakroom and when I had my clothes booked I went to sleep at a friend's house till morning, and when morning came I walked to Llandwrog. But when I got to Tanlan I found the shutters on and door locked. Some-

---

[11] The City of Dublin Steam Packet Company's iron steamer, *Prince of Wales,* sailed regularly between Liverpool and Bangor and Menai Bridge in the 1850s. Thornley, *Steamers of North Wales,* 14-16. Advertising in the local press, it was stated that the *Prince of Wales* left 'Menai Bridge on Mondays, Wednesdays and Fridays at ten o'clock in the morning: returning from George's Pier Head, Liverpool, on Tuesdays, Thursdays and Saturdays at eleven o'clock in the morning'. Reduced fares were advertised 'Cabin 4s, forecabin 2s., children under 12 years old, half-fare'.

thing struck me that perhaps my mother was dead. I knocked at the next door, but a stranger to me came to the door so all was altered. But on enquiring for my mother this woman held out her hand and told me she was my brother Tom's wife and that my mother was with my sister at Chester. I had only poor clothes, not fit to go to chapel with, so my brother rigged me out in his best clothes which made the people to pass remark 'how well I looked'. The next day I went to Carnarvon for my clothes and went to the station by a back way in case Mr. H. would see me. A friend came with me & went to the luggage office for my clothes while I hid myself behind the door in the waiting room. Presently someone opened the door to look in and in the face I recognized Mr. T. Hobley but he did not look behind the door & therefore did not see me. I got clear & in a week's time I left for Chester & from there where I saw my mother and Gainey, Ellin & Jane, the two latter in service, I came back to Portdinorwic where I had relations and here I worked on the fields with the servant till I got a berth in a schooner called the *Ward Jackson* where I shipped as O.S. for £2. 10. & from this time to the present I have always left my mother some [of] the money I could spare.

The *Ward Jackson*[12] was bound to Hartlepool with a cargo of slates, where we arrived all safe, and after discharging took in a cargo of coals for Nantes in France, where we also arrived, discharged and took in ballast for Portdinorwic. But we met with a little mishap this passage for in coming into Portdinllaen, West of Carnarvon Bay, with [sic] failed to give the point a wider berth & a strong ebb tide carried us on a rock but as it was fine weather we did not do much damage although we remained there one tide & she made some water. However the next day we got to Portdinorwic where the voyage was up and of course all left.

My brother Edward was now expected home in the ship *Donald Mackay* where he acted as under steward on a voyage

---

[12] Details are not given in *Lloyd's Registers* of several of the ships in which Thomas served during this period, most of them being foreign-owned. The *Ward Jackson* was built at Dumbarton and owned in 1860 by Jackson and Company, plying mainly in the Hartlepool-Hamburg trade.

to Melbourne & back. She was then one of the finest ships afloat & in the passenger trade flying the Black Ball flag.[13] My brother arrived home all right & after staying home some time we both went to Liverpool for a ship.

Edward got a berth in the *Ocean Chief*[14] where his late mate was master and bound to Queensland with passengers but when they came to sign Articles they would take no O. Seamen and I would not sign as A.B. So after all my brother & me had to part and we have never met since. She arrived in Australia after a long passage and she got on shore there. My brother also left her and has never left Australia since.

I tried hard to get a ship in Liverpool, but it was a very hard times there, double the men to the number of ships so of course the wages were low. However being at the Shipping Office one day, I heard a call for two O. Seamen for Newfoundland and as I could not wait or afford to choose a ship I made a jump & got in & signed to go to Harbour Grace N.F. with a cargo of salt. After signing I went to see her and I was truly sorry I had signed in her as she was an old Brig & very small, her forecastle where we lived was a small dark hole, and not even decked over, the coal locker being underneath, & a few planks here and there to stand, but I could not afford to back out for indeed my advance would not be sufficient to pay my debt at the boarding house. So I sailed in her in few days. She was called the *Heidee*. We had a fair run across but she was a regular wet dirty little brute and three or four of us had fully made up our minds to run away whenever we could. And the first night in gave us that chance. We were moored to a wharf alongside of a Schooner who had a boat astern. This boat we managed to get & brought under our bow into which we passed our clothes & rowed to the

[13] One of the best known of all sailing ships and named after her eminent builder, the *Donald Mackay,* 2,408 tons, had been built in America in 1855; owned by James Baines of the Black Ball Line, she was later managed in the 1870s by Captain William Williams, whose offices were then in 36 Fenchurch Street, London, but who at one time had also served as a master in the ships of the Davies brothers of Menai Bridge. A Eames, *Ships and Seamen of Anglesey,* 256-258; M. Stammers, *The Passage Makers* (1978).

[14] *Ocean Chief* was also one of the Black Ball Line of ships.

other side of the harbour where we had bespoken a house where to keep our clothes. It was a poor widow's house, Irish. There was four of us, one being an ordinary seaman & the other two A.B. The O.S. belonged to a place in Anglesea close to Beaumaris.

When we had left our clothes at the widow's house whose name was Mrs. Coney, we left the town or village as it was not safe to stay there for there surely would be a strict search. So we took a tramp to another small place called Carbonear or such name, one of our number being an old hand in Newfoundland and knew every one about. We got to this place by morning and managed somehow to get some thing to eat. We then retraced our steps by not the main road as we came to a plantation where we laid down & fell asleep but were sometime afterward roused by hearing voices which turned out to be of some men passing but seeing us asleep were talking about us & wondering who we were. We did not enlighten their curiosity but make tracks across the plantation & soon put a good distance between our friends & ourselves. Some time in the afternoon we passed a small farm house and being very tired & hungry two of us were told off to try our luck at the farm. I was one of the two and after knocking at the door we asked for a drink and after drinking this we hinted that a crust of bread and butter would not be refused. The poor woman who also was Irish asked us in and apologised for not having any bread in the house but if we would wait half an hour the load which was then baking would be ready & she would in the mean time get some tea ready. This was I do [be]lieve the greatest kindness that ever I met with. This woman's husband was a common fisherman who was then away at Labrador for the season, leaving his wife & four or five pretty little children at home to look after the small farm in his absence. We very willingly sat down to wait but the other not half liking to see us being fed &c. made their whereabouts known by sundry yells & coughs &c. We explained to the poor woman how matters stood and our whole story, on which she called the other two in as well and at last we made a hearty tea. A goat being called ran in & was milked on the floor, the milk being put in our tea. They make tea here as on

52

board of a ship for the sailors, the tea & sugar being put in the kettle together.

This was not enough for the woman to make but she managed to send a word to another old Irish lady that lived a little way off and lived in a larger farm. This old lady came to us some time before night & invited us home with her where we again got plenty to eat and a bed in the hay house on some birch branches and some green old Irish quilts to lay over us. Next morning we had breakfast and then not deeming it safe to stay here too long we went up a mountain at the back where we could see the harbour & the *Heidee* which we expected everyday to leave as she was only going to discharge part of her cargo, taking the rest to Labrador where she was to load fish for Brazil. After getting on the hill we saw on the other side a fine pond about two or three miles long & having nothing to do we went down to it for a bathe but when scampering about in the water some women from the town came there and as there was a very thick small trees growing round the lake they did not see us till they were close to us. I cannot say who were the most frightened, them or us, but I know we scrambled ashore pretty brisk & into the thicket pretty smart, while the women being quite as bad never even turned to look back but ran to town and soon spread the news that there were some wild people in the wood &c.

When we had ran a mile or so with clothes under our arms we dressed ourselves and going a bit farther we layed down under the spruce trees bushes and, it seems, fell asleep, and first thing we knew was a bell ringing close to us. Never did four men jump up smarter than we did, but not being quite wide awake we did not know which way to run, but after taking Dickens advice to count 25 before getting into a passion we took a careful survey of all around and there close to us were some cattle grazing and as usual in places like this one of them had a bell fast round the neck to tell their owner their whereabouts in the thicket. We had a good laugh over it and as the day was far advanced we retraced our way back for the old Irish Lady's farm where we found tea ready for us as if we were regular boarders· We went on like this for another day or two when the Brig sailed and we then ventured down to town where we found our clothes all right and the landlady happy to see us again, and she told us the Captain had been there to look for us, but the old lady having a former quarrel with him to settle, it seems he did not stay long.

In a day or two the two men shipped in a schooner and Dick & me got a job at a fish warehouse to dry fish &c. at 4/- per day, so we were now in a position to pay Mrs. Coney some of our bill. One day the captain of a Barque called the *Fleetwing* called on us as he wanted some hands to work on board and when ship would be loaded to go on the voyage in her, so we went on board to work till she was ready for sea, but by some means another [*sic*] we did not sign articles nor went with her. Next day we went to work on board the Brig *Mary* of Carbonear & went with her with ballast and empty barrels to Labrador with the intention of loading herring for Quebec and after laying there three weeks we had to leave as the season was over and the fishing boat[s] leaving for home, but we had no herring as there were none caught that summer. We arrived again at Harbour Grace discharged our empty barrels and sailed for Sydney, Cape Breton Island which you will find in your Geography the S. side of the entrance to the Gulf of St. Lawrence. Here we discharged our ballast & took in a cargo of coal for St. Johns, Newfoundland where we arrived all right & left the *Mary*. Our voyage being up and winter coming on we thought it time to leave such a frosty cold country.

St. Johns is one of the snuggest Harbours in the world and very narrow entrance between perpendicular rocks about 100 yds wind [*sic*] leads to a splendid harbour with high hills all round and the entrance being so narrow makes the harbour smooth as a pond. The entrance is also deep to the very rocks and when in the possession of the French had a cable chain across the inner end of the entrance to keep an enemy from entering. The bolt where the chain was fastened to were still to be seen when I was there 1862.

We stayed in an Irish boarding house here and stayed here two or three weeks having a little money in our pockets now.

One morning a Brig hove to outside from the Labrador bound

to Oporto for orders and in want of three hands where Dick & me shipped & joined her in a boat. She was also a Brig & called the *Brooking*.[15] We called at Oporto for orders which we got for Nantes in the Mediterranean where we again arrived all safe. Of course our cargo was dry codfish which we discharged here. The authorities in here as in most places in the Mediterranean are very exact with Bill of health &c. Indeed they will not get hold in the papers when we are first visited but have a long stick with a split in the end in which the captain puts the papers and which are then carried in that style to the shore & fumigated in case a disesase may be lurking within its folds. The mate having a scratch on his nose, a mere nothing, but the health officer did not think so as he had be sent on shore in ship's boat & to land at the Quarantine wharf, on which he landed & conveyed to the presence of the doctors. His nose was overhauled and his whole body went under the closest inspection. In the meantime every stitch of his clothes were smoked or fumigated &c. and at last he was pronounced to be in a clean state & fit to appear and mix amongst mankind. This was all nonsense no doubt, especially for a vessel coming from such a healthy climate as Newfoundland. I am sorry to say that I was a bad boy here again for I took it in my head that I was not properly used and took a fancy of joining a Man of War. I refused in company with a foolish Irishman on board to work and after getting on shore we found our way to the officers of a Man of War then in port, but providentially they were full & required no men. We then after loafing about two or three days went to work again. A good cane on our back would have done us good as we were well treated and had plenty to eat on board. It was here I spend my fourth Christmas at sea. The fruits are very cheap here, also currants &c. For a few coppers we had currants for our duff for a long time after leaving.

We took in ballast here & sailed for Naples for orders. I will say nothing about Naples to you as it is so well known to

[15] *Brooking*, brig, built Dartmouth, 1852, 205 tons, owned by Brooking, master in 1860, Summers, Liverpool-Newfoundland trade, *Lloyd's Register*, 1860.

everyone that read on account of Mount Vesuvius being close to it.

We arrived here and got orders to proceed to Malaga in Spain to load a general cargo for Hamburgh. In Malaga we had to go through a strict process by the health officers, & we were put in quarantine for several days with a quarantine officer on board to see that we hung our things up in the rigging everyday and who also everyday smoked the cabin and forecastle, and at last we were declared clean animals fit to mix amongst other clean animals.

My dear child perhaps it will be well for me to tell you something about quarantine.

For instance suppose at ——* there was some contagious disease it would be inserted on our bill of health and of course a ship coming from such place must be put in quarantine. There is in every harbour a certain place for ships in quarantine to lay, and no one from shore can go on board. But fresh meat or anything can be taken alongside and sent on board, but nothing from the ship shall go onshore, not even a letter in some cases & who ever from shore such as a pilot &c he must stay on board till the ship is out of quarantine. A man is generally put on board with some chemicals &c to fumigate the ship all over. The sign of a ship in quarantine is a yellow flag on one of the masts. A bill of health is a paper given to the captain before sailing for a foreign port. It's an universal law of nations, and without producing which a captain cannot enter his ship in a foreign port nor in England from a foreign port. Some countries demand two, one from the Custom House and one from that country's consul at that port. For instance, sailing from England for Rio Janeiro there will be two required, one from C. House & one from Brazilian Consul. Most bills of health between nations is in Latin but when you get older you can read of these things.

Well we got out of quarantine, discharged ballast & took in a cargo of oil, raisins, wine &c., and after a fair passage we arrived in Hamburgh where we expected to be discharged but

* Indecipherable.

56

captain would not do so as the articles were worded that we were to return to Newfoundland for which place we were now loading bricks & hard biscuit. But one day I was taken bad with the ague and the captain being constantly drunk I went to the Consul who gave me an order to the hospital where I stayed for about two weeks. It was the first and to the present the last hospital that I have been in as patient, but I have been in a great many at foreign ports. It's a most dismal thing for a young man to go to a foreign hospital as in my case. Now there was not one in the ward which could talk English & not an Englishman in the hospital except one and myself.

This was a very large hospital and a very free one, plenty to eat and a pint of porter for every man per day! It was as much of an almshouse as it was an hospital, there being great many old people here living quite comfortable, clean and tidy and nothing matter with them except old age. There were inside the building a grocer shop, baker shop, beer shop &c. Any eatable could be bought for same price as out side. Hamburgh was then a free state & everything very cheap, but it's now a part of Germany.

When I came out I went to the consul who informed me that the vessel had sailed and of course my money left with him. The next day I took a passage in a steamer for Hull, and from there home by train with above five or six pounds in my pocket off my long voyage· And so ends my term in the Newfoundland ships & fisheries.

I stayed home for a while as sailors before the mast generally do till all the money is gone. So I went to look for a ship again and at Portdinorwic shipped on board the Schooner *Dart* of Carnarvon bound to Montrose with slates.[16] We went north about, viz. through the Pentland Firth and after discharging there we took in ballast for Newcastle, where we again loaded coals for Dublin. We went again North about & had a long passage on account of head wind. After discharging here we sailed in ballast for Carnarvon, where we arrived all safe on

[16] *Dart*, schooner built Chepstow, 1826, 92 tons, owned and commanded by O. Davies, Caernarfon, Bangor coasting trade.

a Sunday morning so I was home at Tanlan in the afternoon. This was in the fall of the year 1863 for in September I joined the Barque *Queen*[17] of Liverpool bound to St. Johns, New Brunswick, with a general cargo of iron, anchors, chains, wire rope, hemp & manilla ropes &c. and all things for the use of new ship. St. Johns was then in its prime at shipbuilding; it was common to see a dozen large ships there at the time & just off the block or being getting rigged. We left Liverpool about the beginning of October and had a fair passage out but bitterly cold. The crew were almost all Welsh and mostly young men like myself thinking of getting on in the world. Many of them did try & some succeeded, but as far as I know I think of those alive today that I am far higher in position than [any] of them, but it would be too personal to name any of them now here, but may mention these that's gone on a voyage from which even a sailor never returns. The Captain died soon after, the mate also & second mate. Steward & Boatswain died also shortly after, at least in less than three years. Some of the others got to be master, one of which, the Captain's son, died at sea when master of a ship from Carnarvon. Of the others I am sorry to say that the greatest kindness to them is to close the chapter.

We discharged the cargo and loaded a cargo of deals for Liverpool, and I believe this was about the hardest work I ever had. The deals were brought alongside in scows or square flat-bottom boats· Most of these were waterlogged & frozen, & to get the deals adrift was a job, for every one were frozen one to the other, so that crowbars & pickaxes had to be used to get them adrift and then all the ice & snow had to be scraped clean & swept, for if we stowed them away with any ice on them it would in the hold melt & cause the cargo to shift. Our Whiskers were one mass of Ice – and in spilling it would hardly be down before it was a lump of Ice. We wore flannel mitts & canvas on that again to handle the deals and we got loaded a day

---

[17] *Queen*, probably the barque built at Rye in 1847; 225 tons, — 21.1/13.3, in *Lloyd's Register* 1863-4. According to *Lloyd's List*, the *Queen* sailed from Liverpool for St. John's. N.B., on 2 October, 1863, and her master was named Hughes.

before Christmas day and hauled out to the stream where we spent my 5th Christmas on board a ship.

We were very disappointed to haul to the stream a day before Christmas for we all had an invitation to someone's house over Christmas day, and there was no neccessity for it, especially after us working so hard and all always sober. Christmas morning after pumping her out, for she was very leaky, the steward called us to have some grog, the first glass that had been offered since we joined her. It would do good (if ever grog does any good) when we were half frozen up handling the deals. We however refused the grog for it was supposed to be only a bait to get us to work on this Christmas day, thinking no doubt a little grog would cover all notions about working on a Christmas. However we all one and all refused to work, which even to this day I do not blame myself.

But same time we had no right to refuse work, but it was an act of tyranny to ask us to work for we were all respectable young men and had worked willingly & hard throughout that bitter weather and if we had ran away as every ship's crew were doing the owner of the *Queen* would have had to pay £7 a month to new hands and a high figure to a stevedore for discharging and loading the ship. The consequence was we had a day's pay stopped of our wages and a bad discharge for conduct on the voyage. I leave it to the Great dispenser of justice whether it was right or wrong and will say with the Irishman 'God rest his soul.'

We arrived safely in Liverpool after pumping all the way. Here we left her, most of us never to meet again.[18]

After getting my discharge I went home and went to school at Llandwrog to learn a little more about arithmetic,[19] but as is always the case with big boys I suppose I got to be too big to take lessons and the consequences was I left the School.

[18] The *Queen* sailed again from Liverpool on 9 March 1864, *Lloyd's List,* 9 March, 1864.
[19] It was common practice for adult seamen to return to the local school to learn mathematics and navigation, and at Nefyn, Pwllheli, Porthmadog, Caernarfon, Bangor and Amlwch many future master mariners first learned the rudimentary knowledge of their calling from the local schoolmaster or schoolmistress.

I was engaged to a captain to go with him in a month or two as steward, so I still stayed at home till beginning of March when I went to Liverpool to join the ship *John Davies* of the firm of Messrs. Hughes & Co., Menai Bridge, and in whose firm I have remained ever since. It is now 19 years for it was March 1864 when I joined the *John Davies*. We sailed from Liverpool in few days bound to Quebec where we arrived all safe,[20] but it was a bitter cold passage, it being so early in the Spring. We got among field Ice but were not detained. And now I want to inform you the difference between Ice bergs or Ice Islands and field or pack Ice. Field Ice is the sea itself frozen up in the North where it is very cold and in the beginning of summer it breaks up and is carried to the southward by the polar current, melting by degrees as it gets further south. To look at it is just like looking at a large plain covered with snow. It is not smooth as a frozen pond at home, for you must remember that when it is formed the sea perhaps is rough and lumps of Ice floating about, but the cold fasten all together.

An Ice berg is quite a different thing. I have seen some of them much over a 100 feet high & two or three miles in length & breath, and you must remember that when 100 feet of iceberg is above water 300 feet must be under water for it floats heavy. Some have been seen much higher & there are accounts of some over thirty miles long.

Now my little girl will at once see that these cannot be formed of salt water for the sea could not heave its billows to the height of 100 feet. So you must understand that these mountains are formed on the land and in this manner. The land at the poles is very high and always covered with Ice & snow. The rain, sleet & snow is driven down towards the cliff on the Sea Shore

---

[20] The *John Davies*, named after the eldest of the Davies brothers, who managed the shipowning business in the early years, was a wooden ship, 924 tons, built in 1851 at New Brunswick; she was bought new by the Davieses in 1851 and plied in the American trades until 1869 when she was sold. On the voyage to which Thomas refers she sailed from Liverpool on 3 April, 1864, arriving in Quebec on 13 May. The dates for the sailings of the Davies ships which follow have been compiled from a notebook which their clerks kept in their Menai Bridge office, U.C.N.W. Bangor MSS 3531, cross-checked against the entries in *Lloyd's Lists* and *Lloyd's Weekly Shipping Index*.

and freezes as it moves, and it is supposed that in the summer time the snow on the mountains thaws and runs over these layers of Ice, which also freezes till the mass grows and grows every year till there is a whole mountain of Ice on the face of the land, and when it get too heavy it falls off into the Sea and is carried by the current to the Southward.

There is no doubt but they are formed in this manner. They drift down south till very often they get aground on the Banks of Newfoundland where they melt by degrees till they are light enough to float over it. They then come in contact with the Gulf Stream, a warm current coming out of the Gulf of Mexico which runs along the American coast till striking on these Banks it sweeps away across the Ocean, strikes the British Isle, runs up English Channel & round the North of Scotland towards Norway &c. And you must always remember that if it was not for the Gulf Stream England would be a frozen up country in the Winter time & even the Summer would be so cold & short than nothing would grow on it, for it is just in the same latitude as the Labrador where hardly a blade of grass grows and is frozen up in Winter. Don't forget my dear child the wonder and wisdom of The Great God in arranging things like this.

The Gulf Stream is first formed in the Antarctic Ocean, runs from Cape Horn towards Cape of Good Hope, some of it striking there, turns to the Northward along the West coast of Africa where it is helped along by the South East trades, stops its course & then it find its way right across toward the West Indies & into the Gulf of Mexico, and overflowing this it runs away to the N.E. out of the Gulf into the North Atlantic, scattering there. Some runs North as I said before while the other portion runs across till it gets to the influence of the N.E. trades which again sends it away toward the S.W. to the main stream.

Well the supposed & indeed the positive reason of its warmth is the long time the stream is in the tropics and the Gulf of Mexico is a very hot place so that the water gets quite warm and retains that warmth to the coast of Europe, and it's this stream which eventually melts the Icebergs. They first melt under water till they gets top heavy, then they tumble over &

so on till there is none left. They are very dangerous to ship[s].

My dear child I have informed you enough to form some idea about Ice &c. and now about Quebec which you must remember is or was then a timber port. Nothing else in the shape of cargo could be got there.

Quebec is on the River St. Lawrence & one time was a French colony till taken by the English. The history of this battle you will find very interesting. The people still talk French amongst themselves but they are very loyal to the British Government. The country is called Canada.

The timber is brought down from a long distance up the river in large rafts, viz. lassoed together & then under the charge of few men it drifts down the river. Some are brought down rough as it grows and some squared off ready for shipment. The Canadians are very smart on a log of timber. They will stand on it & turn it whichever way they please with their feet, & some of them will cross the river on a log without wetting a foot.

We loaded a cargo of timber and sailed[21] for Menai Bridge where we arrived[22] all right & in the Middle of summer on a Sunday afternoon, some hundreds of people looking on the Sea shore for it was a rare thing in those days, especially on Menai Straits to see a large ship. We also fired our cannon in rounding Beaumaris point & cheered. But it was a mistake to do so on a Sunday.

When the ship discharged I joined her again bound again to Quebec·

My mother came on board this time & came out as far as Puffin Island[23] & went back in the steamer which towed us. I was now getting good wages and able to keep my family at home independent of every body.

We made this voyage again successfully & came to Bristol to discharge[24] and here all left her, even the mate after the cargo

[21] 5 June, 1864.
[22] 26 June, 1864.
[23] 12 July, 1864.
[24] Arrived Quebec 27 August, sailed 17 September, arrived 19 October King Road Bristol, in dock Bristol 30 October, 1864.

was out, but I stayed by her all the time for after discharging she went to graving dock and after that had new masts & rigging. It was while laying here now that the Clifton Suspension Bridge was opened, one of the finest Bridges in England at that time, and as we layed alongside the street where the procession passed I had a bridge of flags across the street, from our masthead to a window on the other side. In the evening there were all kinds of amusement, the principal sight being showing a magnetic light on the Bridge, but it proved a failure on account of the rain.

After repairing & getting new masts &c. we left Bristol for Cardiff (towing of course), but after we got here we had to stay in the roads for several days & including my 6th Christmas afloat.[25] After docking I left the *John Davies* to go home and I took this opportunity to visit your Aunt Ellin Roberts home in Montgomeryshire, quite an inland place. I had the pleasure of singing a carol here in a little chapel, the first publicly since at sea.

You must remember that in those days carol singing was very popular about Christmas, for when I was a child there always was a service at Llandwrog Church on Christmas morning, and composed mostly of carol singing, but often attended with much riots, which put a stop to it. And then it was held in the evening, and this again had to be stopped on account mostly of riot, for in those days there was no limit to time of closing public houses. Indeed it was common for people to make it a night of drinking and toffee making and only went out to attend the church at 4 a.m. Carols were not sung that [*sic*] by whole choirs but by single individual which very often I am ashamed to say were half drunk. After this carol singing came more in fashion at chapel and I have seen several carols sung at Bwlan Sunday evening next after Christmas. Your uncle Edward & me sang at Bwlan & were then obliged to mount the seat.

Christmas was then kept as a merry making day, no service being held in any place of worship. If I remember right it was

---

[25] Sailed from Bristol, 20 December, 1864, arrived Cardiff 27 December, 1864.

a great day for sliding if there was any frost & a great plum pudding day. I often wonder how it was that plum pudding got so popular. On board a ship we generally get it three times a week instead of once a year then. My belief is that Christmas ought to be kept as a day of rejoicing & prayer. By rejoicing I mean that every one ought to make themselves as happy & joyful as they can in a Christian manner, doing everything to the Glory of God.

May you, my own darling child, see many a happy Christmas without a cloud of doubt or unhappiness in sight. I have seen some hard times of a Christmas in gales in wet & cold, in broiling sun amongst heathens, amongst ungodly people and very often amongst drunken sailors.

I am writing this page of my passage in *Merioneth* from Rio to San Francisco & have just come out of very very heavy weather. June 15th 1883. Lat, 32.S. Long 92. West.[26]

After staying home a short time I again went to Liverpool to join a new ship with my old captain & in due time we sailed [2 Feb., 1865] from Birkenhead for Point de Galle in Ceylon.[27] The ship's name was *D'Israeli* or *Israeli*. After having been out some time the small pox broke out amongst the sailors. The first attacked was an Irishman and he had it very heavy. All the men left the forecastle and left him by himself. He soon got quite blind and delirious and one night got up & took a razor and shaved himself quite smooth. The next morning he was in an awful state, his face all raw after shaving. His head was like a lump of jelly and smelling fearful & I and another man volunteered to cut his hair, which was indeed a fearful job. However, the man got well and to this day I believe he saved

---

[26] The *Merioneth* had sailed from Rio for San Francisco on 12 April, 1883. The heavy weather to which Robert Thomas refers could therefore have occurred in the vicinity of Cape Horn or in his stated position in the Pacific on 15 June, 1883. They eventually arrived in San Francisco on 3 August, 1883.

[27] Sailed from Birkenhead 2 February, 1865. The *D'Israeli* was a wooden full-rigged ship, 989 tons, 177.7/36/22.4, built at Richibucto in 1864, a new vessel registered in the name of Robert Davies, Bodlondeb, Caernarvonshire. Her master for this, her maiden voyage, in 1865, was J. Williamson, with whom Thomas was to sail again in the *Superior*.

his own life by shaving his face although delirious as he was at the time, for it cooled his head and he soon got well but heavily marked.

Two more got it, one very lightly but the other rather heavy but not half as heavy as the Irishman. The poor fellow before he got properly well & strong went up one night to stow *main royal* and fell overboard and was never seen. This was off Cape Good Hope and on a dark & dirty night. I sent the account to the *Herald Cymraeg*[28] which duly appeared, my whole letter and name in full.

We arrived[29] out all safe after a quick passage & where we discharged our cargo except 500 tons which we took to Calcutta to same company, the P. & O. Co.

Ceylon is an Island to the south of Hindustan a very fruitful place & celebrated for coffee. Of course you will know all this when you learn to read. Point de Galle is the Southernmost part of India & therefore a great place for steamers, for then the mail steamer from home would here distribute her mails, some for Australia, some for China &c. & the original for Calcutta, Madras &c. Ceylon like all India is a British possession.

Calcutta is up a long river the Hougly and it was then a very sickly place but now I believe it's as healthy as any other place and a very large place We discharged our remainder of cargo & after laying in the river some time we took in a cargo of linseed & poppyseed for London.

There is a curious custom in Calcutta in regard to meat, for a captain contracts with the native butcher to supply the ship in meat and vegetables at so much per head. About /6d per man per day is about the price of beef, vegetables & potatoes. It is of course very hot there, being so far inland for inland towns are always hotter than towns on sea shore. When we left here we took two invalids sailors on board sent home by the government, and both died on the passage. The captain was ill and the reading of the burial service fell on me, and a solemn

[28] The *Herald Cymraeg*, a Welsh weekly newspaper, would have been eagerly read in North Wales and by the Liverpool Welsh community.
[29] 29 June, 1865, at Point de Galle. Arrived Calcutta 16 July.

duty is was. You must understand, my darling child, that it would not do at sea to bury anyone in a coffin for it would float. Therefore the rule is to sew the body up in canvas and putting weight of old iron, coals or stones if procurable by the feet the corpse is then laid on a plank held on the rail feet out, men holding it steady while the service is being read, & when the reader comes to the part 'we commit his body to the deep' the end of the plank is raised and the body slides out & sinks to the deep. And what a deep grave it often is, about 4 miles deep, as far as from Carnarvon to Glynllivon. But Christ will raise it again for judgement for all must appear before that awful Great White Throne. No skulking back there. All must appear.

My own dear child how will you and me feel on that great day? 'And the books were opened and another book was opened which is the book of life, and the dead were judged according to the things which were written in the book according to their work'. May God give you grace to walk & live a godly and righteous life, that you may be able to look with pleasure on him that will be sitting on that Throne and say this is the God in whom I hoped. What a fearful day that will be to the wicked. We arrived in London[30] after a moderate good passage & left the ship and I may mention here that this ship was lost the second voyage after this on her passage home from India. There is no account how or where she was lost. She was a fine little ship and new when I joined her.

When home this time I went to school[31] to learn navigation and pass the board as second mate, which I did in Liverpool. My brother Edward sent home this time from Australia begging for money to pay his passage home, as he was very ill, but as I was under some expense to pay for schooling &c. I had to

---

[30] 22 January, 1866. The *D'Israeli* sailed again from London for Bombay in March, 1866, thence to Callao and Teneriffe, a voyage of 14 months 17 days, returned to Newport for a coal cargo, sailed Penarth 5 October, arrived Point de Galle 27 January, 1867, Akyab on 27 March, and was lost after sailing thence on 19 April.

[31] Thomas probably attended the school of Mrs. Edwards at Caernarfon where most of the more ambitious young seamen studied navigation, cf. A. Eames, *Ships and Seamen of Anglesey*, 373-4, 468-9.

borrow money to send which I paid on coming home again. Another incident this time threatened to cause me trouble. My old employer Mr. Hobley found me out & demanded pay for clothes received from him when in his vessel. This came on me very hard this time for I could ill afford to pay any money except what was actually required to pass. I paid them the half for a receipt in full & this was my last transaction with the Hobleys.

When I had passed the board all right I applied to my old employer Messrs. Hughes & Co. Menai Bridge for a situation as second mate which they could not then give me but offered me a berth as 3rd Mate on board Ship *Superior* then at Hamburgh loading and taking in German passengers for New York. I thankfully accepted this berth and once more took the old passage to Hull. But I had travelled too much of the world now to get astray on an English Railway so I got to Hull all right but had to stay there two or three days waiting for the boat and I fell in with the mate of *Superior* going to join her like myself.

When we joined the ship we found all as busy as possible taking in cargo & preparing bunks for the passengers of which it appears we were to take about 600 souls, and who came on board in good time and we started on the voyage· The German law is not so strict as ours with emigrants, for here they were all mixed, men & women & children with indeed no partition of any kind to separate them. Four people slept in one bunk. In one bunk four young men and in the next four young women with only a foot board a foot wide to separate them. They were almost all farming people and all country people, very quiet and jolly.

My duty as third mate kept me entirely engaged amongst the passengers, serving out provisions &c. and I got very friendly with them all. They were divided into messes about 30 in each so I could serve out provisions to each mess. The very first day out or indeed in the river one poor woman died and was taken ashore at Crookshaven.[32]

[32] Finished loading and left Hamburg 9 May, 1866, sailed Cuxhaven 13 May, 1866.

We had been out about two weeks when the small pox broke out on board and in a week's time there were about 150 laying up with it and three or four died. It was a fearful sight as we could not separate them, but God be praised we got to New York all right, but had to lay in quarantine for a week, the sick being taken ashore to the hospital.[33] We had very good times of it here, plenty of music and dancing according to the ways of Germans. But although there were not about half of them of that nation for there were almost every country in Europe represented amongst them. We found it very lonesome after them and when all the sailors ran away we were left all to ourselves.

New York is a very large place, but you will be able to learn more about it in a geography book than I could tell you. We discharged our cargo and took in ballast. Shipped new hands and sailed for for St. Johns & N.B.

On the passage the cook was taken bad with diarrhoea, which again caused us to be put in quarantine at St. Johns, and when the cook died we had to Whitewash the ship inside all over and then allowed to enter the port, the body of the cook having been buried on a small island outside, the ship's crew having to dig a grave & bury it there· All our crew ran away here again. Indeed it is or it was then the common practice of every crew to run away in these ports.

We layed here about three weeks in discharging ballast and taking in a cargo of deals for Liverpool. After loading and shipping fresh crews we again started for home,[34] but coming on very thick & a fresh contrary wind we lost ourselves & got on a reef, when she knocked a few times and sailed over it, but she leaked a good deal afterwards. However, we got to L'pool all right & paid off crew.[35] I stayed by the ship working by the day, but somehow by not having friends and influence I did

[33] For discussion of quarantine regulations and emigrant problems, *Parl. Papers*, 1860, LX 529-30. The *Superior* arrived New York 14 June, 1866, and remained there until 17 July, 1866, whence she sailed for St. John's, arriving 30 July.
[34] Sailed 31 August, 1866.
[35] Arrived 26 September, 1866.

not get the berth of second mate of her although the old one (my old friend Capt. Roberts, Bangor) was promoted mate of her. But I could not afford to leave her as I had my mother depending on me for every cent, and the owners promising me the very next vacancy so I stayed by the ship to tow round to Cardiff,[36] where I left her to go second mate of Ship *Northumberland* loading coals for Montevideo. She belonged to same firm as *Superior*.[37] We had a long passage out and when close to river Plate lost our rudder in a gale of wind and now you must know that to lose a rudder is indeed a sad thing for nothing can be done with a ship without a rudder. However, being not far from our destination we got a kind of a temporary affair fixed which enabled us to manage her safely into port, and here we found a great deal of trouble to get another fixed on account of heavy sea which always is experienced in an open bay like this. The gudgeons were gone but I suppose to make you understand I will call them hinges where the rudder works on. Well the low one of these was gone and only 4 feet from the bottom of the ship. To get a big ship up that high is very hard, as an ordinary ship of her size say from 1000 to 1400 tons never draw less than about 12 feet, so you will understand that it was a great job to put ballast in one end to lift the other nearly out of the water, especially in an open roadstead like that, for there is no dock there as we have in England. We had divers from British Man of War but water was too muddy for them to see to work. However we got all fixed and a new rudder and sand ballast bound to Callao. I found at Montevideo none

---

[36] The *Superior* left Liverpool on 20 October and arrived Cardiff 24 October, 1866.
[37] The first *Northumberland* owned by the Davies family was a 377 ton barque built at Prince Edward Island in 1840; she was sold in 1849 after her voyage from Menai Bridge to New Orleans and back to Galway. This second *Northumberland* was a 1,168 ton vessel built at Miramichi in 1864, 181/37/24; in *Lloyd's Register,* 1866-7, her master is named Humphreys. According to the Mercantile Navy List 1867 she was owned by Robert Davies, Bodlondeb, Caernarvonshire, but curiously she is not entered in the Sailings Book (U.C.N.W. Bangor MSS. 3531) with all the other vessels and it may be that Robert Davies operated her independently of the firm's other vessels. In the 1868/9 *Lloyd's Register* there is a note against her name 'wrecked' and she does not again appear in the Register.

of my old friends although I found many I have no acquaintance with. The Hotel I had worked in I found converted into several dwelling houses and many other alterations in the neighbourhood.

When all was ready we sailed for Callao, Peru, and where we arrived after a very smart passage. This was my first voyage round Cape Horn which is the Southernmost part of America and in the 56th South Latitude & consequently very cold. It is also considered a very stormy locality which I can well answer for having passed it many times since both out and home. Cape Horn itself is on an Island, The Hermit Sd.[38] The main land is called Tierra Del Fuego and peopled by savages, but now most of the tribes are quite harmless, but still as savage in their way of living as ever although so cold they have but little clothing, often nothing at all, neither men or women. They do not build houses or even tents, merely making a kind of an arbour of branches and their only covering when they have any is a sealskin or otter skin just hove over the shoulders. Mrs. Brasey in the voyage of the *Sunbeam* mentions a canoe coming alongside with a man, a boy and a woman in it who parted with every rag of skin they had for tobacco &c.

They are of a very dirty habit, never wash themselves and live on fish, seals & birds or anything that comes in their way. There was once a missionary ship amongst them the *Allan Gardiner* but they surprised and murdered all on board except the cook. The vessel is now owned by a man in the Falkland Islands who often goes over to T.D. Fuego with her for a cargo of small fir trees for sheep hurdles, so I believe now there are only a few savage tribes which a white man cannot deal with. It's a wonderful thing that they do not migrate to the northward to Patagonia[39] as there is only a narrow straits between, the Straits of Magellan, but I suppose they like this kind of life & weather and may be are afraid of the Patagonians who are reckoned the biggest men in the world while the Tierra del

[38] Is. Hermite.
[39] Attempts had been made by Welsh emigrants to settle in Patagonia during the period, but curiously Thomas, writing in 1883, does not mention this.

Fuegians are of a very low stature. It's wonderful how different races like these are scattered over the world. Where did they come from? How did they get to this cold dreary corner of the earth and how did they settle there? They are reckoned about the most miserable and lowest of the human race except the old natives of Australia who are in intellect very little superior to the monkey. They have not sense or understanding to build a house for themselves, no[r] have they left a particle of anything as a monument of their lives to future generations except a heap of rubbish & shells which they leave as a common midden whenever they halt for any time. I have never heard of their having any kind of religion whatever.

But we must not forget that God made them as well as us and we ought to be more thankful for a greater share of common sense and more of the things of this world, for when God had finished the world and all therein the testimony of the Bible is 'And God saw everything that he had made and behold it was very good', and who or what are we to find fault with His works.

(so much for Tierra del Fuego)

To resume my story we arrived in Callao after a very good passage, 33 days I think. Callao is the chief seaport of Peru. Lima is about 8 miles inland and of course Callao is the mart for all foreign goods.

The weather on this coast is no doubt the finest in the world. It never blows hard here nor does it ever rain here. The weather is mild, neither too hot nor cold. Always in the night it's just cool enough for a person to require a blanket to sleep under. All kind of fruits grows here but most of it is brought here from neighbouring states : beef, potatoes, cabbages &c almost all comes from Chile also the flour &c. The people are too lazy to cultivate their land. This country was once peopled by a race of Indians called the Incas and by the forts &c. left after them is an evidence that they were far advanced in civilisation. The Spaniards conquered them & got a fine booty of gold and silver and tyrannized over them that the race was exterminated and what real Peruvians there are now are at the back of the

71

mountains, but the old Incas are no more. The Spaniards kept the country as well as Chile under their government till about the beginning of this century when they gained their independence, but they are a most corrupted countries even now. Might triumphs over right, money will do anything here, murder or buy off a murderer. Callao bay is formed by a large Island about 10 miles long called San Lorenzo and the old tradition is that it rose from the sea in an earthquake in one night. A fisherman out fishing found himself next morning on top of an Island 800 feet high, so it was called after his name. Whether true or not I cannot say (it sounds dusty). However without the Island Callao would be a very bad harbour, having no shelter at all. I ought to have mentioned that the wind is always from S. East here (S.E. trades).

Callao was then the great centre of the guano which was got on Chincha Islands 90 miles South of Callao and about 15 miles from the Mainland. There were three Islands 'North', 'Middle' and 'South' Islands.

Guano is a strong manure about 20 per cent of the best being ammonia which caused it to be very strong, so strong indeed that a person could not stay in the hold more than two or three minutes, and sometimes in the morning when there was no wind it was like putting one's nose in a smelling bottle. It was a fearful work to turn it in the ship's hold. I have seen men's noses bleed through it·

To give you some idea how the guano is on the Island, you must just think of a high barren Island and covered over about 100 feet deep of soil (or guano). Where it was very thick it was worked in terraces of 20 or thirty feet each and it was nearly as hard as cutting a road on the land, powder & dynamite being often used to blast it. Running against the bank were railway wagons which being filled were pulled away by mules to the cliff where it was emptied into large troughs, perhaps 150 feet often more above the Sea. From here were canvas sheets rigged to convey it down to ship boats & lighters.

...away... *emptied into large troughs perhaps 150 feet often more above the sea. From here were Canvas Shuts rigged to convey it down to ship boats & lighters*

guano

rocks

It was a fearful work to go under these shoots in rough weather, for soon as the boat was fast a trap door would be opened which let the guano down so fast and at such a rate that they would [fill] a twenty ton launch in few minutes, and the dust was that thick that nothing could be seen, and the only way to know when the lighter was full would be by putting the hand outside and feel the water. But this was not the only danger, for besides the suffocating nature of guano a big sea might come in & smash the tackles which would be the means of the lighter dashing to pieces in a few minutes against the high rocks, and the chance of life would be small for the dust would be that dense that no one in the offing could see those under the shoots. And I do not think I am saying too much to say that thousands were drowned at Chincha Island by this means and in swamping on their way to the ships. I have myself been witness of lighters dashing to pieces against the rock and crew lost. Some shoots were worse than others according how they would be exposed to wind and sea. It was a regular competition work also, for the first launch under in the morning would get first load and it was common for launches to be kept under all night and very often dashed to pieces in the night for the heavy swell raises very sudden and at full & change of the moon it is often too rough to load up at all. But they would hardly ever knock off for good till some launches were lost & lives as well. They generally commenced work at 4.30 or 5 a.m. and left off at same hour P.M. The guano was mostly winched up from lighters to the ships, & some passing it up in baskets.

The workmen on the island were all Chinamen, brought to Peru to make their fortunes they thought, but were nothing better than slaves indeed they were slaves for seven years when

73

they were reckoned free, but very very few lived to see the 7 years ended. They were very badly used. I often saw them getting whipped with a horse whip far worse than a horse is allowed to be whipped in England. Now indeed I have often seen it done out of bravado & with no earthly need or excuse when we would stroll up to see the working, only just to show the tyranny of one man over the other. It was pitiful to hear the poor fellows yelling. These gaffers were generally their own countrymen, promoted, and of course they must show what they excelled in, namely cruelty. My dear child, I did not at first intend to write all this but it may be instructive to you & interesting.

When the Chinee emigration was put a stop to they had to get labourers elsewhere which they got by employing free Chinamen and any other labourers, but at a higher wages than the slaves, & when the slaves had all served their seven years, they were most induced to stay at so much per day, which was quite a fortune to them, and having been used to slavery for seven years the labour was only like play to them. When free Chilean labourers were also introduced, as hard a set of rascals as ever walked, but would work well for a month out of pure necessity but after the pay at the end of the month these would be only drinking and fighting for a week after. The Peruvian is too lazy & proud to work in guano. In fact anything but work, it did not matter how mean or degrading the job as long as there was no sweating of the brow about it.

A ship then chartered for guano had to go to Callao to get surveyed &c. Her sides would be overhauled if she required caulking and pumps sealed for 24 hours to see that she made no water, & such formalities had to be gone through as if her cargo were to be gold & passengers. When all these were strictly gone through, including a mark on her side being the depth she was to be loaded to, she would then be deemed fit to load guano and a permit accordingly given the captain to take with him to the Island. The time for loading was 90 days and after that had to go to Callao again to be again surveyed &c. But after the guano on Chinchas has finished a ship was often latterly always despatched home from loading port, which gave the official at the place a chance of making few dollars by allowing a ship to load a little deeper than the mark &c.[40]

There has been a great deal of argument about guano, what it is. Some say rotten stones, others that it was the bottom of the sea & the Island, volcanic. But the true and now acknowledged fact is that it is birds' dung, dead seals, dead birds &c. When we consider the thousands of years it has been accumulating & the millions of birds, mostly boobies & pelicans that live on it and the millions of seals about these Islands and which always crawls up on land as high as they can to die, it will not be incredible. I have seen birds' eggs dug out 40 feet from the surface and bird & seal bone are often met with in the very heart of it, and as it never rains there it get time to dry & accumulate. On these guano Islands there is nothing at all growing, not a blade of grass. So all the provisions is brought from the main land, even water as there is not a drop of water on any guano Islands. Indeed on the main land of Peru there are large tracts of land along the seashore without a drop of water nor consequently a blade of grass. All on the Island are on allowance of water and all the ships had to contribute or pay for water to the Island at the rate of a ——* per 100 tons register. Cattle were brought over alive and killed on the Island.

We loaded here with the *Northumberland* went back to Callao and then sailed for home. Made rather a long passage. Called at Queenstown for orders which we got outside for New Castle where we also arrived all well, which terminated the voyage and my first as second officer. We arrived in the Tyne[41] a day before Christmas but I am sorry to say our watchman went to sleep instead of watching our *plumduff* and the consequence was the pudding got fast to the boiler and got burnt, which in a great measure spoiled our dinner, but still I enjoyed

---

* Indecipherable.

[40] The overloading of sailing ships to which Thomas has scattered allusions throughout his narrative was a matter of grave concern to all who cared for safety at sea during this period, and many of the losses of ships by Welsh companies were directly attributable to this practice.

[41] *Lloyd's List,* 24 December, 1867, *Northumberland,* Humphreys, ma., arrived from Callao. This is the only date for this voyage I have been able to trace.

myself as we were now in England and could take a ramble on shore after dinner. After getting my discharge I went home and after a while to school at Carnarvon and afterwards to Liverpool to pass my examination as first mate which I did the second time, having failed the first time, and when I got through I went home, but first calling at Menai Bridge to apply for a berth again, and I believe the very next day at home had a letter from these gentlemen offering me a berth as second officer of my old ship *Superior* which I thankfully accepted. She was at London loading a general cargo and passengers for Melbourne[42] and in a few days I joined her.

She took in a cargo of manufactured iron of all kinds. Also beer, brandy, porter, pianos, hops, salt &c. including 15 tons of powder. This last named we took on board in the river below Gravesend, all fires on board being put out when this is taken in. We had about 50 steerage and one cabin passenger. We arrived out right and all well but made a rather long passage and latter part of it extremely rough, the ship being loaded far too deep. We discharged our cargo at Sandridge just below Melbourne. I shall not attempt to say anything about Melbourne as in any modern geography you will learn all about it in a far clearer manner than I can write but I may add that I liked it very much. From Melbourne we went in ballast to Callao. By going East we were going round the world, for you know even at your age the world is round, so by sailing East from here we were going round the world. We made a quick passage of 35 days to Callao – which was considered very good. From Callao we went as before to Chincha Islands and loaded as before, coming as formerly to Callao to clear out. Had a fair

---

[42] *Superior* was one of 14 vessels entered outwards (date of entry 21 February) from the Port of London for Port Phillip, and Geelong in *Lloyd's List,* March 11, 1868. Her master was named Williams and the brokers Mackay. She sailed on 12 May arriving at Melbourne on 29 August, 1868. Leaving Melbourne on 3 October, she was at Callao 6 November, sailing six days later for Chinchas Island where she arrived on 18 November. They remained there until 13 February, 1869, sailing first for Callao and thence for home on 18 February. The *Superior* was at Queenstown by 2 June and arrived in the Port of London on 16 June, 1869.

passage home and got our orders at Queenstown for London where we arrived all well & safe· I may add that we spent our Christmas at Chinchas this year. In London all left except me. I stayed by her thinking this time to get a mate's berth but was again disappointed. Another man had her. When cargo was out I left her to go home on my holiday and did not join her again for three weeks and in the River Tyne where she had gone from London.[43] There was a new captain & a new mate on board. In fact I was the only old hand. The captain was my old captain of *Disraeli* and *John Davies*. Of course it was another that was in *Disraeli* when she was lost.

We loaded a cargo of coal here for Coquimbo in Chile and sailed with a fair wind but which soon came foul again. So we made a very long passage and I believe this was about the most miserable voyage I ever made.

The captain was always drunk when he could get drink. The mate was as great a scamp as ever when on board of a ship. The little principle he had was so little that I would defy all the microscopes in the world to find a trace of it. We lost an anchor outside the harbour.[44] We put 14 men in jail who would not work, all through the fool of a mate and no master to control.

Consul turned mate ashore and all hands went to work. But I for pity sake brought him aboard again on the quiet, but again soon as the men found he was interfering with the ship they all knocked off, went to jail where we left 14 of them. The captain was only as a child on board for he had undermined his constitution with drink that when he was even sober he was like a child. I had to do everything. Even the steward could not go to market for meat without getting drunk, so that job also came to my lot. I had to do all. And only for regard to this man for former kindness, and to my owners I owed a duty else I would

---

[43] The *Superior* sailed from London on 6 July, arriving in the Tyne on 8 July, and sailed thence for Coquimbo on 22 July, 1869. The name of her master is not given in the appropriate entry in *Lloyd's List* 24 July, 1869, but from Thomas's comments which follow it must have been Captain J. Williamson.

[44] Arriving at Coquimbo on 29 Noember, 1869, the *Superior* remained there until 14 January, 1870, when she sailed for Callao.

certainly have left her here. We at last and at great expense got her discharged and took in ballast, and a cattle merchant from Callao who was down here shipped about 50 head of cattle on board, sending a man to look after them. They were splendid animals but very wild and wicked. We had them on top of the ballast. By leaving so many men behind we were very short handed and no men to be got there. So we had only 5 men before the mast, but of course we were only to run down the trades and distance about 1500 miles. We arrived in Callao[45] all safe and as if we had a whole crew. I believe captain promised each man so many dollars extra so where there's will there's generally a way too. After survey &c. we left Callao for Guanape Islands for guano,[46] which were to the north of Callao, and taking with us several men to work as sailors to load the ship and be discharged on return to Callao. The guano on this island was not so strong as that on Chinchas but the weather was much worse, a thick fog setting in very often and the dampness making the guano slippery and nasty to work in. And although I saw men getting drowned here still I don't think it was so dangerous as at Chinchas except one shoot and no one would go there unless it was fine. But still I believe I never had a narrower escape under a shoot as I had here, but my tackles were good and held on else we would certainly have been dashed to pieces. As it was a boat towed us out half full of water. The Chinamen were very badly used here and often commited suicide. Everything was also much dearer here than at Chinchas. I saw two vessels on fire here, one an American the other Italian. I believe both were put on fire purposely to gain insurance.

After loading here we proceeded for Callao, but it was not so easy to get there from here as from Chinchas for we were now to the leeward of Callao 500 miles, so we had a head wind and a strong current against and I believe it took us of three weeks to beat to Callao,[47] after losing

---

[45] 24 January, 1870. *Lloyd's List* 18 March, 1870, gives date of arrival as 25 January, sailing 29 January after survey. The master is named Williamson.
[46] Arrived 2 February, 1870.
[47] Arrived 28 May, 1870.

78

great many sail for the trades was remarkably strong that time.

It was at Coquimbo I spent my Christmas this year.

We paid off our 'choulos' as they are called and shipped a fresh crew who came on board mad drunk & fought amongst themselves till morning and most of the following day, which was Sunday. Monday ship ready to sail but sailors refused to work as the boarding master had not given them enough out of their advance, for it was then a custom at Callao to get two and three months' advance of wages which was almost all pocketed by their boarding masters, which were the greatest scoundrels in existence, the very lowest scum of the lowest society. Some of these men had only left their previous ship the day before in these boarding masters' boats. Were on shore one night blind drunk, next day put on board of *Superior* and three months advance and all the sailor got of these would be plenty of cheap stuff to get drunk, a pound of tobacco, a bar of soap and maybe a pair of cheap shoes.

The wages at Callao was from four to five pounds a month, so these men gave the boarding-master 12 or fifteen pound for taking him from his ship & whence he often left a lot of wages besides.

It's surprising that there are such fools in the world, but this is nothing new for a sailor to do. We have always in such ports as Callao to keep a constant watch that the men don't run away in a runner's boat which are always prowling about. I have seen good decent men do it often. However it is that the evil one gets such an upper [hand] over men puzzles me. Same man will do it over & over again, leave a good ship and wages behind after having been in her for months, get on shore to a boarding house for few days. Most of that time he is blind drunk and then is shipped on board some 'hell afloat' as the wild American ships used to be called, where a man was drove about and treated worse than dogs, and for all this he leaves to the boarding master his advance of wages of 12 to 15 pounds. But things are geting a little better now for respectable men don't so often run away now as formerly, and as there are less men running away there are also less boarding masters and runners. A runner is the man or two generally which goes to steal the men from ships and in Callao they got from their master, the boarding master, 15 dollars for every man brought to the house.

These men we had would not work but the boarding masters and runners came off and put the ship underweigh and came out with us outside the harbour and then they rushed on the men that would not work and beat them unmercifully, dragging them out on deck, and swore if the ship came back on account of them not working they would murder every one of them. So those that could went to work while some of them layed up for weeks from the effects of beating they had. But my dear child to put an end to this miserable and disgusting voyage let me just add that we got home all right,[48] and had our orders at Queenstown for London again, where I was indeed glad to see her moored, and where I left her. The owner promised me a mate's berth this time, so I went home to wait and recruit [sic] after this great voyage.[49]

And I must acknowledge the great mercies of God towards me this voyage, for indeed it was through this mercy we were spared, for often were we close to the land of which no one had any idea of. The captain was drunk half the time & the mate was rejoicing in same, but had not the sense to see the danger.

To Thee Oh Merciful God we owe our safety and preservation that voyage. This was my last voyage in *Superior* and I look to the time I served in her with horror or as some frightful dream. She always leaked badly since that time she got on the reef in the Bay of Lundy as noted in a previous page. There were different captains in her each voyage viz : 'Williams'

'Davies'

'Williamson'

After staying home few weeks I received a letter from Hughes & Co. offering me a chief mate's berth on board the *Minnehaha* which I of course accepted and joined her at Cardiff where [she]

[48] Sailed Callao 6 June, 1870, arrived off Kinsale 5 September, Victoria Dock, London, 9 September, 1870. The clerks in the Davies office at Menai Bridge recorded this voyage as just another line in the Sailings Book, 14 months 23 days duration.
[49] Discharged 29 September, 1870.

was loading coal for Callao. We made a very quick passage out, especially for her as she was a very slow sailer.[50] After discharging cargo and taking in ballast we sailed for Guanape Islands again, but as I was now mate I did not have to go in the launches for that is always the work of the 2nd mate. After loading and without any mishap we sailed straight for home, not having to go to Callao to clear out. We made a fair passage home to Falmouth where we got orders for Hamburgh, where we also arrived all well and paid off the crew, myself of course staying by the ship till all cargo was out and arrived all safe and well.[51]

Hamburgh as you know is on the river Elbe and a long way up. There are some shallows in the river that loaded ships can't get over, so have to lighten at a place lower down. Ships drawing over 17 feet can't go up to Hamburgh without lightening, but that does not take long for a gang of men comes down in the lighters and at the rate of discharging from 100 to 200 tons per day they soon lighten a ship.

[50] The *Minnehaha*, a wooden ship, 845 tons, built New Brunswick 1857, 158/33.7/22.4, was commanded in 1870/71 by H. Roberts. *Lloyd's Register* 1871/2. She commenced loading coal at Cardiff on 17 October and had completed by 22 October, 1870. She then sailed on 1 November arriving Callao 31 January, 1871.

[51] 18 March, 1871. Arrived Guanape two days later and, having loaded, sailed again 4 May, arriving Falmouth 8 September, sailed 9th for Hamburg, 23 September in the Elbe, 25 September commenced discharging, finished 17 October, 1871. Total length of voyage 13 months 2 days, 332 days at sea. Thomas had reason to be pleased with this voyage for the clerks in the Menai Bridge office duly noted the following times for the company's vessels on similar voyages to the Guano island during 1870/71.

Ship	To	Time at Sea	Total Length of Voyage
Glenmonarch	Macabi, Callao, Guanape	456	16 months 16 days
Curlew	Callao, Macabi	388	14 months 25 days
British Princess	Callao, Macabi	339	13 months 8 days
True Briton	Callao, Ballestas	410	15 months 16 days
British Empire	Callao, Ballestas	391	15 months 15 days
Caspian	Callao, Ballestas	391	15 months 23 days
Ajmeer	Callao, Guanape	375	14 months 27 days
Minnehaha	Callao, Guanape	332	13 months 2 days
Superior	Callao, Guanape	355	16 months 4 days
Canute	Callaõ, Ballestas	334	12 months 16 days
Magnificent	Callao, Guanape	348	14 months 28 days

Lloyd's List 15 March, 1871, indicates that the *Ajmeer, British Princess* and *Curlew* were at Callao together.

There are no docks at Hamburgh and ships have to lay in the river moored to dolphins, which are a number of posts drove into the ground and then fastened together in squares. About 200 posts forms one dolphin. Hamburgh is a large place and was a free state till lately when all these states were attached to Prussia and then all combined are called the German Empire. Things were very cheap here when it was a free state, but quite different now for Germany has according to her size and greatness to keep a large army on foot which costs money, and to obtain money there must be taxes and to pay taxes, articles must raise in price. Hamburgh was one time indeed till few years ago divided by a wall and a gate. One side of it was the state of Hamburgh while the other was a part of Denmark, and different languages were spoken on each side of this boundary. This gate was closed at a certain hour of the evening, and guards always keep guard. But in a war between Prussia & Denmark, the Prussians gained the day and got this land of Schleswig Holstein. So both Hamburgh & Altona, which was the name of the Danish part of the town, passed into the hand of the Emperor of Germany (then King of Prussia).

When you learn to read you must read all these histories in a good geography for there is nothing that looks worse in a[n] educated person than ignorance of Geography.

But mind at the same time on no account to forget or neglect the history of the Bible. Let that always have the preference for it gives you the history both of this world and the world to come. Passed this Christmas off R. Plate. From Cardiff[52] I went home for my holidays and then again joined the ship and after taking in a cargo of coals sailed for Callao again, where we arrived all safe and well. After discharging cargo & take in ballast, we sailed for Guanape, loaded there and sailed direct for Antwerp, where we arrived after a good passage.

[52] The *Minnehaha* sailed from Hamburg 19 October, arrived Cardiff 4 November where she commenced loading on 11 November and completed 24 November. On 25 November, 1871, the *Minnehaha* sailed for Callao (in *Lloyd's List,* Tuesday, 28th November, her master's name is Roberts), and arrived there on 14 March, 1872. She sailed from Callao on 25 April, arriving Guanape 28 April, and remained there loading till 15 June when she sailed for Antwerp, arriving 2 October, 1872.

Passed this year's Christmas on passage out about Equator. I had been now two voyages as first mate, so the owner let me leave her at Antwerp to go home to School and pass for master. I stayed home a while then went to Liverpool where after two failures I passed as master and then I went home, and when home this time I first met your good mother. It was a curious thing for it was the first time I had been in the house of Glynn for years, but ever after I always went there & lately by invitation of Mr. Wynn. The ship went from Antwerp to the Tyne (Newcastle)[53] which I again joined her as mate and it was here I believe I got the first letter from my dear Kate, and we corresponded ever after. We loaded coals here for Callao again but with another captain. We made a long passage out & spent one Christmas in the Channel going out and another outside the Channel coming home, viz. 1873. We went from Callao to Guanapes again, loaded, and arrived in Falmouth all right, where we got our orders for Dublin.[54]

Sailed from Falmouth with a strong breeze from N.W. and we had on board a channel pilot by the name of Volke. All went well till Saturday night when the wind came fair but with very thick weather and we were then shaping a course between Scilly Islands and the Wolf rock which lay right in middle of channel. About two a.m. Sunday, Jan. 18th, 1874 we saw the loom of a light which we made out to be St. Agnes on the Scilly Islands. Immediately after the man on lookout calls out 'land ahead', but it was too near to do anything but try to get boats out for the ship was running at the rate of 8 knots an hour when she struck and almost immediately sank till Mizen top was awash aft and bowsprit forward.

I myself was in the act of turning up a boat when a big sea washed it out of my hands, but I made a jump and got on the bottom of it, for it was bottom up, and where I clung while the

[53] She sailed on 4 November from Antwerp, was reported off West Kapelle (Walcheren) on 5 November, and arrived at Shields, 12 November, where she commenced loading on 27 November. Thomas therefore rejoined her towards the end of November or the beginning of December; she had finished loading by 5 December and sailed on 12 December, 1872.
[54] She did not reach Callao till 12 May, 1873, arrived Guanape 17 June, and sailed again on 20 September. She arrived off Falmouth 14 January, 1874, and sailed on 16 January, and was wrecked on 18 January, 1874.

boat went out. But another wave brought it against main rigging where I held on and climbed up on topsail yard.

When we got a little composed I found there were ten of us saved and clinging to different masts, but eventually all came to me on topsail yard and I found I was the only one from aft that was saved unless the captain could get on the rocks for I found he had swum from mizen top for the shore but he was never seen again. It was bitterly cold on the mast head as we had neither shoes or jacket and some only a shirt & drawers. We hailed the shore all together, but there was no answer & it had now cleared up fine and we could see that the ship's bows were nearly right against the cliffs, but the sea was breaking all round. About 7 a.m. we thought the sea did not break so much forward so we slided down top gallant stay to the foremast, a hard job at best of times but doubly so when half frozen & weary, but we got on the fore all right and there down the jib stay on jiboom and from where through the mercy of God we could swing on a rock and climb up the cliff and we were safe· First thing we did was to kneel down and offer thanks to God for our wonderful delivery. Then we ran about to warm ourselves and eventually found a path which we followed and as the day was dawning we saw the town just below us where we got before any one was astir. But in a few minutes all the inhabitants were astir. We got to a public house and had a good stiff glass of rum which gave us a little warmth. I left the men here and again went to the wreck and as the captain was lost I was the man in charge and so in conjunction with receiver of wreck put men on to save what could be, and they saved some of the sails and few things washing ashore. Next day in answer to my telegram the owners told me to stay there and look after their interest, which I did.[55]

[55] *Lloyd's List*, 20 January, 1874: Scilly, 11.15 a.m., 18 January. The *Minnehaha*, Jones, from Callao and Falmouth for Dublin, struck on Peninis Head, south part of St. Mary's, this morning at 2 o'clock under full sail; master, Falmouth pilot and eight men drowned; mate and eight men saved; ship lies with jibboom over rocks; forecastle in wash; hull nearly under water, at low water; ship will soon break up. Wind W. fresh, thick. 19 January, the masts of the *Minnehaha* are still standing but the ship and cargo will be totally lost. Wind today W. strong and dirty. 20 January, masts of *Minnehaha* all went yesterday, her hull is fast breaking up; no portion is visible at low water.

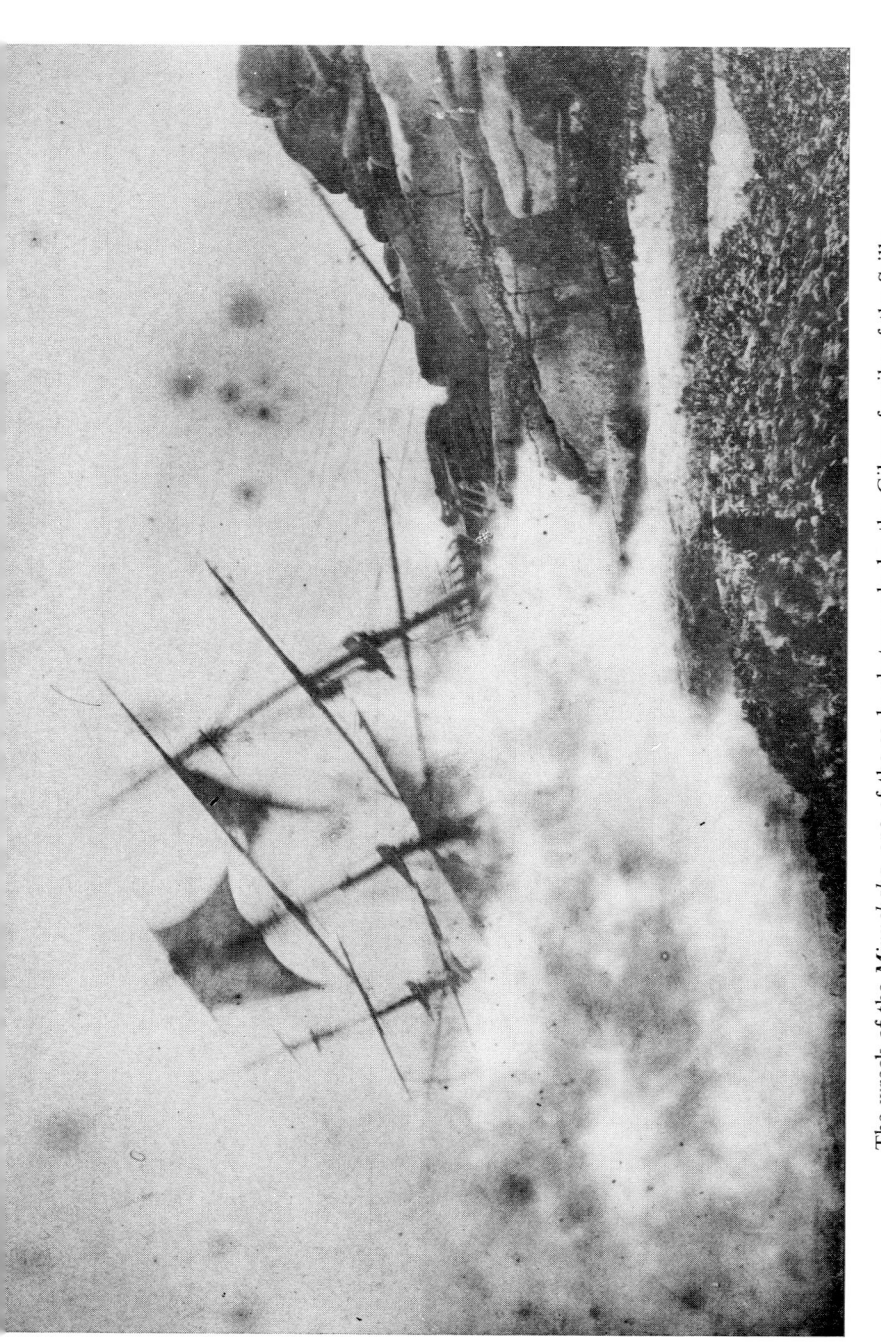

The wreck of the *Minnehaha*, one of the early photographs by the Gibson family of the Scilly Isles. Captain Thomas has written on the back of the original copy: 'Wreck of the ship *Minnehaha* of Liverpool on St. Mary's Scilly, January 18th 1874 on her passage from Falmouth to Dublin by which ten hands were lost and ten saved'.

I believe I stayed there about a month and went to Penzance to give evidence on the Board of Trade enquiry there.[56] Saved out of the wreck about £300. When I came home I called at Menai Bridge and saw the owners who were very kind and promised me a ship the first vacancy, but would employ me ashore for awhile to look after their ships with the overlookers.

And after looking in Cardiff *Curlew* I was sent to London to look after *Ajmeer* and *Conway Castle* and finally sent to

---

[56] The court of enquiry was held at Penzance before F. Boase and H. C. York, J.P.s, assisted by Captain H. Harris and Vice-Admiral C. G. E. Patey as nautical assessors. Their report stated that: 'The *Minnehaha* arrived safely on 14 Jan. 1874 with a cargo of guano from Callao, and having received orders to proceed to Dublin sailed again on 16th having taken on board a person named David Volke in the capacity of pilot. The weather appeared to have been moderate with the wind at N.W. At 4 a.m. on the 17th the Lizard Lights bore N.E. by N. at a distance of 20 miles. The ship was tacked to the Westward and made a W.S.W. course till 4 p.m. When she was again tacked to the Northward, and stood upon a N. to N.N.E. course till 3.30 a.m. on the 18th when she struck upon Penninis Head, and became a total wreck, the master, pilot, and eight of the crew being drowned. The remainder of the crew, ten in number, took refuge in the top and escaped from the jibboom when daylight broke.

The court were of the opinion that the vessel was lost through neglect of the lead. The weather was represented as very thick for some time before the casualty and the ship had been heading for 11 hours prior to stranding down upon the land. No land was seen after the Lizzard was lost sight of on the morning of the 17th and no sight had been obtained from either latitude or longtitude. Under these circumstances the court considered the omission to take a cast of the lead was most reprehensible and was doubtless the sole cause of the deplorable loss of life that occurred by the wreck.' *Parl. Papers,* 1875, LXX. 362. In John Fowles's admirable collection of the photographs of the Gibson family of Scilly, there is a photograph of the wreck of the *Minnehaha* and the story (possibly apocryphal) that the master called out, as he tied a rope round his middle and prepared to jump into the waves, 'Follow me and I will save you all.' Robert Thomas, who could not swim, and those who clung to the rigging were the only ones saved. J. Fowles, *Shipwreck* (Kenneth Allsop Memorial Trust).

Liverpool to take charge of *Glentilt* as master.[57] This was in
May 1874. I went from London to Liverpool to join *Glentilt*
and I found her in the London Graving Dock undergoing
extensive repairs.[58] After which we took in ballast and proceeded
out to sail to Cardiff but coming to blow I held on the tug till
he got me into Holyhead where we laid for a week, wind
blowing a gale from South all the time.[59]

From Holyhead Robert Thomas wrote to Catherine Jameson,
his future wife:

Holyhead Harbour
July 3rd 1874

My dear Jameson
   Sorry to have been so long without writing to you but
the heading of this will explain most of the fault.
   I left L'pool at midnight Tuesday night in tow of a
steamer. Wednesday morning came on to blow very hard
and through strong winds and very dirty weather we
reached here in the afternoon as we could not get any
farther, and you may be sure that I am very glad that
we are here now as it is blowing very hard. I have not
been ashore yet, nor have I any message there as I have a

[57] The *Curlew*, a wooden ship, 1,224 tons, 188.5/36.8/23.9, built in Quebec
in 1867, had put into Falmouth, damaged, on 20 December, 1873, after
a voyage from the guano islands, and had finally discharged her cargo
at Antwerp in mid February, 1874. She was in Cardiff loading from
5 March to 10 April, 1874, when she sailed for Rio and San Francisco.
The *Ajmeer*, wooden ship, 1,163 tons, 189.2/37.9/23, built in 1861 at
St. John, had finished discharging her cargo on 19 May, 1874, and
sailed from London 27 May for Shields whence she sailed again on
12 July for Rio and Callao. The *Conway Castle*, a 1,299 ton wooden
ship, 188.6/38.3/24, built New Brunswick in 1866, finished discharging
her cargo in London on 8 June, 1874, and sailed the next day for
Cardiff where she arrived 16 June, 1874, and loaded coal again for
Callao, sailing on 31 July, a day after Robert Thomas left in his new
command, the *Glentilt*.
[58] The *Glentilt*, a wooden ship, 991 tons, built Quebec in 1865, and
according to the Mercantile Navy List she was owned by Robert
Davies, Bodlondeb, Caernarvonshire. She had been built in Quebec
in 1865, 170.9/35/22.9, *Lloyd's Register*, 1874-5.
[59] *Glentilt* had completed discharging her cargo on 23 April, sailed from
Liverpool on 30 June and put in to Holyhead on 1 July. Here she
remained until 6 July: *Lloyd's List*, Thursday, July 2, reported, 'It is
blowing a gale from SSW at Holyhead', and on 3 July communications
between Liverpool and Holyhead were reported 'interrupted'. The
Glentilt arrived Cardiff 12 July, 1874.

boat hired for attending the ship at 10/- per day. This is rather a poor beginning for me in my new capacity, but can't be helped. I am glad to hear you like Brighton, it seems you like everywhere better than Llandwrog, also glad to hear Miss Emily is to be spliced. I wish her success and happiness. It's time more of you about Glynn were married. Hoping you are well and still enjoying yourself.

I remain with kind regards,

Yours &c.

Robert Thomas

Ship *Glentilt*

P.S. I don't know when I shall be able to post this but shall do so if possible tomorrow. I am writing it today ready as the boat does not stay any time. Sorry you have no friend at Bristol or Cardiff. Please write with this address but goodness knows when I shall get away from here. Anyhow, write beginning next week. If the wind comes fair I shall only be about 2 days going down to Cardiff.

<table>
<tr><td></td><td>R. Thomas</td></tr>
<tr><td></td><td>Ship *Glentilt*</td></tr>
<tr><td>goodnight</td><td>4 Louisa Street,</td></tr>
<tr><td></td><td>Cardiff.</td></tr>
</table>

When it moderated I sailed and in a day or two got into Cardiff where we loaded smelting coal and coke for Coquimbo.[60] All went on well until the ship commenced to leak, but we still got on all right till off C. Horn when the rudder head split & of little good for it was damaged so much that we could not move the helm with it at times. This was a very serious case but we rigged some guys and tackles to help it and still kept on although bad weather and contrary winds. But one morning the mate came and told me the ship was on fire. I got out pretty smart and on going to the forehatch I found smoke coming up and by crawling on top of cargo we at last found a place by main hatch quite hot and from where apparently the smoke was coming, opened main hatch and hove some coal on deck, but smoke getting so thick we had to leave off and heave some tons of

---

[60] The loading of coal was completed by 29 July and the *Glentilt* sailed on 30 July, 1874.

Fire Insurance cases

I went from London to Liverpool to join Glentilt
and I found her in the Sandon Graving dock.
undergoing extensive repairs. after which we
got in ballast and proceeded out to sail to
Cardiff but coming to blow I held on the
tug till we got in link Holyhead. where we
laid for a week. blowing a gale from South
all the time. when it moderated I sailed
and in a day or two got in to Cardiff.
where we loaded smelting coal and coke for
Coquimbo all went on well untill the
ship commenced to leak but we still
got on all right till off C. Horn when
the rudder head split & of little good for
it was damaged so much that we could
not move the helm with it at times.
this was a very serious case. but we
rigged some guys and tackles to help it.
and still kept on although bad weather
and contrary winds. but one morning
the mate came and told me the ship
was on fire. I got out pretty smart
and on going to the forehatch I found
smoke coming up and by crawling
on top of cargo we at last found a
place by main hatch quite hot and
from where apparently the smoke was
coming. opened main hatch and hove
some coal on deck but smoke getting
so thick we had to leave off. and hove
some tins of water down and battened
down the hatches. next day no smoke

Extract from the 'Diary' 1874; voyage of the *Glentilt*, Cardiff to Coquimbo.

Easter Tuesday.   ☾ 6ʰ 30ᵐ A.M.   Easter Sittings begin

visible, and we were in hopes it was put-
out, but two days after it came on worse
than ever and gas which made every one
sick and next day had to abandon the
cabin and forecastle, and managed to
just get room enough to eat our meals
and some time lay down in the coal
locker and carpenters shop, on deck.
the men were one after another getting
insensible by laying within doors. where
the gas was like death itself.
so this, I deemed it prudent to look for
our lives, and so abandoned all idea
of holding on any longer. the Falkland
Islands being the nearest place where we
might get succour. we squared away and
before a gale of Westerly winds we soon
sighted the Falkland. I think it was on
the 5th day.
A ship could hardly be in a worse fix
leaking, on fire. and rudder gone.
we bored holes in the deck. above when
the fire was and worked at poring water
down there night and day. the water
coming up the pumps was quite warm
which enabled us to stand it better as
the weather was cold down south.
it was a fearfull thing to see the charred
timber coming up in pieces through
the pumps. the very ship we stood on
was burning away under our feet.
but by poring water down we kept the

Extract from the 'Diary' 1874; voyage of the *Glentilt*, Cardiff to Coquimbo.

water down and battened down the hatches. Next day no smoke visible and we were in hopes it was put out, but two days after it came on worse than ever, and gas, which made every one sick. And next day had to abandon the cabin and forecastle and managed to just get room enough to eat our meal and some time lay down in the coal locker and carpenter's shop on deck. The men were one after another getting insensible by laying within doors where the gas was like death itself. So this I deemed it prudent to look for our lives and so abandoned all idea of holding on any longer. The Falkland Islands being the nearest place where we might get succour, we squared away and before a Gale of Westerly winds we soon sighted the Falkland. I think it was on the 5th day.

A ship could hardly be in a worse fix, leaking, on fire and rudder gone. We bored holes in the deck above where the fire was and worked at pouring water down there night and day. The water coming up the pumps was quite warm which enabled us to stand it better as the weather was cold down south. It was a fearful thing to see the charred timber coming up in pieces through the pumps. The very ship we stood on was burning away under our feet, but by pouring water down we kept the fire in the bottom.

On the 16th day after the fire broke out we got into Port Stanley, Falkland,[61] where we scuttled her till there was 12 feet of water in the hold and this we kept in for three days. After discharging most of cargo into a hulk we found the ship badly burnt. A long piece of Kelson was burned and not far from heel of mainmast which would have caused the mast to go if it had burned few inches more.

I went to Montevideo myself, leaving the ship in charge of the mate. At Montevideo I wired the owners but Capt. Jermain our overlooker arrived and we decided to charter two smaller vessels to take cargo on to destination, and Captain Jermain came back with me, and after discharging all the cargo to the other ships we repaired the ship as well as could be done under the circumstances & without a graving dock, and decided to take

[61] Arrived 11 November, 1874, Falkland Islands.

her on to Callao,[62] as we had a very good charter of 75/- per ton, and where I arrived in 34 days.

I had wired my owners on arrival at the Falkland, which will account for Capt. Jermain being there at Montevideo so quick. From Callao we went to Point Lobos in Lat 21 South to load guano. This was my first cargo off main land. But on account of a dispute between charterer and the Government we had a very long delay, about 9 months, and a dreary place it was for nine month and everything very dear· But at last we got loaded and sailed for home and arrived in Falmouth all well where we got our orders for Hamburg, where I left her to join *British Princess*.

Before he left Point Lobos Robert Thomas wrote again to Catherine Jameson:

Point Lobos C. Peru
Augt. 3rd 1875

My dear Jameson,

Yours came to hand last Saturday. Many thanks for all the news. I am afraid you will have to be satisfied with less from me from this cursed and barren land. My dear Jameson I am extremely sorry to hear you have left old Glynn, but of course you know what was best for you and I sincerely hope that you will be comfortable in your *new home*. You said if you stayed longer at Glynn you should be as bad as Miss E. herself. Well if you thought that I would much rather come to see you to *even Scotland* than to Denbigh Asylum for it would grieve me greatly if I were to come home and not to have a chat with you. Do you remember the quiet walks and the old chat we used to have towards the hill, minding everybody's business *except our own*. I am in hope that we shall have a similar walk again.

I shall surely come to see you even to *Scotland* if the Guano Loading Company will ever give me a load and the Almighty to spare me to see the iron walls of old England again. I am sorry to tell you that there is no

[62] Sailed Falkland Islands 26 March, 1875, arrived Callao, 30 April.

prospect of getting away from here for some three months longer; therefore, please answer this again by return of mail and don't forget to enclose that card this time. This place is a new deposit and therefore they are very backward with the works. There are over 100 vessels here now, most of them empty like the *Glentilt*.

You will be surprised to hear that I am a great teetotler here now. Some Americans started a meeting, signing not to drink any spirits nor any intoxicating drink while on this coast. So the Welsh they started another and now every Welsh captain and most of the officers and many of their men signed this pledge and we hold a meeting every week. There are 15 Welsh ships here. Your humble servant is one of the conductors, but I would sign for only 6 months for you are aware that I have always been very steady and it's to benefit others here that I joined at all. Great good may it do them, I say. I hope you won't forget your Welsh there nor learn Gaelic. You must let me know which will be the best way for me to come there, but it will be time enough to do that when I arrive home. You never said anything about Miss Wynn in either of your letters. Is *my old friend* still with her? Do not forget to write me a long letter with all the news in your next, also *report of survey* of that *outlandish* place you are now in.

I was surprised to hear of the new arrivals at the Fort and the Garden house. Whatever was the matter with them? Perhaps it was a bet. *Does* the Ladies ever bet like that? I saw several very nice persons from Dumfries at Falkland. Perhaps when I come there I shall be able to trace their friends out. I suppose I can venture there without pistols or any murderous weapons.

If you do not hear from me again from here (for a letter might go astray), write to Falmouth, about Christmas. You may send as many as you please there, address

Captn. Thomas
Ship *Glentilt*
at Mr. Toms
till arrival of   Sailor & Draper
ship   Falmouth

I do not know why you should scold your Brother for getting married, the man had a right do as he liked. I hereby enclose a copy of our programme at the next meeting :

Temperance meeting on board ship *Malabar* Wed. evening at 7 p.m.

Conductors. Captn. Evans & Captn. Thomas

          Captn. Davies *Teresa* Chairman

1. Hymn & prayer by O. Roberts, *Glentilt*
2. Speech by Captn. Owen B. *India*
3. Song ('Come to the Mountains') *Teresa* choir
4. Speech by E. Evans *Glentilt*
5. Song ('Ash Grove') *Malabar* choir
6. Speech by Mr. Edwards *Dusty Miller*
7. Anthem ('Glory to God in the highest') *Teresa* choir
8. Song ('Gwendolen Pugh'), Capt. Thomas, *Glentilt*
9. Speech by Captn. Roberts, *Duke of Rothsey*
10. Song ('Annie Lizie') Miss Williams, *Eastern Light*
11. Address Captain Evans, *Malabar*
12. Hymn & prayer H. Williams, *Leonore**

          God Save the Queen.

And now my dear friend I must conclude with kind regards and best wishes and hoping you are enjoying the same.

          I remain
            sincerely yours
              Robert Thomas
                ship *Glentilt*

    R. Thomas
      Ship *Glentilt*
        Papellon de Pica
     care of Bryce Grace & Co.
         Callao, Peru
          S. America.

---

* The *Malabar* was one of the first of the large ships owned by William Thomas, Liverpool. She was built in 1874 in Quebec, 1,355 t, 206 × 36.7 × 22.5, and at this period, as a new ship, was commanded by Capt. David Evans of Nefyn who was later to become Thomas's Marine Superintendent, a man whom all the masters respected for his ability, honesty and integrity. According to the official report, *Parl. Pap.* 1888, xc, the *Malabar* was lost on a voyage from Cardiff to Rio de Janeiro. By that time her master was Capt. J. Griffiths, and neither he nor any of his crew of 23 were seen again after they had passed Lundy on 4 December 1886. The *Teresa* belonged to a London company, another large ship built in New Brunswick, with Capt. D. Davies, master, according to *Lloyd's Register* 1875-6. The *Eastern Light* and the *British*

Continued on next page.

My dear child perhaps a few remarks about the Falkland will be interesting. All the commerce here is in Ships in distress and hide & wool for they don't grow anything here except potatoes, which are always at about /2½ per lb. The Islands are overrun with cattle and although in a manner wild still they are all owned by different parties who kill them for the sake of the hide alone, for bringing the tallow and bones to port would not pay. But it's a great pity to see so much good beef wasted like this. The best beef or mutton can be had at 2½ to /3d per lb at Port Stanley. Fish are in abundance but meat being so cheap fish is not caught except on rare occasion.

It's a great country for sheep farming which thrives well. Wild geese are plentiful indeed. On leaving I had 50 wild geese hanging up after one day's shooting or half a day shooting with two guns. There are no roads nor of course any carriages for everybody owns a horse and ride every where.

They are a hardy breed of small horses and will go on a slow trot for very long distances. There is a great deal of peat land here which is very teacherous in some places the surface being under mined, but there is no danger when riding for the little horse looks out for these and will pick his own way to clear it. I have been on one occasion with a party out shooting about 30 mile from the settlement and came back loaded with game.

There is a Schooner trading between here and Montevideo making eight trips per annum, and they generally load two

Continued from previous page.

India had both been bought in 1873 by the company formed by Capt. Thomas Williams of Criccieth and W. Roberts, a ship store Liverpool Welshman. Both Williams and Roberts had been associated with James Baines of the famous Black Ball Line and had purchased some of his ships following the latter's financial downfall in the late 60s. (For further information on the Black Ball Line see M. K. Stammers's admirable study *The Passage Makers* (1978).) John Owen & Co., Caernarfon, were the owners of the *Dusty Miller,* a ship which was very well known among Welsh seamen, as was the barque *Duke of Rothesay,* which belonged to J. B. Jarrett's company, Nefyn. The ship *Leonore* was owned by W. Hughes & Co., whose address is given in *Lloyd's Register* as North and South Wales Bank, Caernarfon. She, too, had been built in North America; this was the decade in which there was a very considerable investment by North Wales and Liverpool Welsh shipping companies in large wooden North American built ships.

small trading barks with wool & hide every year. Most of the settlers are Scotch, all the Shepherds being Scotch.

All repairs to a ship can be done here above water but there are no graving docks, every thing of this kind is very expensive.

I stayed there from November to March and I can only say that it was a very happy time under the circumstances. The people are very good and homely. I spent one Christmas here and another at Point Lobos with the *Glentilt*.[63] This is the true account of my first voyage, long & disastrous throughout·

When I left the *Glentilt* which was for sale I went home by steamer to London. I called at Menai Bridge on my way home and found that the *British Princess* was almost ready to sail from Cardiff and that I could not have more than three days at home. And my poor dear sister Ellin died within four hours after my arrival home. She had been ill a long time, and she was praying all along to be spared to see me, which God granted for she was quite sensible to the last. She had seen much hardship and had toiled hard for her living as long as she could and I am certain a more unselfish woman never breathed. She was all heart and would share her last crust with anyone in need.

God rest her Soul.

My dear child my Kate your mother was then in Merionethshire with the ladies and then when I wired her that I had to go away in three days she came to Glynn for a day and so we were able to see one another. And we agreed to get married on my return off this voyage. I believe it was mutual love that brought us like this to agree to marry, for we were in a manner of speaking perfect strangers one to the other. They say marriages are ordained in heaven and I believe it was God's will to bring us together for I do not think either of us has ever had any occasion to regret our union.

---

[63] *Glentilt* sailed for Pabellon de Pica, 8 May, arriving 29 June, Point Lobos 30 June; remained Lobos from June till 29 January, 1876. Arrived off Falmouth 7 June, 1876, Gluckstadt 17 June, Hamburg, 26 June, 1876, and she had therefore been almost two years on this voyage.

[64] The *British Princess* sailed from Cardiff on 11 July, 1876. Thomas had thus had a very long and difficult voyage of nearly two years and had only been home for a few days before he set sail again for Callao.

95

I left home Sunday evening and arrived at Cardiff the following morning and found the *British Princess* was out in the roads & only waiting for me. So after signing some papers, bills &c. I went out to join her and sailed next morning with a cargo of coal for Callao. Made a good passage out of 95 days. Discharged there for the P.S.N. Co. Laid here over Christmas day and sailed for Huanillos to load guano & where I arrived in due time.[65] Huanillos is in Lat 22 South & near the border of Peru & Bolivia namely River Loa, a small stream but unfit to drink as it runs through saltpetre beds. Still I believe the fishermen sometimes are glad to get it. If it had been good it would have been a great blessing in this part for water is very dear all along the coast and what is obtainable is condensed water made at a great expense. Of course you must understand that condensed water is the steam of salt water made in large boilers full of salt water and the steam from this is let out through long pipes coiled in cold water to convert it into water which runs out by the pipe into large tanks and is a splendid water, very pure but to drink it is quite tastless.

Shipwrecked sailors on barren Island have been known to exist a long time by boiling salt water and spreading a shirt & bag &c. over the vessel to catch all the steam and then wrench same into a vessel. The steam from salt water is always the best of fresh water and chemists when experimenting with chemicals must have condensed waters for use for in that state alone it is pure. Well my dear child you must see therefore that water must be very dear here when you consider that all these boilers and coal &c. must be brought out from Europe at a great expense.

Huanillos is like Point Lobos on the main land and the guano is greatly mixed with stones which are to be accounted for the earthquakes which are so often felt on this coast, which causes the rocks to roll down off the high mountains close to the guano bed and rising almost perpendicular to 4 or 500 feet and every earthquake shakes some of these stones down which happening

[65] Arrived Callao 15 October, sailed thence on 28 December for Huanillos, where *British Princess* arrived 23 January, 1877.

for generations causes these stones to be found in the very heart of the guano beds. After being loaded I sailed for Falmouth for orders and arrived all well after a passage of 86 days.[66] It was two month after I left Huanillos that a great earthquake and a tidal wave visited this coast which drove great many ships ashore and great many were lost. It was a fearful time for those on shore, the rocks rolling down from the mountain on one side and a wave of 50 feet high on the other. And all the houses that were within that height from the water were washed away, all being of wood had at first shock of earthquake got on fire by the capsizing of lamps &c. When the wave broke in it carried away house & inhabitants, many of the houses still on fire. It looked like a floating town on fire. It will never be known how many were lost on this coast that time. Some of the ships were lost at their anchors by knocking one against the others but most of them parted their cables on the very first, some of which drifted out to sea while the others sank under the cliffs where they had hammered to pieces. It was in the night but there was no wind so that but very few of those belonging to ships were lost as they got in their boats. One of my owners' ships was lost there, a fine wooden vessel called the *Conway Castle*.[67] At Falmouth I got my orders for Browershaven in Holland where I arrived and discharged my cargo.[68]

After taking in ballast I sailed for Cardiff and two days after arrival[69] I went home and met your mother and your Antie Ceilia who it seems had travelled on same train as me from Menai Bridge. She was coming to our wedding. We took a car from Carnarvon to Glynllivon.

We got married on the 16 Augt. 1877, took our breakfast at Tynllan & afterwards to Carnarvon en route for Glasgow. The late Mr. Jones, Tynllan, my old schoolfellow, gave away your

---

[66] Sailed from Huanillos 10 March, arrived Falmouth, 6 June, 1877.
[67] Telegrams reporting the earthquake were published in *Lloyd's List* 19, 15 May, 8 June and fuller account 15 June, 1877. The *Conway Castle* was among 20 or so vessels reported as total losses, 40 others were damaged. The sea was said to have risen 60 feet in some places and Iquique was reported 'completely ruined'.
[68] Arrived Browershaven 16 June; discharged cargo 20 June, 1877, 340 days at sea, voyage 13 months 20 days, according to the Davies clerks.
[69] Arrived Cardiff 6 August, 1877. Home 8 August.

mother. Your Auntie Celly was the bridesmaid and my staunch old friend H. Jones, Nursery formerly, as best man. Our wedding party consisted of my brother Thomas and Sister Jane, my cousin Henry Jones and his (now wife) Polly Jones — also her brother and W. Roberts gardener, now forester at Glynn. All went very quiet and all came to Carnarvon & some even to Bangor with us. We had two carriages from Carnarvon. We did not get to Glasgow till next morning. We had taken the wrong train and had to wait at Preston for several hours in the night. We stayed at Glasgow for about a week, raining continually. From there we went to Shrewsbury to see my sister Gainey & stayed there some days and from there home to Tanlan & thus ended our wedding trip.

At this time Robert Thomas received the following letter from Capt. Ferguson, the overseer of the Company, which reflects their attitude to ship masters:

92 Windsor Pl.

L'pool 2nd Sept. 1877

Capt. Thomas

Dear Sir,

I received your letter yesterday. I am glad all is to your mind onboard. She has cost a deal of money and has a fair prospect to repay it. Any little help Captn. Pike can give you he will. He is to relieve Capt. Williamson on his arrival and you must thus do your best, get to know shippers and the agents and coast workers and do all you can with Capt. Pike to get her loaded and away about 21.8 or 21.9. She is to load in East Bute, U.K. I can't get a 2nd mate to suit me. They are all boys or very old men that I can find. I must send the best I have on hand unless you have any one good at Cardiff. I hope the 4 men you have may give satisfaction — that's my wish. I am sorry about the detention. Hurry shippers up all you can. See Mr. Reid Coal Tips, also Foreman of Glamorgan Mr. Mews and Mr. Duman. Capt. Pike knows them all. Hurry all up you can. I send this c/o Capt. Pike that you may get it early. Write me how things works and prospects and about the soundings of the pumps as Pike will be busy at the Elbe I hope.

I remain

Yours Truly

John C. Ferguson

P.S. I quite forgot to wish you much joy and happiness in your new life. May God bless you & her to be a Comfort to one another and shall together always and be of one mind in all that pertains to good.

J.C.F.

We stayed at Tanlan for couple of weeks more and then went to Cardiff to rejoin my ship[70] which was loading for Rio Janeiro which place was then and is now at times very unhealthy. The yellow fever is the general kind and what a multitude it has carried away not long ago. Ships were laying there without a soul aboard of them, all dead, both captain & men & a great number of captains and sailors were sent out from England to take charge of these. So you may think how loath I was to go to Rio and your mother was also very sad over it, but what could I do? I could not afford to leave my ship for it would have been a poor recomendation to look for another after leaving a ship because she was bound to Rio.

So of course I sailed and on arrival at Rio[71] found no sickness there though all were in dread of it. The yellow fever is more prevalent in the West Indies and South America than any other parts of the world and is as deadly here as the Cholera is in India. It first comes on with pain in the head, back & limbs which soon turns to a burning fever. The skin gets hot and dry till it soon kills the patient. The remedy is on first sign to get the person to sweat. The best plan for this is to have a bucket of hot water & plenty of mustard in it over which the person must sit and cover himself up with blankets in a manner that the steam of the hot water will make him sweat. Force must be used if the patient won't stand it. After a good sweat, roll him up in blankets & put him to bed till all is wet from sweat. 12 hours after give him half a tumbler of castor oil & 24 hours after he is likely to be all right. But these things must be done at once to kill the fever.

Well I found no sickness there for it's not every year it does

---

[70] *British Princess* had arrived Cardiff, 6 August, and sailed again 26 September, 1877.
[71] Arrived Rio 15 November, 1877.

99

break out. Rio is one of the finest harbours in the world. The entrance is very narrow between high land (fortified on all points) after which it opens out into a large Bay studded with small Islands. The far end of it cannot be seen from the shipping. This is the seat of the Brazilian Government which is a very large country & governed by an Emperor from the royal family of Portugal, Don Pedro III. He is now, 1883, an old man but quite brisk. I have often seen him driving through the streets generally with six horses to his carriage. He is well liked but simply because he lets them be or lets the government be ruled by bribery and corruption and to put down which in the Brazils must cause a great deal of spilling of blood, although there is not a country in the world that requires reformation more than this one. The population of Rio is now over 300,000. The town is built on the side of the hills but there is a large space of level ground between the hills & the water and where the business part is the streets are narrow, so narrow that two carts can not pass one another without getting on the side paving. The houses are built 5-6 & 7 story high so that the streets are well shaded and very cool, for the narrow street draws a current of air which makes it quite pleasant even when an umbrella is required in the sun. But in wet weather the streets are like rivers, the water running down in strong force and for this cause all the streets are lower in the middle than at the sides, so a person walking along cannot cross the street without being carried or getting wet. It's quite a trade for some porters to carry people over. No fever comes when there is plenty rain. It's the dry hot parching and cloudless sky for weeks that bring the fever & small pox.

So much for Rio Janeiro.

After discharging here I took ballast for Callao and where I arrived all well and after a good passage but after some mistake in a telegram I had to wait here some time (Spent Christmas this year 1877 – two days out from Rio).[72]

From Callao I went to Pabellon de Pica[73] to load guano,

---

[72] Sailed from Rio 23 December, 1877; arrived Callao 7 February, 1878.
[73] Sailed from Callao 9 March, arrived Pabellon de Pica 31 March, 1878.

which place is a little northward of Point Lobos. And it was at Pabellon de Pica that I came to know of the birth of a young lady afterwards called Catherine Bruce Thomas, daughter of Robert & Catherine Thomas, which event had taken place at no. 1 Gladstone Place, Glasgow on the 21st May 1878 & that was you. My own darling child I was very happy to hear you were born and both you and your mother doing well. She wrote the letter with a blacklead pencil two days after your birth. Your health was drank by all hands on board.

I must here tell you that after I had sailed from Cardiff your mother went home to Glasgow as we had no house then ready, but soon after your birth our new house got ready, Penrallt, by Groeslon, where we afterwards lived for over two years, and it was my first home coming to my own house to Penrallt.

We sailed from Pabellon de Pica for Falmouth[74] & arrived all safe at Plymouth as it was blowing too hard to fetch Falmouth. I got my orders at Plymouth for the River Tyne, and after a hard passage of about 12 days I arrived in Shields.[75]

Following the arrival of the British Princess *at Shields, this letter was sent from the office of the ship's owners at Menai Bridge:*

Menai Bridge
Nov. 7th 1878

Capt. Thomas,
  British Princess
Dear Sir,
    We have your yesterday's letter and hope the ship is by this safe in discharging berth. We note that you had a good passage from Plymouth to the Goodwins & a hard beat from there to Shields. What was the amount of inward towage you incurred? Please let us know.
    With regard to outward pilotage from Plymouth, as you state Messrs. Fox should have informed you that the same was subject to a reduction on account of steam being employed. We also observe your remarks in reference to the distance money & quite agree with you that the weather

[74] Left Pabellon de Pica 23 July, 1878, arrived Plymouth 28 October, 1878.
[75] 5 November, 1878.

was exceptional at the time you reached there, but it would be well for you to bear in mind hereafter should you at any future time put into Plymouth that being in the vicinity of Falmouth the same rules and regulations in regard to the Pilots exists at both places.

The Tyne Dock Co. of course (as Capt. Ferguson has informed you) take the discharging of the cargo & Capt. Ferguson will also have named to you 2 or 3 check clerks who offered their services and advised you which best to engage & shall thank you to let us know the arrangements you will have made in this respect, & also to see that in addition the Mate keeps tally of the Cargo and that both have desks formed in a convenient part of the deck for the purpose, also that they compare notes every noon and night or oftener to see that their tally correspond, & if there is any difference to have the error rectified then & there. But Capt. Ferguson may have desired you to keep the check clerk only tallying the cargo & the Mate to be constantly watching the scales to make sure that the ship gets fair play & that no overweight whatever is given. If so, we are quite agreeable, but please note that the mate is to attend in either one or the other of the above ways exclusively to the discharging of the Cargo during working hours, & you will of course inform us of your exact managements & let us know what kind of scales are used for the purpose & how many bags are weighed at a draft, & we require in addition, that you yourself should keep a *strict watch* upon the scales to ensure the ship having fair play and also to satisfy yourself at the outset that both scale & weights are perfectly correct and that the ship does not deliver a single hundred weight of Guano but what she gets freight paid upon, & be most particular to see that no bag is allowed to pass the scales into the warehouse without being weighed as is sometimes the case.

Enclosed is table of her previous discharging of Guano at Hamburg in 1876 for your guidance in checking her present output, and you will fill up the blank form attached to send us at the finish.

Should you have any damaged Guano on board or any having the appearance of being damaged from its different colour to the rest, we trust you will be able by *good management* to get the greater part mixed up with the sound and if there is to be any deduction on account of such damaged guano you must be careful to see that what is weighed of the *damp* for average is a *fair specimen of the whole* of the damaged and do not agree to their bushelling the heaviest portion of it. In like manner that the dry Guano weighed for average is taken from *the middle of the hold* & a fair sample of the bulk of the Cargo & not selected from the lightest of it, but on the contrary try to get them to choose *this* from the heaviest portion you can so as to make the difference in weight between a bushell of 'damaged' & the same measure of 'sound' as little as possible.

We learn that Guano of various shades of colour is now being shipped at the Islands. Therefore be careful that none is allowed to be classed as damaged but such as is really so & don't let them persuade you it is damaged simply because it is different in colour. So be on your guard & keep the second mate, or some other reliable member of your crew constantly in the hold to watch that the men do not select a single bag as damaged that is not really so, also that they do not tread the cargo under foot, which is sometimes done in order to bring it in as damaged. Keep supervision over this yourself as much as you can & in case there is any damaged be careful that you are present at the time when the bushelling takes place.

We hope the cargo is free from stones, but should there be a few small ones intermixed with the Cargo, we trust you will be able to get [letter ends, incomplete].

I had wrote to your mother to meet me at Newcastle & leave her address there at the general Post Office. Soon as the ship was fast at Shields I took train for N. Castle, although late, but I got your mother's letter & took a cab for her lodging. She heard and knew my voice & soon ran down stairs to meet me. When we got up to the sitting room she introduced me to you, my own darling, & what a fat little dumpling you were & so very good. It's seldom you ever cried. You were then about 6 month old. A few days after we left this lodging and went to live on board of the ship at the Tyne Dock.[76] From thence we went home to Penrallt for my holiday. We travelled all night, leaving New Castle about 8 p.m. We were in Penrallt about 6 a.m. Your mother had wrapped you up in Shawls and you

---

[76] *British Princess* finished discharging 21 December, 1878. Voyage recorded in Sailings Book as 405 days at sea, total length of voyage 17 months, 1 day.

were so good, either singing or sleeping all the way. There never was a sweeter darling than you were & so old fashion.

I had about three weeks at home and then went back to rejoin and bring the ship round to Cardiff to load. Of course your mother and you did not accompany me this time as the ship was almost ready to sail, but were to meet me at Cardiff.

I spent this Christmas 1878 at Newcastle with Mr. Hughes, Ship Chandler, who you have often seen at Cardiff, but who then lived at Newcastle.[77]

I arrived in Cardiff in due time[78] and although late I got on shore & soon found you and my Kate in lodging in James street, where we spent a very happy fortnight. But it was very hard to leave this time. You were about 8 month old and had to come to know me so well & had got so friendly together that it made it doubly hard to leave you two this time. It was so very cold this time and we had such a cold bedroom that we had to put you in the middle in bed to keep you warm. I never felt such a cold place as this lodging was but the people were very good and kind and the landlord was such a man for children he would often nurse you on an evening when your mother & me went out shopping &c. These people's names were Lakes and I am sorry to say they are gone backward in the world since, and I am afraid on account of drink. I stayed at Cardiff for about two weeks this time and then sailed for Callao[79] with a cargo of coals & made a good passage out. But when I got out I found that the Peruvians were at war with Chile and on account of this I layed in Callao bay for about six months, & then went down to Lobos d'Afuera, about 600 miles northwards of Callao to load guano.[80] But when we had about 600 tons on board the Chilean Squadron came & put a stop to all the loading by setting fire to the shoots & take all the launches away to sea where they scuttled them.

We all (Shipmasters) went on board the Admiral's ship &

---

[77] Sailed from Shields, 30 December, 1878.
[78] Cardiff, 12 January, 1879.
[79] 28 January, 1879.
[80] Arrived Callao Bay, 27 April, 1879; sailed for Lobos d'Afuera, 17 October, arrived there 22 October, 1879.

begged hard to be allowed to finish our loading, but he said his orders were to destroy the loading facilities & which he did.[81] They afterwards sailed away and providentially the next morning almost all the launches were recovered, for although holes had been made in them and some of them fired by means of parafin oil &c. still they did not sink, & everybody put out their boats to save the launches and which was accomplished.

The fire about the shoots was also put out and in a week's time all was ready again for loading. But the governor of the Island would not allow us to load till he had communicated with the Government. So the answer in time came not to go on with loading till further notice. This was a great blow to us, but could not be helped, and I in company with other two shipmasters went over to Etten, a little town on the main land, & from which we could wire to Callao for instructions, & in the meantime all the ships sent their crews on shore to collect stone ballast & carry some on board in case we had to go to another place. This was a hard & tedious work for they had to roll the stones down from the top of the hills & brake them &c.

When at Etten I lodged with an old Irish lady well known in the guano deposits. We used to call her Irish Kate but her right name was Mrs. Ball. She had a family of two sons & two daughters. She was a very rough tongued woman, very vulgar & a rogue to boot, but had made a great deal of money by letting launches out to ships on hire to load guano. Hers was the only house at Etten where we could lodge.

We slept in different beds but in the same room, and in the morning we found our beds were laid on some Wheelbarrows &c. although the outside looked clean & tidy. Getting an answer from Callao I returned to the Ship in a little steamer & in about two weeks more an order came down from Callao to go on with

[81] *Lloyd's Lists* contained many reports of damage done and interference with loading the Peruvian guano deposits — e.g. 'On January 28, 1880, the Chilean admiral visited this deposit and wholly or partially destroyed everything within his reach'.

the loading and in about two weeks more I was loaded.[82] I spent this Christmas of 1879 at these Islands and had very good times of it on the whole.

There was an American missionary and his wife staying on board of a ship here and services were held on board my ship every Sunday and one evening in the week. I had such a large fore cabin & we had it fixed capable of seating 200 people & it was well attended. We also had a temperance meeting once a week which did some good. Mr. & Mrs. Gillebaud were real good people but carrying religion to my fancy to extreme. They spoke against almost everything as unchristian, even against gold ornaments of every description, such as shirt-studs, rings &c. But they were good earnest Christians. He had no salary of any kind but we supported them voluntary as Mrs. G. was near her confinement. They left for Callao and I have not since heard of them. But I am afraid they will find that living by voluntary subscription will be hard to bring up a family.

We sailed in due course, about eight of us together for Falmouth and arrived there all well.[83] I was the 3rd in the fleet to arrive & here again we were detained for about two weeks owing to some dispute about the cargo· And so I wrote to your mother to come to Falmouth, which she did and brought you with her of course, quite a big saucy girl, able to talk like an auctioneer. I was quite surprised for you were only eight month old when I had left. You were the laziest and the most

[82] *Lloyd's List,* 17 March, 1880, contains report from Callao, 11 Feb.: 'Since our [Lloyd's agents] last report loading at these deposits [Lobos d'Afuera] has gone on uninterruptedly, and about 9,000 tons more shipped up to Jan. 31. Not only have those vessels which were partly loaded been rapidly completing their cargoes, but those in ballast have begun to load. The following vessels finished loading on or about the dates given below: *North Star* Feb. 1st, *British Princess* Feb. 1st, *Arabella* 6th, *Woodfield* 7th, *True Briton* 9th, *State of Maine* 9th, *Willie Reed* 9th, the *Caroline Beha* and *Augustin* having been dispatched, there only remain seven vessels to complete cargoes, and as the quantity shipped averages about 700 tons a day, these too will, we trust, soon get away'.

[83] The *British Princess* and the *True Briton,* the two Davies vessels among the fleet which sailed togther from Lobos d'Afuera both left on the 13 February, 1880; the *British Princess* reached Falmouth on 6 June, 1880, and the *True Briton* arrived six days later. Both vessels sailed on 16 June for St. Nazaire where they arrived together on 21 June, 1880.

impudent little girl that ever was spoiled. How my back use[d] to ache in carrying you.

We first stayed at the Globe Hotel, but it was too public & so we took private apartments in a very nice place with people called Jenkins and we spent very happy time here. Capt. Edwards, *True Briton,* was also here & with his family stayed close to us.

Eventually both of us got our orders for St. Nazaire, France, & in the Bay of Biscay. But we could not take our family with us so we sailed in the ship & our familie[s] went there to meet us by the Southampton & St. Malo route, & were in St. Nazaire some days before us. But it was very nice & happiness to see you & my darling wife on the pierhead waiting for us, and came on board in the dockgates and where we lived nearly all the time. We stayed there, the *True Briton* being close to us.[84] We were very comfortable. Indeed I believe we never spent happier times than we did this time for about six weeks. It was the midsummer & every evening after Tea I used to take you both in a small boat to the shore & then for a long ramble on the seashore, & several times we just were in time to stop a certain little girl on the ladder going to the boat by herself, and it took us all our time to watch that naughty little daughter of ours.

We had to employ a doctor for you there as you were greatly troubled with the worms, but he knew nothing at all about it. Latterly, the *British Princess* was sold and we had to go to an Hotel to make room for the new Master, and I could not go home till all was settled. We had good times of it at the Hotel, although very dear and a certain little girl used to drink her wine at the table like a native and Kate growling at the old man for stuffing the child up with that nasty rubbish.

When we got through all business we took passage in a French steamer for Cardiff where we arrived all safe on the 3rd day.

---

[84] The *True Briton* commenced discharging cargo on 23 June, the *British Princess* on 26 June. As Thomas indicates in his account, the *British Princess* was eventually sold after she had finished discharging her cargo at the end of July, 1880. The *True Briton* made one other voyage, from Cardiff to Singapore, and was then sold when she returned to Greenock in 1881.

But your mother was very ill all the way and the captain & mate were so good & kind, especially to you, the cabin boy playing the concertina for you on the Bridge & captain making you dance. We stayed one night at Cardiff and then went home to Penrallt & spent some very happy time there. You & me had to go to Plasmawr everyday for milk and we used to have great games about that little river and sometimes we would fall out, especially if you wanted to bathe in the river without undressing, and although I was saving you from being drowned many time, still you generally got Kate to side with you & the old man blamed. But my dear child this was a very happy time, although we did perhaps not enjoy it as we ought. After having been home for a short time, we went to Glasgow on a visit, but did not stay there long as I had to go to London on some business & from there to Liverpool where you & your mother joined me. I had engaged very nice lodgings in Everton, 52 Stanfield Road.

Meanwhile Captain Thomas received the following letters, the first from a relative by marriage, Captain Malcomson, and the other from the office of the Davieses telling him they no longer required his services:

Oswald Mordaunt & Co.
Ship Builders,
Southampton 5th August 1880.

Captn. Thomas,
Dear Sir,
   Your favour of the 24th ultm. was forwarded to us here, and I note your remarks.
   I am not surprised to know that you declined to keep command of the *British Princess* on the terms you name, but the simple fact is the timber trade is such a poor trade at best, that it can neither pay a first class ship or ship master.
   We are both here at present and will be here all November. I am superintending ship building, and being here since the 8th of April am out of the way of knowing what is doing in Liverpool, except among our own ships, and I am sorry to say that we have no openings in our employ at present or is likely to have for some time. We sold the Barque *Per Ardua* recently and the Captn. is going in this

ship as soon as she is ready. He is an old servant who has risen from mate in our employ.

I should and shall be very glad to assist you promote your interests in any way in my power, meantime situated as I am in a remote place like this I find myself powerless. But situated as you are with a good character and long service in one employ your late owners are honour bound to assist you in getting a ship, but of course you will have to be on the look out as well as them. Meantime should I hear of anything suitable or that I think suitable I shall not fail to let you know.

Mrs. Malcomson unites with me in kind regards to Mrs. Thomas & Babe and accept the same for yourself, hoping this will find you all quite well as it leave us here at present, and hoping also you will soon be suited with a ship and remuneration more in conformity to your own ideas than the one you are leaving.

But you must bear in mind a 2nd class ship cannot afford to pay a first class salary to a ship master.

I am
Yours Respectfully,
Wm. Malcomson.

Menai Bridge 18th Sept. 1880

Captn. R. Thomas,
Dear Sir,

In reply to your note we beg to certify that you have served in our ships from 1864 to 1880 as A.B. in ships *John Davies* & *Disraeli,* 3rd mate in *Superior,* 2nd Mate of *Northumberland* & *Superior,* three voyages as Chief Mate of *Minnehaha* into West Coast, South America, & during the last six years master of ships *Glentilt* and *British Princess,* 991 tons & 1401 tons regn. respectively. As we are parting with the wooden vessels & not replacing them are sorry we can at present see no prospect of a vacancy for you, at same time, beg to say we part with you with much regret as you have always given the greatest satisfaction & should, from any unforeseen cause, a vacancy occur, while you are disengaged we shall only be too happy to give you the appointment.

Trusting you will soon be suited and bear in mind, we shall have much pleasure in replying to any enquiries respecting your character &c.

Yours faithfully,
Hughes & Co.
R. C. Jones

I took on myself to look for a ship here as my owners had none in view,[85] but our greatest trouble was your getting very ill here, & we had a doctor who did not understand it at all. But when we got another who did know what was the matter with you we soon had the pleasure of seeing you all right again, but it was a very narrow escape for you had got so weak. When you got well we went home as my late owners said they had a ship for me. After staying some time at home I was ordered to Cardiff to take charge of the *Merioneth*.[86] Your mother came with me but we left you at home with Nain. We stayed this time in Mount Stewart Square, Cardiff till the ship was ready to sail. This was the first iron ship I had ever been in but she is a fine strong ship and a good seaboat.

I left Cardiff bound to Singapore[87] and made a long passage out and at Singapore[88] I heard of the Birth of your sister Celia which happened on the 16th March 1880. I was very glad to hear the news for it would have been a weary time on my homeward passage if I had not heard the news first. And I may here mention that this year Christmas was spent on the passage out about the Equator in the Atlantic.

From Singapore where we stayed only 9 days we sailed for Bassein in Burmah where we arrived in 19 days[89] & loaded a cargo of Rice for Bremerhaven. Bassein is a small town about 90 miles up a river of that name. It is a Rice port & nothing else. A very expensive port. I have nothing to write about this place for a scholar like you must learn all about these countries

[85] Letter from owners quoted above.
[86] The *Merioneth* was one of the group of iron ships (named after Welsh counties) built by Roydens of Liverpool in the 1875-77 period. An iron ship, 1,366 tons, 231.4/38.9/23.6, she was built in 1875 and her masters before Thomas are named as J. Perrin and — Thomson. Robert Thomas's obvious confidence in her as a good seaboat was amply justified, and it was this vessel that became probably the best known of all his commands. cf. B. Lubbock, *The Last of the Windjammers*, Vol. 1, 203.
[87] The*Merioneth* had arrived in Cardiff from Bremerhaven on 19 October, and sailed for Singapore on 19 November, 1880.
[88] Arrived 17 April, 1881.
[89] Sailed Singapore for Bassein on 27 April, arrived 17 May, 1881.

in your geography book at School. All the Port[s] of Burmah are under the British Flag.

At Breverhaven[90] your mother came to me, bringing two big daughters with her, one of which I had never seen before. We commenced & even did live on shore for one week in private apartments, but it was so uncomfortable that we had to shift and were very glad to go on board of the ship to live where we lived very comfortable for about three weeks, the only drawback being Celia so ill indeed I thought sure we should lose her. But we had a good doctor who was very good and kind although he could not talk English nor could we talk German, but we had a Stewardess who could talk each and I expect you still remember Bremerhaven and old Emma the Stewardess, & Mr. Segar the weigher &c. When nearly ready to sail I sent you home by the London boat and I was very sorry to learn afterwards from your mother the trouble she had as the steamer did not go alongside in London but to the Stream & your mother had to take you and Celia on shore in a small boat and home same day, at least as far as Bangor where she stayed at Capt. Edwards' house for the night. I left one part out here, namely before I joined *Merioneth,* we had bought our present house in Carnarvon & called it Tanlan Cottage and soon as I sailed your mother & you shifted there so that Celia was born there. So she is a thorough *Welshman* while you are only about half.

You will perhaps remember Penrallt. It was a most miserable house and in such a lonely place that I now wonder however it came for us to live there at all, but somehow I had never lived in town and had a great liking for the country. But it was no place for your mother all alone and had we stayed there while you children grew up we would have had to send you to Carnarvon to School. So I am very glad we took & bought our own little house which I am very fond of. We have on Lease of 75 years & when that's up your Mother & me will be

---

[90] The *Merioneth* sailed from Bassein on 7 June, was reported to have passed St. Helena 3 September and arrived at Bremerhaven 8 November, 1881.

low enough in our graves, & if you are spared my own darling child to see that day you will be 30 years older than I am now in 1883. May God protect thee my own child & guide thy footsteps along this path in this wilderness of life and oh my child how concerned I am sometime about your future. What temptation & snares there will be laid to trip thee my own child. Your little body & soul are now in the full bloom of health, beauty, innocence and mirth, but care & trouble of mind will crawl in bye & bye that nothing can save & help thee but the love & grace of our Heavenly Father, who you must always look up to in time of tribulation. Live a life of spotless purity & in the love of Christ and live by faith in Him to keep at all times both in this life and the life to come. Hebrews VI, 19 verse. From Bremerhaven[91] I brought the ship round to Cardiff, and fearful weather we had of it. I never experienced worse, but we arrived in Cardiff the day before Christmas 1881, and as we could not dock we had to lay out in the roads over Christmas & docked day after Christmas. (All Carnarvon thought the ship had gone & 2 of the old Captains came up to our house to try to break the news to us.) And the day after I came home to Carnarvon by last train at night and I was near to be left there all night as I had a carriage all to myself & had fallen asleep, but your mother who had come to meet me happen to see my head & so woke me up. And when I got to Tanlan Cottage Brusey Thomas was up waiting for the old man, so we had quite a jolly time of it.

I stayed home about four weeks and I joined the chapel in Turf Square with your mother and for the first time had you to go with us to chapel. But I am ashamed to have to say, although it is the unvarnished truth, that every Sunday evening Miss Catherine Bruce Thomas always went to sleep in my arms at the beginning of the sermon, and I must own that in the

---

[91] Finished discharging 6 December, sailed from Bremerhaven 7 December, arrived Cardiff 24 December. The length of time taken to reach Cardiff underlines Thomas's comments on the weather. *Lloyd's Lists* for December, 1881, with accounts of very stormy weather reported from a wide range of British ports, reports of vessels missing and damaged, bear out in melancholy fashion the concern that must have been felt for the safety of vessels such as the *Merioneth*.

Sunday School I found her fighting with another young lady. I was quite shocked but when I told my daughter of it afterwards she only laughed at it. So I suppose it is quite the fashion, but I am a crabby old sailor and don't know the rule of polished life (There's one you old girl). After having been home for about four weeks I was ordered to Cardiff to join my ship bound this time for Rio Janeiro. You & your mother came with me but we left Cecelia at home with nain & the servant. After about a week at Cardiff we sailed[92] & made a moderate good passage out of 44 days. After discharging at Rio I took in ballast & had a telegram from my owners to proceed to Rangoon. It was very healthy in Rio this time, not one case of yellow fever, so I spent a very good time there, all my crew staying by the ship. I was very comfortable. That is, I was as comfortable as any one could be under the circumstances, but if I had my little family with me I would indeed have been comfortable. I met some very nice people there. One was Capt. Bailie of the *Prince Umberto* who was an old friend & had now got married & had his wife with him, a very nice lady. Perhaps you will remember them having tea with us in Liverpool at Mrs. Brown's.

I made the passage from Rio to Rangoon in 72 days,[93] being rather long, but the ship bottom was very foul after laying in Rio for about 40 days. You must know that iron ships are very bad for getting foul in tropical countries. In a very short time big shells will grow on them & this will stop a ship from sailing. Wooden ships are sheathed over with copper which keeps them clean, for no shells can get fast to copper. There are all kind of patents for putting on iron ship bottom but none so far has been invented to keep off shells & barnacles & grass.

My ship had got very foul at Rio this time but Rangoon River being fresh water they all got killed so that I had a clean bottom again to start for home, & bound this time for Liverpool.

Rangoon is in Burmah, but under the British Flag. It's a large

---

[92] Sailed from Cardiff 26 January, 1882, arrived Rio 12 March, sailed 20 April for Rangoon.
[93] Arrived 2 July, 1882.

town & well laid out, splendid avenues miles long, well shaded. The Burmese are of a copper colour and very intelligent people & hospitable. They are far above their neighbours in every respect & they are very proud & independent. It's very seldom any of them condescends to work as a labourer. Coolies & Chinamen does all the work. The Burmese do not increase very fast & they have been trying amongst themselves to have a law compelling young people to marry at a certain age, so as to increase the population. Some of them are in very high offices at Rangoon, both in the employ of the government & merchant offices, & are very trustworthy.

The British had a very hard fight to take Burmah, especially Rangoon, & the British General was surprised at the inventions of the enemy to oppose his land. The upper part of Burmah is still under the King of Burmah who lives at Mandalay, the Capital of Burmah. The present monarch is a very bad, cruel man & has murdered nearly all his relations.

All the houses are built of teak wood, very plentiful in this country but very dear in all other parts.

I loaded a cargo of Rice here for Liverpool[94] where I arrived after a passage of 112 days, nearly the best that season. I wired to your mother from Liverpool & she arrived in Liverpool about 6 p.m. with her two big saucy daughters & my mother with them. The first thing my eldest daughter asked me was 'ydach chwi no lew.'[95] Did anyone hear of such a thing? I had no idea she could talk Welsh. We drove from Lime street to our lodgings, 93 Upper Hill Street, my ship being in the Wapping dock. Nain went to Shrewsbury after being in Liverpool few days, but my daughter used to come to the ship very often, taking charge of the cabin, especially the hard bread locker. After paying the crew off &c. we went home to Carnarvon where we enjoyed ourselves for about a month. And then I went to Liverpool by myself to take ship to Cardiff & left on Christmas day

---

[94] Sailed from Rangoon with rice cargo 5 August, arrived Liverpool 27 November, 1882. Completed discharging 12 December, 1882.
[95] 'Are you well?'

1882.[96] We towed from Liverpool Christmas Sunday but on Monday in Cardigan Bay something got wrong with the tug boat (for we were towing) so we had to run back for Holyhead. The second time the tug broke down again nearly in same place so we again ran for Holyhead. Another Boat was then despatched from Liverpool but strange to say this one again broke down. We came back the third time. After this another Boat came and towed us round. We got into Penarth Dock about 3 A.M. and I at once came over to Cardiff to look for my little family and your Mother knew my knock at once & came to open the door. I woke you up & after a great deal of kissing & loving you went to sleep again.

Cellia when she woke just remembered me and no more, but instead of kissing me she only gave me a slap accross the face. But we soon got friendly. I was very sorry to find both of you had the whooping cough very bad and great trouble we got with you, your Mother hardly ever getting out, and it was very hard to keep you both in the house, & Cellia was very naughty some time. One day she opened the tap & let all the water from the boiler out till everything was afloat. Then she ran up to the garret to hide. But my poor child was too ill to be reproved. I sincerely hope that next time I come home you children will be in good health. But almost every time I have been home either one or the other has been ailing. But I am not growling nor grumbling as long as we are able to get you what you require. How hard it must be on poor parents to see their little ones sick and unable to get them what they ask for or require to get well. I thank God that as far as you two are concerned you have had everything for your good. Expense has been no object at all and the attendance you have had from your good kind mother is something that I cannot express, & had you been the children of the Queen you would not have been cared for better nor indeed half so much.

We were in Cardiff for about three weeks and then sailed

---

[96] *Lloyd's List* December 27, 1882, *Merioneth* was one of 22 vessels which sailed from Liverpool December 24/25 period. Put into Holyhead 26 December, and again 28 December. According to *Lloyd's Weekly Shipping Index* arrived Penarth 5 January, 1883.

again for Rio Janeiro[97] but we came first to anchor in the roads on account of the weather being too bad to go to sea. We laid there for five days & then went out to sea. You left Cardiff same day as I left the dock. You went to Glasgow but slept one night I believe at Shrewsbury. I got out to Rio in 44 days,[98] but the weather was fearful for the first part. Great many ships were lost in same gales, but Thank God we got out all right. When I got out I found the yellow fever very bad there, but by paying for discharging I got away very quick, viz. 20 days & had a telegram from my owners to proceed to San Francisco.

I met at Rio our old friends Capt. & Mrs. Baillie, but they went to Calcutta. I made a very long passage out to San Francisco,[99] 112 days & had fearful weather, losing all my sail and ship springing a leak, & the loss of one pump, but we got out all right, but had to go to drydock to stop leak which we did satisfactory in 24 hours, after which we went up to a place called Port Costa to load. This is up the Bay about 30 miles. After being loaded I came down to S. Francisco to clear out and in four days sailed bound to Liverpool with a cargo of flour mostly. Left on the 20th Sept. 1883 and have had rather light winds up to now, 5th October. And now my darling child this is a short sketch of life up to now, which had I not wrote it down you would never learn it. I have had to trust to memory entirely but all of it is the faithful truth but the dates are

[97] In Roads, 30 January, sailed 5 February, 1883.
[98] Arrived Rio 23 March, 1883. Thomas's comments re weather confirmed in *Lloyd's Weekly Shipping Index*, e.g. LWSI 31 Jan., 1883, Milford Haven: 'The Schooner *Cadwaladr Jones* of Port Madoc, Cadwaladr, from Liverpool for Clare with coal, put in last night with main boom, gaff and mainsail cut away, vessel having been thrown on her beam ends'. The heavy gales appear to have been general, e.g. *Kirkwall*: 'Capt. Williams of the steamer *North Durham* which put into Longhope disabled has come to Kirkwall to execute repairs. He reports that his steamer was on her passage from Newcastle for North America and when 300 miles west of Orkney during a fearful gale the vessel narrowly escaped foundering, the fire being put out, and the firemen working up to their middle in water. For five days the captain was never off the bridge of the vessel. Also a considerable number of steamers and sailing ships reported missing or damaged'.
[99] Arrived San Francisco 3 August, 1883. Sailings Book confirms loading at Port Costa and also exact date of sailing from San Francisco, 20 September, 1883.

wanting.[100] I hope you will keep this book as a treasure in memory of your affectionate father.

R. Thomas.

Oct 5th 1883

Lat 14N Long 123W

From this point the 'diary' continues in the form of a series of letters, presumably copies of those sent by Captain Thomas to his daughters.

Sunday 7th Oct. 1883 Lat 9N Long 122W

My darling children Brusey & Cellia,

I am now in what we call the 'doldrums', just between the two trade winds. The prevailing winds along California coast about San Francisco this time of the year is Westerly & light & dry. Never rained one shower while I was in Frisco. After which generally the wind hauls more northerly as we come south and about 25 to 30th Latitude the N.E. trades is picked which carries a vessel to about 10N this time of the year and S.E. about 5 North. So we are now in the variables between the two trades. In this Latitude we generally get very wet & squally weather & you will as you get older often read about tropical showers of rain which are very heavy. And we save all the water we can in these Latitudes for the weather is very fine except a squall at the commencement of the rain. Old sailors when they had only casks to hold their fresh water depended a great deal on the tropical rain for water, but now ships all have iron tanks to hold enough water for the voyage and do not care much about saving water only for washing. You would laugh if you were on board of a ship on the Equator in & after a heavy

---

[100] *Lloyd's Lists, Lloyd's Weekly Shipping Index* and the Davies Sailings Book in fact confirm the remarkable accuracy of Captain Robert Thomas's account.

117

shower of rain. Every man in the ship is almost naked, saving water and washing clothes and a free licence is given everybody to wash away as long as the water lasts. You on shore have no idea about the value of fresh water for on board of a ship everyone is on allowance which is very barely enough without talking about washing.

The two of you but especially Brusey will know what the tropics are. It is the distance the sun goes from Equator North or South, about 23-27 North in June when it is summer in England, and 23-27 South in December when it is winter North of Equator & summer to the South of it. The sun does not stop on this hardly anytime but soon as it reaches that Declination, which is the distance of the Sun from Equator on either side it commences to move back again, and when you grow older you will learn that it is the earth that moves & not the sun.

The N.E. & S.E. trades meets between equator and Lat 10N and the air getting condensed causes the rain in these Lat. But my little girls are too young yet to understand these things.

I was just looking in my Bible your ages and I see Brusey is going on six & Cellia going on three years old. Why you are getting to be big girls all ready and a lady who you both know and love wrote to me to San Francisco to say that Brusey said one day that she could eat like a *donkey*. What an expression from a young lady, and I am grow[n] puzzled what I am going to do with big girls that eats like *donkeys* for the mischief is although they eat like donkeys in quantity I find they won't eat like donkeys in qualities. I don't know what I can do with them unless I fill them up with sailors' Duff & Peasoup. But there is one comfort, that their mother is able to make porridge for breakfast. But the discipline I am afraid is wanting to make these two little donkeys of mine eat it. So don't think I can do better than come on the Peasoup & Duff. So look out little Daus.

I wish my two pets were with me now for it is so lonesome & miserable to be always alone like this with no one to talk to. How I would play with you if you had been here now. But somehow this passage home is a little more encouraging than passage out for now every hour brings me nearer. I am also very

118

uneasy about your mother for she expects another little Donkey home ere this. God grant that she has got fairly through.

Your loving father,

R. Thomas

Lat 5 N Long 124 West 14 Oct. 1883

My darling children Brusey & Cellia

It's with a weary heart that I take up my pen to write these few lines at the close of this blessed Sabbath day.

All the week I have only made about 300 miles which with a good breeze could be done in 24 hours.

I am really very downhearted for it seems as if fate was against me on all sides. The ship is clean after the dry dock & I am expected to make a good passage, but what can I do when the winds have been quite contrary for the last eight days which make a big gap in my passage. I have tried to pray but cannot as I ought to but I find myself grumbling very often at my ill luck.

May God help me & give me fair wind for this is almost unbearable. It is weary enough at sea at best of times, but have extra worries like this is awful.

May God forgive me.

Your affectionate father

R. Thomas

Merioneth

Oct. 21st 1883

Lat 7S Long 128 West

My Own dear Wife,

I would have dictated some of these letters to you before this but when I write to you I consider it too sacred for anyone else to see it at all. I am thinking a great deal about you these days. You know the reason but I trust you are all right.

I got into the S.E. trades four days ago and have done very well so far, but the week before has upset my passage so much that unless I get good winds from here home I must make a long passage. We are doing all we can to creep up, spreading every yard of canvas we can and I hope these trades will carry us well to the Southward and if we could get to Cape Horn in 50 days from Frisco we may yet make a respectable passage. I look anxiously to the time when I can meet you at Lime Street Station, and I supose I must look for great alteration in you all, especially Cellia. How curious it will be to hear her talking for when I last saw [her] she did not speak much. But she was a good hand at slapping the old man in the face and not as fun or pretending as Brusey used to say, but for regular tyranny.

Your beloved husband,

R. Thomas.

Oct. 21st 1883

My darling children.

You will se by 'Mama's' letter that we have better winds today than the last one and consequently I am in better spirits today. I know that it is very wicked to grumble & get out of temper because the Almighty does not always give us fair wind and always everything according to our own ideas. We are now in the Southern Latitudes running down for C. Horn which is in about 56 South. We have a long way to go yet even to C. Horn, but few days of fair wind does wonders if the wind is also fresh & making between 200 & 300 mile per day. Our day at sea is 24 hours & commences at noon & goes on by hours till noon next day which is 24 hours.

There is now about eight hours of difference between your time & ours. When it is 9 a.m. with us it's 5 p.m. with you, so you see the sun eight hours before us here & we see it 8 hours after you. But as we come more East we shall shorten the difference in time till we are in the same Longtitude as you. No matter what Latitude our time would be the same. The Longtitude as I think I said before is the distance east or west of Greenwich. The nearest land to us today is the Marquesas Islands, distance about 600 miles. I wonder if my eldest daughter is geographer enough to find this out on a South Pacific chart or on a map of the world. They were discovered by a Spaniard called Madidana. Some of them are large and fruitful but missionaries have not been very fortunate in civilizing the natives. The French Government for some time took charge of them but they abandoned them again, being too expensive & no returns. What a tedious life this is sailing about on the trackless deep all by ourselves. The same thing over & over again, the same routine from day to day & month to month. We are now 31 days out and in that time have seen neither ship or land & will perhaps see neither for some time, but if wind keeps fair I shall try to sight an Island 900 miles ahead just to see how my Chronometers are, for you know that by the Chronometer we are able to know our Longtitude, that is between Chronometer & the Sun for neither are of any use without the other. A Chronometer is a time piece like a watch, very expensive. Mine is worth £30. It is supposed to show the exact Greenwich time all the voyage & the difference between which & the time of the place by the Sun is the Longtitude. An error of 1 minute is an error of miles.

Your loving father,

R. Thomas

Sunday 28th Oct. 1883.

My dear Brusey & Cellia.

We are now again out of the S.E. trades & have today a light westerly winds.

We had a very poor trades all through, very light & lost them two days ago, since which we have had a great deal of rain, thunder & lightning but very little wind. I am afraid I am going to make another long passage, as it will take us all our time to get to Cape Horn in 20 days more. We must take the winds as we get them & do the best we can & what [sic] I have done that I have done my duty.

My dear children I have nothing new to write about today. We are now abreast of the Society Islands, Tahiti &c. These Islands are about the most interesting in the South Pacific. They were discovered by De Quiros a Spaniard in 1606, and the first Englishman to see it was Captain Wallis in H.M.S. *Dolphin* in 1867 and Capt. Cook landed here in 1769. The Missionary ship *Duff* came here in 1796 with Missionaries & Bibles and soon converted all the natives. But the French land[ed] some priests here & they disagreed with the other

121

Missionaries so that today they are of a mixture, some Protestants & some Catholics. The French Government also took charge of the Islands although still retaining the Queen on the throne, but little more than in name.

Pitcarn Island is a little to the southward of us here, a small Island but a very interesting one. It's only $2\frac{1}{4}$ mile long by 1 mile broad.

H.M.S. *Bounty* in 1789 went to Otaheite Island to tranship the bread fruit tree to the W. Indies. The vessel stayed here some months till the crew got very friendly with the natives and after sailing they mutinied & turned the captain & few men adrift in a small boat. They then turned the ship back & returned to the Island, but after a time a part of them again ran away with the ship, taking some native women with them, & of these nothing more was heard of for 19 years, when they were found living on Pitcairn Island living a good religious life & simplicity, the Island being very fruitful.

The Captain of the *Bounty* sailed for thousands of miles in this small boat but landed all safe & when the account reached England a man of War was sent out to look for the mutineers & few of whom were found on the Society Islands, taken home & few were hung. But the others were not found till 1808 on the Pitcairn Island. A pardon was sent out to them and this Island is still inhabited by their descendants which few years ago had got so numerous that the British government sent some of them to Norfolk Island, giving them Norfolk Island as a gift. You can some day see all the interesting account of the Mutiny of the *Bounty*.

This day, as every other, especially Sunday, I have been thinking a great deal about my little girls at home and I would give anything for just a look at them. I am wondering where they are now this minute. It's noon here so that is about 8 o'clock in the evening with you. So I hope you are about coming home from chapel like good little girls. I have never had the honour of the company of Cellia in a place of worship yet, and I do hope she is good in chapel just as good as Brusey always was (but not so lazy and sleepy), for Brusey never heard a sermon in the evening for she always made herself quite comfortable

on my lap for good nap & a good snore. And when we got
outside the first thing would be 'Caly me Lobat', meaning
'carry me Robert' & there she would snore again and of course
I had to do it all for your mother would always side with you
and sometime would give me a help if I was good. But it was
all very jolly and I wish I had the chance of carrying you
tonight. I don't think I would grumble.

Sunday evening.

8 P.M. nearly bedtime and nearly time for Miss Brusey &
Cellia Thomas to be up and doing for it is past 4 a.m. Monday
morning at Carnarvon and in four hours more I hope both of
you will be on your way to school and I trust with a mind to
learn & not to play. I am so pleased to hear you are so fond of
one another. This does look well with children to be fond of
each other & whenever you see brothers or sisters not fond of
one another it at once shows a bad bringing up or bad children.
Little girls should always make their mother their confidant in
everything, and to her sister as well, providing they are like my
little girls not seeing their father only about once a year.

Another thing that makes children mean and disliked by
everyone is telling falsehoods, and I trust I shall never hear my
little ones telling an untruth. Whatever wrong you have done
and in whatever manner it is done, always tell the truth at all
cost. Learn it when young and you will never depart from it.

No matter how trifling always admit the truth. My little girls
will have no excuse whatever for they never heard their parents
telling falsehood, and may God guide both of you on this path.
There is something grand & noble in a child owning at once
to any fault committed for children are bound to do many
things wrong & sometime naughty but still quite unintentionally
of doing wrong so that they can always be excused for confessing
the fault. Another thing I want my little daughters to use themselves to is punctuality. Always try to be punctual, and which
brings us to its neighbour, promise. Never promise to do anything
without you are sure to be able to accomplish it. It looks so
mean for a man, woman or child to make promises of things

which they do not think of fulfilling, and often not able if they would.

Never go into bad company. It's easy to tell when you are in bad company by the talk & manner of the company. Never stand & listen to filthy language, no matter by whom. A gentleman or a lady are never guilty of a slang or filthy words. So you can always know the tree by the fruit thereof. A gentleman once on parting with his son said 'always keep company with a better man than thyself.'

And may God bless my darlings this good night.

Your loving father

R. Thomas

23S 128 West.

Sunday, 4th Nov. 1883

Lat 30 S Long 125N

My own darling Children Brusey & Cecelia

We have done but little since my last on account of light winds & calms. Last Sunday night we had a terrific squall with thunder and lightning & heavy rain and I lost some sails & the three following days had much rain with thunder & lightning and afterward very light winds, but fair. Today there seems to be a change and I am in hope we are getting to better winds. This is indeed miserable these light winds day after day and my passage already getting long to C. Horn. How miserable these long passages makes a man and we can do nothing only wait & depend on the wind.

How wicked also it makes one's heart always grumbling and growling at the wind and I often find myself blaspheming. May God forgive me and not take me at my word for I often say & call for such winds that I would be sorry to see coming. How much harder it is for people in trouble to live a good & godly life to what it is to persons who are strangers to trouble & suspense. A Sailor's cup of grace must be very full when he is able to live a godly life but there are some people of such a nature that nothing can trouble them ,and are always happy and contented. I often look with wonder at my own sailors, so happy & jolly together, playing & skylarking together like

124

children while I am sad and almost weary of life, and what a contrast there is in one position in every respect.

I often wonder whether this is nature or wickedness. I can remember when no one could be more jolly than me but somehow higher I get in the world the less comfort I feel. I never knew what real anxiety of mind was till I got command of a ship and indeed there is much responsibility on a ship master, more I think than any other class of servants in the world. They have a vast amount of property under their care and a very slight deviation or mistake may cause the loss of his ship, lives & cargo, or on the other hand the loss of his certificate & situation. He may act faithful & honest & do everything well in his own mind which may after all turn out a failure & loss &c. He has to act by himself so much. He is not like a shore servant, always able to ask his master's advice &c. But a shipmaster has no one only himself and must act according to his good Judgement, whether right or wrong it will turn out. An owner of the ship also always expect good passages and do not always take into consideration that the man has to depend on wind and weather. A ship well fitted out does not always secure a good passage as now in my case.

My darling children I do not know whether I am right in pouring out my feelings like this to you who are as yet too young to understand it, but although I dictate this to you I know who will read it to you and I know she will understand it & sympathise with me.

I am now reading the *Quiver,* a very good monthly paper and what a lot of nice '*stoleys*' there are in it. '*Lobat*' will have to tell you some of these '*stoleys*' when he gets home.

We have seen neither ship or land since we left 45 days ago. How would my little girls like to be so long without seeing land. I am afraid they would want to go back to Tanlan Cottage again.

It's now November and getting cold there, so I expect there will not be much school again till next summer, and I expect Brusey is quite a scholar by this time. I shall expect a letter from her very shortly now. There is nothing like a girl to be a nice letter writer and I hope some day to have great pleasure in reading my children's letters. And such long ones full of news.

Your affectionate father

R. Thomas

ship *Merioneth*

Nov. 11th 1883

Lat 42 S Long 115 West

My Own darling Brusey,

I wonder where my little girls are today and what they are doing. I trust that have kept the Sabbath a Holy day to God and have been good little children in chapel. I wish I was able to go to chapel now, but there are several thousands of miles between me and a place of worship. When I was about your age it was very seldom I could go to chapel on a Sunday on account of not having clothes good enough, but in these days it's very few there are in the country that have not got clothes to go to chapel. The wages are so much better now, for at that time 2/- a day was a tradesman's wages & labourer's at about 10/- per week, & very little difference in the price of provisions. We had no trains then so when we wanted to go to town we always had to walk.

No one thought of anything else unless there was a farmer's cart going to town. The farmers themselves used to ride & when both the farmer & his wife they would both ride on the one horse, the wife behind. It was quite common then but my little girls would be surprised to see it. Many & many a time I went to town on an errand with a halfpenny in my pocket to buy a cake or sweets.

There always was then two hiring fairs at Bontnewydd every year, for that's where the farmers got their servants and servants situations. Well it's not so now I believe & a good job too for it was a disgrace to a Christian country to see a parcel of men & women in a row on each side of the road and farmers &c. surveying & engaging them as he would buy cattle.

A man on a farm then considered £6 good wages for six month & fine healthy young women at from £2 to £4, and what a life a servant girl on a farm had of it, more like slaves than free people.

126

Bontnewydd being so near Llandwrog almost all of us boys were allowed to go there and generally got few coppers from acquaintances. The road by Llandwrog towards Clynnog was a great thoroughfare then for the people used to walk from even Pwllheli & Nevin to Carnarvon & on a fair day could be counted by the hundreds, and if it was a cattle fair the road would be black of cattle &c. Pigs we used to take to Carnarvon to sell. I have gone with mother many a time to Carnarvon with a pig with a string fast its legs, and if suitable price was not got we had to bring it home again, but if sold the money generally went for small articles of clothing for us children and perhaps a little extra groceries. My darling child I look back with wonder & pain at those days, for now I suppose it would be out of all reason for a woman & children from Llandwrog to drive a little pig to Carnarvon and then stand all day with it in the wet & cold and perhaps after all no one asking what it was for. Well I thank God that the times have altered for the best for the poor in that respect and when my little girls sees a poor man or a poor boy or girl, they must pity them & not despise them.

Tuesday 13th

My dear child I had to leave above written on Sunday as it came to blow hard but fair. So since then we have made over 400 miles while [*sic*] is some consolation, but the wind is light today although still fair and has the looks of a breeze. We are very deep this passage and consequently take a great quantity of water on deck. Indeed we had all through Sunday night to keep her 'right before' the wind & sea.

A ship 'running' in a gale takes a great deal of water and it's in running that ships founder, of which you will often see account in the papers. So you see that to keep a ship running too long is very dangerous, but when it is blowing too hard to 'run' it's very dangerous to 'heave to'. My little girl must as a daughter of an old sailor learn to know the meaning of these nautical names. 'Running' or 'Scudding' is sailing right before a heavy gale. With high seas curling after her & sail enough must be carried to enable the vessel to run quicker than the high seas that runs & curls after her, else they will curl over the stern of

127

the ship & wash everything away, & this is 'pooping', when she takes in the sea over the stern, a most dangerous thing.

To heave a ship 'to' is to bring her head on the sea, but to do this almost all the sail would have to be taken in. A ship is considered as safe as she can be put when hove 'to' and a captain cannot ease his ship or lay her in a safer position than this.

It's the sea that overpowers a ship and not the wind, but of course the wind is the cause of high seas. A very small 'bump' of a sea breaking on board will make a fearful havoc sometime. I have seen it bending a strong iron bar, knocking down men senseless, breaking strong timbers &c.

The wind would be nothing if it was not for his destroying companion the sea. A ship 'on' the wind is a ship going as close as she can to the wind whether under full sail or 'laying to'. When the wind is, say, West the ship's head will be six points from that, say S.S.W. or N.N.W. A square rigged ship can not go closer than that to the wind. A ship on starboard tack would head S.S.W. port tack, vice versa & heading N.N.W. When two ships on different tack meets, the one on port tack has to keep away for [sic] the one on starboard tack. A ship going free, that is with fair wind, has to keep away for [sic] all ships 'on' the wind what ever tack they are on.

We carry lamps in the night, a green lamp on starboard & a red lamp on port side, and a steamer in addition to these carries a bright masthead light so that we are always able in the night to see which way a vessel is going by her lights. A steamer likewise has to give way for all sailing ships. All this is an universal law of nations and is called the 'Rules of the Road'. And now I have told you all about these things which is very puzzling to show people when reading about shipping in the newspapers.

We are now in Latitude 45 S and the weather is getting cold. It is so much colder in 45 S than 45 N in North Atlantic on account of the warm current of the Gulf Stream of which I have already wrote. The stream of water here is very cold & which runs up toward Callao where it is still very cold & helps to keep that country cool although so near Equator, and which would be as hot as India if it was not for this cold stream from the Antarctic Ocean. The stream divides a little farther south, one branch coming this way, another round Cape Horn & away towards C.G. Hope where it again splits, one part going North & in time into the Gulf Stream itself. God bless my little girl tonight.

Your father,

R. Thomas.

Nov 18th 1883
Lat 52S Long 96W

My dear children Brusey & Cellia

Another week has passed & still find us although lonely still all in good health. We have seen no ships since we left but are likely to see some outward bounders in a day or two for the track of outward bound ships are more to the Eastward than we are now, for soon as they get round Cape Horn they endeavour to get to the Northward soon as they can to get hold of the S.E. trades. So the outward & homeward bound ships cross one another's track on a passage to California & vice versa but three times, 1st on Equator in the Atlantic, 2nd off Cape Horn, 3rd Equator in Pacific. The cause of this is the trade winds which is for one ship fair for a straight course, while for the other it is a side wind. So one goes through the middle of it while the other sails along its edge. My little girls will understand this better by looking at a map. The N.E. trades is in the Northern tropics & the S.E. trades is in the South.

We have done pretty well since my last letter and have today a good breeze of fair wind. We are about 800 miles now from C. Horn and had much rain & thick weather all the week. The weather is cold now after coming all at once from a hot climate but the days are long which is a great help & comfort. I trust my little darlings are well today & in good health and may God bless my little family.

Your loving father

R. Thomas

Lat 55 30 S Long 63 W
Nov. 26th 1883

My darling child Brucey

We are now in the South Atlantic having rounded Cape Horn yesterday at a distance of about 10 miles.

I have had very good strong winds since my last letter but fair throughout with the exception of about 8 hours.

Cape Horn is the Southernmost point of America & is on an Island named Horn Island, so that it is not the Southernmost point of the main land. The most southerly cape of the American continent is Capt. [sic] Froward in the Middle of the Straits of Magellan which divides the American continent from Tierra del Fuego which consists of hundred of Islands big & small.

There is a very miserable race of people on Tierra del Fuego. They are small in stature & very ugly, the colour is of dirty copper. They live a miserable life in tribes. They live on wild birds, fish & shell fish, seaweed, seals &c in fact anything at all. They do not wear any clothing except an untanned hides which they do not make into garments but simply wrap themselves up with and even this they will part with for a piece of Tobacco or a piece of iron &c. They have no notion of decency. They hunt with bows & arrows but except birds & foxes there are no game to hunt. Some of the tribes are friendly & some not. I do not think they are cannibals, but same time are treatiously [sic] for the sake of plunder. They once massacred a whole crew of a missionary schooner called the *Allen Gardner*. Those tribes along the Magellan Straits are the tamest, I believe, by seeing so many steamers passing through.

They do not take the trouble of even building huts to live in but simply spread a few branches for a roof. They pass much of their times in canoes, a whole family in one & in summer all naked. It's a great mystery where they came from at first, for the people on the other side of the Straits are a very fine race of people named Patagonians, few of whom are under 6 feet high in stature. The land of Tierra Del Fuego is high, bleak & bare along the sea shore with perpetual snow on most of the mountain. When you get bigger I shall buy you a book, *The Voyage of H.M.S. Beagle,* which gives a great deal of

130

information about these people. Steamers do not these days pass round Cape Horn but go through the Straits of Magellan but it would not do only for small sailing vessels as it is so long & narrow & very few anchorages.

The water being very deep there is a small settlement on the middle end of it on the north shore under the government of Chile called Sandy Point, & there is also a light house on Cape Virgin on East Entrance. We are now at noon in sight of Staten Island, a large barren Island, uninhabited, but I believe the natives come there in summer to gather berries &c. There are some splendid harbours in this Island, but except for a ship in distress are at present of little value. These barren looking Islands may in time become of consequence, for yet but little is known of their inside. I do not believe the Almighty created anything to remain useless and a few nuggets of gold found in these desolate looking lands would soon draw people, and people would soon find a way of bringing it into use.

I have to inform you that we are in company of ships at last, no fewer than five in sight. Have just exchanged signals with one the *Salamis* of Aberdeen from Port Phillip to London, 37 days out while we are 66 days from San Francisco. The other ships are outward bound and too far for a talk.

My little girl must know being such an old sailor that the way we talk at sea are by flags named as follows B C D F G H J K L M N P Q R S T V W. All are different and certain flags means different words. B D for instance means 'what ship is that?' WJGT means *'British Princess* of Liverpool'. MN means 'I am on fire' &c &c. Every ship has a book exactly the same, so we are in this manner able to hold a conversation together.

A little fair wind now would soon drive us to warm weather which I greatly wish for. The difference in the time between you & me now is about 4 hours. So when I am eating my breakfast some little girl that I know & who *eats like a donkey* is eating her dinner.

My little girl can reckon the difference in time between different places if she looks on the map for the Longitude of a place and allow 15 degrees to one hour, so when it is noon in London it's 2 P.M., 30 degrees *East* of London and 10 A.M.

30 degrees *West* of London. Do not forget this for it does not matter what the Latitude is. It's Longitude alone that alters time.

I trust my little daughters are well & good today. I was reading the other day of a little boy who never did or say anything while out of sight of his parents what he would not do in their sight, and I want my little girls to be the same. Take it as a standard, never say or do anything when your mother is not looking more than you would do if she were present.

I need They Presence every passing hour.
What but Thy Grace can foil the Temptor's power
Who like Thyself my guide & stay can be
Through cloud & sunshine O abide with me
                    I am your affectionate father R. Thomas.

Ship *Merioneth* Nov. 26th 1883
Lat 54 S Long 60 West
On the Burdwood Bank

My darling child Cecillia,

My little girl must not think that I think or care more for Brucey than yourself, because I write all the letters to her, but the fact of the matter is that Brucey is able to understand them while you are too young. I will if God spares me write to you soon as you are old enough to understand them. And I have no doubt you will be quite as clever as her at her age, but she has had a great advantage over you by being her mother's companion for a long time when alone at Penrallt, & that's how she got so old fashioned so young. While I was at home one summer before joining *Merioneth* her & me had good times of it running over the fields after blackberries, but we generally fell out before we got home and soon as she was near enough to be heard by Mrs. Cathrine Thomas she would let it out in a good scream which would before long bring forth the above named lady in a great scare and of course it was useless to plead my innocence (for the little girl would not cry unless I had done something to her). So I generally got behind a good sulk for an hour, when all would come square again.

One time I helped her on top of a high fence in (Rhiw) field, then got over myself to help her down on the other side, but while doing that she took it in her head to fall back on the other side and the first thing I knew was a yell from the ditch on the other side. I did not know at first whether to run for a doctor or go & give myself up to a policeman or a coroner for manslaughter, till I heard her calling, and over I went pretty smart & found her none the worse, & after loading her with blackberries & flowers & let her ride on my back & all other condescentions to keep her quiet & Mrs. C. Thomas in ignorance of the fall. We travelled toward home & soon as Penrallt came in sight a good scream was the first salute and you can guess whose voice was the next I heard & the form of whom I saw advancing at double step &c. Well the end of it was a good sulk till it was time to go to Plasmawr for milk, and of course that was my work with my daughter on my back for to tell you the truth she would never walk if she had any one to carry her. So you see what trouble I had with that big sister of yours.

The first news I had of you was at Singapore where I learned that I had a daughter born on St. Patrick's day or very near it. So I am not likely to forget your birthday, especially if amongst Irishmen who always keep St. P's day as a holiday.

I hope my little girl is good & kind to Mama, Brusey & Baby and also Nain, both of them & may God bless my little girl.

Your affectionate father

R. Thomas

Lat 53 30 S Long 57 30W
Nov. 27th 1883

My dear child Catherine Bruce,

I am just wondering whether I am fonder of my little children than anyone else or whether it is a little foolishness to be continually thinking about my family, and after all they are only a little Scotch woman and two big romping girls, half Welsh & half Scotch. I am sure I don't know how I am so soft as to be always thinking & longing for them, but I suppose they make it a point of spoiling me while at home (*that's the reason no doubt*). We have had fair wind since we passed Cape Horn & shall at this rate pass Falkland Islands tonight at a distance of

133

100 miles. We often at sea when near the land catch shore birds which gets blown off the land and are quite worn out, I have seen a score of swallows getting on board and would not leave till they perished or blown away & over board. I have often watched little birds trying to battle against wind & rain to gain a ship & I have seen them soon as they reached the deck fall down dead from exhaustion, the poor little things having spent all their little strength to reach a footing. An old ship's cat is wide awake to all these and will watch them so alight & then it's only an escape from the storm to fall a prey to a cat. But I have seen Pussy paying dear for her cruelty by getting overboard herself to catch a bird.

One time in the *British Princess* I saw an old Tom cat making a jump from the rail to catch a passing swallow & both fell to the water & were drowned. Old Tom did not consider that there was water underneath. Is that not a very good illustration of that old proverb which saith 'Look before you leap' which I hope my little girls will mind to do all their life. Never do anything without considering the result. Great many thing will appear full of goodness and pleasant but when you consider the end or what it will amount to at last all the unpleasantness is driven away at once. A naughty boy I was one time to play truant instead of going to school. It was so pleasant to go nutting & bird-nesting but it was not so pleasant to suffer a good whipping afterwards and more than all to be found so dishonourable as to tell a lie to my parents.

Well I have strayed from my '*Stoley*' with that old Tom cat jumping without looking first and I may here remark that 50 per cent of cats taken to sea are lost in this manner of getting overboard in trying to catch birds.

Yesterday a lot of white birds flew on board about the size of a pigeon. They went to roost on the royal yards (which is the upper one) and soon as it was dark the two boys went up quietly & caught three of them & today they are in a cage eating & drinking and seem to like wheat – but ever old (Betty Jones) the black cat is watching them with one eye & watching me with the other, although she pretends to be fast asleep. But I know her dodge & I know that old Mrs. Betty Jones is only shamming

& watching me to go below, but I won't. There, what good times a cat on board a ship gets to a shore cat. A cat or a dog are nursed like children and often all hands are watching and laughing at a cat playing, what a shoreman would never condescend to notice, but our pleasures are so few that we make the most of everything however small.

The carpenter is making some picture frames for me today to put my little girls' Photos in, & the cook has made two brass buckets for you two, so we shall be able to send you out to fetch milk.

How often I had to tramp away with a pitcher to some farms for milk. Of course farmers always gave the poor people butter milk gratis and I suppose it is the same now in the country. And I can tell you Brusey Thomas that a good basin of buttermilk is not a despicable drink, hot or cold, and I could now just enjoy a good hot buttermilk. But I am afraid my little daughter don't care for it, which is a great pity, but of course you cannot get it so good in town as in Llandwrog.

Your affectionate father

R. Thomas

Friday Nov. 30th 1883 Lat 47 S Long 48W

My dear child Cecillia,

Just a few lines to you this afternoon, being the last day of the month. This time last year I was home with my little family, but what a distance today about 8000 miles as the crow flies, but much farther the way we have to go. I wonder if my little girl will know me. I am afraid not.

My darling we have done very well since my last letter to you and I sincerely hope to do well from here home. Yesterday we passed a ship called the *Roslin Castle* which left a week after me. We passed him quite easy so that to be ahead of me here he must have had different winds to what we have had and I trust to make up for it from here home. There are generally birds following a ship but almost all are different birds to different parts except one kind, viz. Mother Carey's chickens, which are perhaps a very little larger than a swallow & a little darker colour & not quite so smart on the wind, but they follow

135

a ship through all weathers warm & cold, rough & fine, and almost always on the wing. It's very very seldom they are seen sitting on the water. They fly & skip close to the water astern of the ship, just touching the water with their feet & picking up anything small as eatable but never rest to eat it but just jumping on & off the surface. Some time they are called the storm petrel, for they seem to be more at home in a gale than when it is fine weather. Old sailors [used] to be very superstitious and are yet to a great extent, & some of them actually believe that these petrels never go ashore but that they hatch their eggs under the wing. But even my little Cellia knows better than that. I believe that wild Island called Shetland is a great place for them, but their nests are always in such localities that seldom a man can get at them. So a storm petrel is a good name for them after all.

'Albatross', 'Cape pigeons' & 'Cape Hens' are always about a ship down in these cold Latitudes, but they always leave soon as the weather gets warm. We often catch these by means of a fish hook & line, a piece of pork for a bait. They are always hungry & will if fed eat till they cannot rise off the water. I think I have wrote about them in a former letter. Snow birds are also met with down this way, a light grey bird about the size of a snipe but as smart as a swallow on the wing. The Boatswain is another bird met with in the vicinity of Islands. He flies very high above the ship, over which he drops much dirt sometimes. The birds we caught the other day are alive & seem to be all right. Gulls are seldom met with in mid ocean except in the Western Ocean where they follow steamers to new York & back so are always met with in that route. Mediterranean is also a favourite place of gulls.

Your affectionate father

R. Thomas

Lat 43S Long 40W Dec. 2nd 1883.

My dear Brusey,

You can see by above figures that we have done good work since last Sunday and I greatly wish we may do the same this week. The weather is still cold, but better than it was. You can also see by above Longtitude that the difference of time is getting less between you & me. It's now 10 a.m. and I can just imagine two big healthy girls eating their dinner in Tanlan Cottage. How I wish I could listen to them and I suppose they will presently [be] going to school hand in hand. I have no news to tell my little girl today. We passed another vessel yesterday but I did not speak to him as there was a strong breeze on & rather far off too. We passed him at the rate of at least one mile an hour. It's very pleasant to pass other ships and it is miserable to be in a ship which lets everything pass her. The *Merioneth* will keep her own with most ships now as long as we have plenty of wind but she don't like light winds. I suppose my little girl don't know what a Log is so I must try and explain.

A Log line is to measure how many knots (miles) a ship is going through the water. A Log line is marked at about every $23\frac{1}{2}$ feet which is equal to a mile, while the sand glass runs 14 seconds. A Canvas bag is fastened to the end of a long line marked as above and hove over the stern & payed out. As fast as the ship goes the bag keep it in position. When this is ran out a man holds a sand glass measured to 14 seconds and when the last grain of sand runs out he calls out 'stop' and the line is held on the instant. And whatever mark the line then shows is so many knots per 14 seconds, which is equal to so many miles per hour. The log is hove every two hours regular if there is any wind.

I hope my little girl will understand this. Almost all nautical measures goes by fathom. Depth of water goes by fathoms & we measure ropes by fathom. A fathom is 6 feet and an ordinary size man measure a fathom from tip of finger of each hand when the arms are held out straight at right angles. If my little girls remember nautical Phrases, reading nautical *'Stolys'* will not seem to be so uncomprehensive.

I was reading yesterday such a funny *'stoly'* about a little boy who swallowed a mouth organ & he did not tell his mother. But when the little boy sat at the table to *'dinan'* the bothering music began to play in his little belly which made the little [boy] to blush and his mother to wonder where the music was. Then it would stop but would start at such curious times, for when

137

the little boy & [*sic*] just sat down in the school the old music commenced a song the schoolmaster called out 'silence', but more he called the louder the music would play and the schoolmaster not being able to know where it came from got so wild that he whipped every one of the boys, and little James never said where the music came from.

It then stopped for a while and just when they were all nice & quiet at their lesson out came that music with 'Rule Britannia' till the Master got so wild that he took a cane and drove all the boys out of school who all went home crying, & this wicked little boy never said it was him. One Sunday he went with his mother to chapel and sat down so good & quiet, but in the middle of the sermon everybody jumped up on hearing a music play 'Auld Lang Syne' & after that 'Rule Britannia' then 'Beulah Land' then 'Auld Robin Gray' &c. So the minister he got so mad that he dismissed all the people who went home wondering what it was.

But one day he got sick with pain in his little stomach and had to lay in bed and his mother had a doctor who when he came commenced to feel Jimmy's little belly, & just as he was feeling a lump in the middle of the stomach out comes the old music with 'Rule Britannia', which made the doctor jump & say 'bless my heart there is a piano in the little boy's stomach and I don't know how to get it out.' But he called some other doctors & then they thought it best to open him & get it out, & soon as it was out his mother knew it at once, and when he got well she gave him a whipping for not telling the truth and when he went to school the master gave him another whipping, and then the other boys they would not let him play with them because they had so many whippings on his account. And so now he stays by himself, but he always tells the truth now – so by degrees he will be forgiven. And another little boy I was reading of, quite the reverse in character. This little boy's name was Jack, & Jack would never tell lies and he used to tell the other boys how good, truthful & straightforward his mother was. And his favourite way of expressing himself was 'When my mother says No. there is no yes about it.' Was not that a beautiful way of admiring a firm character and how that little boy will admire himself, learned in the same way able to say No when tempted to do wrong. And how many good little girls & boys get into trouble when they have not been brought up to say No when No what [*sic*] the only word in the world to say at the time, & how many good men & women also have been ruined by the same cause.

So my darling child remeber when your Mama says no that there is no yes about it. I pray that my little girl when [*sic*] always continue to be good as she has always been. Then it will be no trouble to her to withstand all wickedness.

Your affection father

R. Thomas, Ship *Merioneth*.

Saturday, Dec. 8th 1883.

My darling child C. Bruse

We have had very bad weather since my last letter, very strong winds & heavy rain & confused sea, and I never saw *Merioneth* taking in so much water on deck. Indeed it was flush with the top of bulwark on one side several times, but I knew I had a good ship under me & nothing ordinary could hurt her. What a fearful thing it must be to be at sea in an unseaworthy ship & a leaky one. When people have to stand at the pumps to their middle in the water & that cold & splashing about by the rolling of the ship no shoreman has the least idea what a sailor has to go through. Why a shore man may live to be 100 years old & never be [in] danger of his life except by natural causes, but a sailor has to face death several times on a voyage & his work very very often is work for life. Suppose also two ships to meet or in anyway get close together on a dark stormy night & to touch one another is certain destruction of both & loss of life to all on board of both of them, & the least bit of carelessness or loss of presence of mind or incompetency is just sufficient to cause this. Even the light of one of them may accidentally get out & which would be sufficient cause for such casualty, & it may sound strange even to my inexperienced little girls to think that any ship owners are too mean to supply sufficient quantity of oil for the voyage to enable those in charge to always carry light in all weathers. But such is certainly the case. Some ships never

139

carry a sidelamp except just in the channel, while others like our owners supply their ships with plenty of oil & orders the captain to carry lights always in all weather. But most of those ships that don't carry lights are generally well insured, so if the ship is lost & all hands as well, Well it won't hurt them.

But there are several other causes that mind [*sic*] cause the loss of the ship which my little Girl would perhaps not understand.

What a poor miserable trade a sailor's life is as before the mast, & what a small pay, only £2.15 per month, about 12/2 per week. A farm labourer is far better off in every respect. I often wonder what ever it is that gets into men's hearts to lead a sea life at first, & although I am in a good paying situation still half of it would be better on land with my little family which would not require a man to write stupid letters like these to his children to keep them in remembrance of him. I told you in a former letter that I am always thinking of you & now I am getting to dream about you.

Two nights ago I dreamed I had you & Celia with me in some town but somehow I lost you both & then in an awful trouble looking for you everywhere, and the ship was ready for sea. I did not know what to do but every day I walked through the town & at last passing a small house what did I see but my own darlings going through their drill by an Italian who had them to go through the street to accompany a hand organ & my little ones were being drilled to dance to the music. Oh how glad I was to find you, & the Italian at first disputed my rights to my darlings. But he soon found out that an old man finding his children was not to be trifled with so I took you away quite jolly and then I woke to find myself trembling and quite nervous.

Well I suppose you will think me a very foolish old fellow to go & trouble my sleep about you. I found the cause of such dream when I began to recall that on the previous day I had been reading a '*stoly*' about a little girl getting lost by being so inquisitive as to want to find out the end of a dark cavern, but her light went out & so she could not find her way.

Your affectionate father

R. Thomas.

Sunday Dec. 9th 1883
Lat. 35 S Long 28W

My dear child Cecillia

We are still coming along fast as ever we can, taking advantage of every flow of wind. Yes wind, wind is all our care and talk. Without wind we are nothing, nor can we do anything. How careless one is ashore of wind. Less wind always the better. But at sea we are continually studying the wind. If the Almighty was to keep away the wind we would never see land again.

Perhaps my little girls have never given it a thought what good the wind is to the world at large. Without wind people in great part of the world would starve for they depend on wind to grind their corn &c. In many places they depend on the wind to turn Windmills to draw water to irrigate the land. If there was no wind to stir up the sea it would come to stink so that all the fish would die in it & the smell of it to get so strong as to kill everyone within its bounds. In the East Indies the wind for six month blows from S. West, which brings heavy rain which causes the rivers to overflow their bank & irrigate land which without it would be of no value. The natives meanwhile sow their crops, rice in land saturated with water ankle deep, and when this rice has taken root the wind comes to the N. East for six months which bring dry warm weather with which the crops grow & get ripe & gets harvested & stored, and so on from year to year from one generation to another. In hot calm sultry weather the wind is sent by the Allwise God to stir up the air & bring life & health with it, and in places where wind cannot penetrate the same Wise God has created flies &c. which flies about stirring & freshening up the air.

My little girl perhaps never thought that the flies which are so mischievous & troublesome are indespensable to pure air & pure atmosphere. Well these are only few visible things that could not exist without wind. We have still fine fair wind and in what a short time I could see my darlings if such wind as this would last. A shift of wind at sea will give a ship's crew work for about an hour to get the ship round & get the sail fixed on the other tack. This is providing that the wind is moderate.

141

Ashore you think nothing of a shift of wind. All you have to do is to shut one door & open the other &c.

A sudden shift of wind near the shore is very dangerous for to one ship in an open Bay at anchor a shift of wind is often a total wreck, and very often a sudden shift of wind is the salvation of another, perhaps on the point of becoming a wreck.

The Lord is good to all & His tender Mercies Are over all His works.

Your affectionate father

R. Thomas.

Lat 27 S Long 21 West
Sunday Dec. 16th 1883.

My darling children

I almost let this day pass without writing a line to my pets but the reason is light & contrary wind which makes me anything but amiable. It is indeed so miserable to have all these light & contrary winds. Here we are a whole week making about 300 miles & passages already long and such a long distance yet to go. Oh what a treasure for a Sea captain patience is. I really wish I had some of it or better still some godliness which would always do the work of patience.

My dear darlings do not think you are forgotten even [if] I nearly let the day slip without writing. I never on a Sunday do any thing except reading a religious book or reading old letters from your dear mother & writing a letter to my little daughters. This forenoon I went over all your mother's letters to me this voyage and afterwards destroyed them all for that is the best in case some one may get hold in them when I came home. I have read them over many many time since I got them and it is a pleasure to do so on a Sunday morning, and I hope it's not a sin for it's nearly all one gets of his dear ones which [*sic*] leading a sea life. And I can assure my little girls that reading them makes me long after them very much. In one you are in Glasgow sick, in another at Carnarvon. In one I find you are gone to Llandwrog and in the next I find you coming up Pool street with the brass band. In the next Brusey is at school & lo & behold in the next one my Celia is also at school. But in this once [*sic*], well, I am really ashamed to have to record it, here is a whole basket of groceries which Kate has just brought home capsized on the floor, eggs & all. Well well I don't know what Kate did or said but I expect my daughters were not much hurted with the whipping. But what, here is another letter of one of them going to Llandwrog in a cart & the other lashed behind the cart in a perambulator and in the next here they are both over in John Jones' field playing &c. Well all this has not helped me any in forgetting my darlings. Here we are now very near the same time & only about an hour & 20 minutes difference. It's now half past four P.M., so my little girls are on the way to chapel, all muffled up while I am here roasting with heat, for we are only 4 degrees from having the Sun right above us. The three little white birds are gone. We cut their wings & let them go about the decks and they got quite tame, but one by one they managed to climb up on top of the bulwark & then overboard. It was so sad to see the little things dropping astern & unable to swim and now we have no pets at all except the old black cat, and she has got too lazy to come for her meals. Indeed it takes the steward some time to remind the old lady that it is time to eat & then unless it's something very nice & tempting she will just turn up her nose & roll over for another sleep.

The carpenter is now making a cradle for Celia for I suppose Miss Thomas is past that now. It's a doll cradle & very smart & strong so it will stand a good bit of tossing about & enable a certain little girl I once used to call bulldog to use her *boxes on*.

I really have nothing more to tell my little girls today, but if I [*sic*] we very soon gets into the trades I shall write another in the course of the week. I had my hair cut yesterday & I am astonished to see how gray I am getting. It seems only like a short season since I was like you two playing about and my greatest ambition was to grow & be a man. Alas to find that manhood is only the top of the hill & the next steps will to downward again to the low valley on the other side. But if a man live many years and rejoice in them all, yet let him remember the days of darkness for they shall be many. All that cometh is Vanity.

Your loving father, R. Thomas.

143

My dear child Catherine Bruce

We have done but poor work since my last letter, barely 600 miles, but we have at last got into the trades although so far very light. I really do not know what to tell my little daughter today for we have barely 300 feet of a deck to collect any gossip. Not like you going down town every day & seeing so many things & so many people.

This is Christmas Sunday and Oh how I wish I was with my little family today. This day twelvemonths we left Liverpool for Cardiff, and what a time we have had since and what fearful weather we have come through since then.

I do not think anyone would ever go to sea if he knew before hand the weather he would have to encounter.

It seems somehow to the Allwise Being fit to arrange the wind very unequal for in some part of the world as Peru &c. it never blows hard nor ever rain or snow, a perpetual summer while in other parts it's little of anything we get except gales.

We know not what what His object was in distributing the winds thus but we know that All that was made was made by Him & everything was done good & proper. We took the trades about 3 days ago but they are so far rather light but I live in hopes to be somewhere about Equator this day week. We are now busily cleaning & painting ship and I have painted my room last week & made it very grand with pictures. I have also made Cellia's doll cradle, very grand & will be a very smart cradle indeed, far smarter than what dolls generally get into, and I hope my little girls will take good care of it.

I suppose my little girls will be very smart today for people do almost all get something new about Christmas and I hope you have a big goose hanging up ready for roasting on Tuesday. Well the 'old man' has got a piece of salt junk and plum duff as usual and maybe he will indulge in a glass of wine & drink to his dear ones at home.

When I was at your age we used to keep account of Christmas months before and every halfpenny that did lose its way & come our property was jealously kept for Christmas to buy treacle

144

to make toffee. The fashion then in the country was for everyone to make toffee Christmas eve & all young people used to flock to one house for that purpose, everyone paying his share.

I believe & I am glad that practice is gone out of use now, and a mercy that it is for it led to much evil.

I hope 'Kate' has manufactured some at home for my little darlings.

Your affectionate father,

R. Thomas.

Christmas Day 1883
Lat 13 S Long 17 W

My Own dear Children

Here is another Christmas day which come as milestones on our journey of life and how quickly they follow one another & shows how fast our life is winded up. I should so much like to have one of them at home with you. I trust & indeed I am quite confident that both of you has been very good today and if there were any service in the chapel I expect & hope you have been regular in your attendance for Brusey is big enough now to go to chapel by herself & take care of Cellia, although that young lady will not readily submit to Brusey's patronage, and I am afraid can back up her independence if it comes to a scratch.

Our Christmas on board ship is but little different to our Sundays, but the sailors had plumduff & ours was perhaps a little richer than usual. I cannot enjoy these kind of days for they give me so much time to be fretting for home.

Now I should enjoy singing a carol at Llandwrog Church this morning and then some good sliding & to be under no constraints but simply as we used to when from 10 to 15 years of age & some of my old pals with me. There used to be in my young days very good sliding in a pool by Gwernafalau and also in Richard Thomas's field at the back of Church Cottages (it's filled up now), and if there was good hard snow with frost we always had a good slide down from Tynllan to Shiop Isaf, and some time we had to go to Morfa to find good sliding. Oh how I would enjoy one of those turn outs now.

It does not seem natural somehow to have hot weather like this on a Christmas. It would be more like old time if it was cold. Well perhaps I shall sometime have a run over the ice on a Christmas day & my little girls with me and if I would not snowball them it's a caution to me. It's now nearly 5 P.M. & consequently about 6 P.M. with you so I expect you are getting ready for chapel.

Our trade winds are still light & now there is no prospect of crossing Equator in 100 days, so the prospect of even a moderate passage is getting small.

I have nothing else to write about today but hope my darlings are well & happy. That's my greatest desire & may God bless you both & keep & protect you to see many many a Happy Christmas.

I am your affectionate father

R. Thomas,
Merioneth.

Sunday Dec. 30th 1883
Lat 2 S Long 22 W

My darling children

You can see by above that I am still to the Southward of Equator but if the wind keeps anyway moderate as it is we shall cross it by noon tomorrow. Our trades have been very light throughout.

This is the last Sunday in this year and this is my last letter in this year and I have been seriously thinking how my doings for the last twelve months could be overhauled & my footsteps for the last twelve month traced. Oh what a crooked path it would prove to be and what useless stoppages there would be found on the way. The crooked paths would prove to be far more numerous than the straight ones.

And if all my wickedness for the last year of 1883 were laid in writing before me what a heap of filthiness it would be, and how it would show our utter helplessness without a Redeemer, for my sins would certainly prove too many & too heavy for foregiveness without the weight of our Saviour's pleadings and merits. And how sweet that promise ought to be to our ears,

146

'The blood of Jesus Christ cleanse us from all Sin'. We are indeed in some need of the cleansing blood of Christ.

I wonder where my two little daughters are today. I know they are good wherever they are. At least I hope so, but one thing I know that they are as near the fires as they can comfortably get while I am just melting with heat. It is very hot & close today but a good breeze of fair wind will soon put us in cold weather after crossing the Equator. The Trade winds have not always the same limits but this S.E. trades almost always goes a few degrees northward of Equator while the N.E. hardly ever comes within from two to five degrees to Equator, & in the summer does not reach to the southward of 15 or 20 N. This time of the year its average limit is about four degrees to the north of Equator, so we are hoping not to have much variables between the two. A shower of rain is very often the only separation between the two, but when the N.E. trades runs to far south the Northward limits of it is far south as well so that we are likely to lose it about 23 North. It follows the sun. When the sun is far south the trade winds are far south also &c.

> Swift to its close ebbs out life's little day
> Earth's joys grow dim its glories pass away
> Change and decay in all around I see
> O Thou that changest not, Abide with me.

I am my dear darlings your loving father

R. Thomas.

Jan 6th 1884
Lat 6N Long 25W

My own darlings

Here is another Sunday & the first this new year. How fast they travel. I sincerely wish my little girls a happy new year & may God keep, protect & guard my little pets for this and many year to come, and may every year be one step nearer heaven (& not from it).

I have nothing new to write about. We have had miserable winds since my last but today we have a strong & pleasant N.E.

trades. There is no doubt but that my passage is to be a long one, but still we may yet do it in a moderate time.[101]

We have seen several ships this week but not one near enough to signal, but we are now on the spot where outward & homeward bound ships cross one another's track.

Hoping my dear wife & my precious little ones are well & happy today.

I am your affectionate father

R. Thomas

Merioneth.

The 'diary' ends here.

---

[101] The Merioneth finally arrived in Liverpool on 9 February, 1884. She sailed again for Cardiff on 11 March, and was at Penarth on 18 March, 1884. Having loaded her cargo of coal, she sailed from Penarth on 15 April for Rio de Janeiro where she arrived on 26 May, 1884.

Capt. Thomas made the following voyages in the *Merioneth* from 1884 to 1891 :

Year	Dept.	Port	Arrive	Port	Dept.	Arrive	Port	Time at Sea Mths. Days	Length of Voyage Mths. Days
1884	16 Apr.	Cardiff	24 May	Rio de Jan.	12 July 13 Dec. 4 May	2 Nov. 29 Apr. 14 May	Sa. Frans. Falmouth Galway	12 28	15 18
1885	22 July	Cardiff	21 Nov.	Sa. Frans.	9 Feb. 24 June	17 June 1 July	Falmouth Liverpool	11 9	13 3
1886	30 July	Liverpool	20 Dec.	Sa. Frans.	16 Apr. 29 Aug.	23 Aug. 1 Sept.	Falmouth Dublin	13 2	14 3
1887	15 Oct.	Cardiff	20 Jan.	Sa. Frans.	4 Apr. 13 July	8 July 15 July	Queenstown Dublin	9 0	10 12
1888	8 Sept.	Cardiff	11 Jan.	Bombay	31 Jan. 4 Mar. 22 Mar. 17 July	2 Mar. 7 Mar. 13 July 22 July	Akyab Bassein Falmouth Bremerhaven	10 14	12 6
1889	26 Sept.	Cardiff	13 Nov.	Rio de Jan.	24 Dec. 26 Mar. 22 May 21 Oct. 9 Mar. 19 July	25 Mar. 4 Apr. 16 Sept. 14 Feb. 17 July 27 July	Akyab Rangoon Rio de Janeiro San Francisco Queenstown S. Shields	22 1	24 12
1891	8 Oct.	Birkenhead	22 Feb.	Sa. Frans.	21 July 10 Dec.	3 Dec. 16 Dec.	Queenstown Hull	14 8	16 17

THE RECORD BREAKER

Robert Thomas remained in command of the *Merioneth* for a further seven years after the voyage in which he had written the 'diary' and it was during these years that, despite many fluctuations of fortune, he enhanced his reputation greatly. Following his return to Liverpool in February 1884 he sailed again with a cargo of coal from Cardiff for Rio de Janeiro and San Francisco. As many readers will know, the Crew Agreement Lists, or 'Articles' as they were called by seamen, have been dispersed, some to regional Archive offices and others to the Memorial University of Newfoundland, but a ten-year sample is held in the National Maritime Museum, and the *Merioneth*'s crew list for this voyage which began in Cardiff on 16 April 1884 is available.[102] It will serve to illustrate the type of crew which sailed with Captain Thomas in the *Merioneth* during these years. The mate, Robert Griffith, whose birthplace, like that of Captain Thomas himself, is given as Caernarfon, was a year older than the master and had sailed with him at least on the previous voyage, as had the Second Mate, Alfred George Thorndike, aged 44, a native of Whitby; their respective wages were £7 and £5 a month. Evan Jones, the ship's carpenter, also from Caernarfon, aged 27, received £5.5 a month, L. S. Wetherade, a Dutchman aged 55, the sailmaker, £3.10, and Evan Jones, the cook, a native of Cardigan, aged 44, who had also sailed on the previous voyage, £4. The bosun, Richard Hughes,

---

[102] The Record Offices of the Gwynedd Archives Service have a fine collection of Crew Agreement Lists of vessels registered locally, but unfortunately those of Liverpool registered ships (which inevitably includes the majority of the larger vessels owned in North Wales and by the Liverpool Welsh Shipping Companies) have ben dispersed. Even in the case of the ten-year sample at the National Maritime Museum it must not be assumed that all the Crew Agreement Lists have been preserved — the *Merioneth*'s Crew Agreement Lists, for example, for 1895 are missing.

aged 28, of Caernarfon, who received £3.10, was another who had sailed with Captain Thomas before, as had the A.B.s John Thomas, aged 19, of Holyhead, Charles Thomas, aged 20, of Bangor, and an ordinary seaman, David R. Stephens, of Newport, aged 17. There were two other Newport men aboard, David H. Williams, A.B., aged 23, and David Higgson Jones, aged 18, cabin boy, who received a wage of £2.5 a month. There were four other Welshmen among the A.B.s, Edward Rowland, 38, of Aberystwyth, Henry Evans, 21, and David James, 18, both of Newquay, and Robert Price, 29, of Aberdaron, Caernarfonshire. Six Swedes, one Dane, one Pole, one German and a native of Jersey, all A.B.s, completed the crew; all the A.B.s being engaged at £3 a month. The total complement of twenty-six was probably fairly typical of the crews who manned the *Merioneth* from 1875 to 1905 when she was sold to a Genoese shipowner, G. Mortola.

The voyage to San Francisco in 1884/5 was also probably fairly typical – arriving at Rio in May and sailing again in July, the *Merioneth* arrived in San Francisco on 2 November 1884. There Captain Thomas had to report to the British Consul the death of one of his crew. John Habinette, aged 20, one of the Swedish A.B.s, 'fell overboard from the rigging and was drowned on 31 July', in a position given as 41° 25′S, 51° 30′W. The full details were recorded in the official Log Book and the Consul's office noted that 'His balance of wages and effects will be accounted for by the master at the ship's final port of discharge in U.K.' This was duly done when the *Merioneth* reached Galway on 19 May, 1885. There the balance of wages paid to the crew varied considerably, indicating how much had been paid elsewhere – the A.B.s had between £9 and £27 due to them, the young John Thomas of Holyhead having most, £27.15.10d, but the carpenter and sailmaker had obviously hardly been ashore. The Dutch sailmaker was paid a balance of £32.19.2, but thrifty Evan Jones, the Caernarfon ship's carpenter, had £62.5.5 due to him, much more than the mate or second mate. At Galway most of the crew were discharged, and the *Merioneth* was brought to Cardiff by Captain Thomas, Griffith, the mate, H. Evans, D. R. Stephens, Evan Jones, D. H.

Jones, with a group of Galway men as 'runners' for the brief voyage. Captain Thomas must have been aware of some of the problems with 'runners' for he inserted a special clause in the Articles: 'If vessel is detained in Cardiff Roads over 48 hours, crew to be paid at rate of 4/- per day or discharged at Captain's option. Crew should be on board when vessel is ready to leave the Dock and to obey all orders given by the Captain or any of his officers during the voyage, and not to leave the ship in Cardiff until she is moored in dock to the Captain's satisfaction'. The voyage of 1884/5 to San Francisco had probably been a happy one for Captain Thomas, with no desertions, unlike that of his friend the master of the *Merioneth*'s sister ship, *Flintshire*, Captain Owen Pierce who had lost several men through desertion at San Francisco about the same time, including William Roberts, aged 22, of Menai Bridge, John O. Griffith of Caernarfon, William Jones of Newborough, and John Williams, aged 20, of 'Anglesey'.

Whilst the Davieses' wooden North American built ships continued to be sold by Charles Pierce in the 1880s – the *Superior* in 1880, the *True Briton* in 1881, the *Curlew* and the *Arizona* in 1885, the *Edinburgh* and the *Etta* in 1887 – the iron built 'county' ships continued to ply to the Far East and particularly in the San Francisco trades. Within a matter of weeks of berthing at Cardiff, Captain Thomas and the *Merioneth* were off again to San Francisco with a cargo of coal, leaving Cardiff on 22 July, 1886 and arriving in San Francisco on 21 November. He had had a rough passage, which was reported in *Lloyd's Weekly Shipping Index* for 18 December, 1886: 'San Francisco, November 25. The *Merioneth,* from Cardiff, reports that on November 16 the wind was blowing hard from S and SW with terrific squalls, and by midnight of 17th it blew a perfect hurricane. On the morning of the 18th the wind lulled, but again blew very hard in the evening. She lost and split a number of sails'. The terse account underlines what was everyday routine for seamen of Captain Thomas's generation, but where he survived others of the Davies fleet did not. Much nearer home, the *Malleny,* the first of the iron ships to be built for the Davies family by Thomas Royden, was outward bound

152

for Rio de Janeiro with a cargo of coal from Cardiff when she was wrecked one mile from Ogmore Point and the Tuskar Rock 15 October, 1886. Other vessels in the area, such as the steamer *Jersey City,* reported meeting hurricane force winds : 'The captain who is an experienced man describes the sea as terrific'. An inquest was held at the Greyhound Inn, St. Bride's Major, and Captain William Thomas Germain, the marine superintendent who had been summoned to assist Captain Robert Thomas in the battered *Glentilt* in the Falklands some years before, was one of the witnesses called. He was one of the Davies family's longest serving masters, having commanded the *Bacchus* in the early 70s, and his evidence at the inquest, quoted in *Lloyd's Weekly Shipping Index* for 25 October, 1886, underlines both the hazards of the weather which Captain Robert Thomas and his contemporaries faced and also the attitude of the Davies family towards marine insurance, already noted earlier in the case of the wreck of the *Victory.*

'William Thomas Germain, Newport, Pembrokeshire, said he was marine superintendent for Messers. Hughes and Company of Menai Bridge, the owners of the *Malleny.* She was a ship of 1036 tons register. She sailed from Cardiff on Thursday morning, 14 of this month. She was laden with 1366 tons of coal and was bound for Rio de Janeiro. She went out with everything looking prosperous. She was towed out by a tug belonging to the Clyde Shipping Company, a very powerful boat. The captain was Hugh Richards, and the crew consisted of 20 hands all told. On Tuesday last he saw the four bodies at the Greyhound. They were in coffins and numbered. He recognized the coloured man as the cook of the *Malleny.* His name was Francis de Gomez, a native of Goa in India. He had seen various articles of wreckage on the beach to satisfy him that it was the *Malleny* that went down on the Tuskar. She was built in 1868 and was an iron vessel, classed A1 100. Neither the ship nor the cargo was insured. The proprietors never did insure'.

Captain Hugh Richards was almost certainly well known to Robert Thomas for they were almost the same age – Richards was two years younger – and had served in similar Menai Straits

153

ships during their youth – Richards in the small Beaumaris coaster, *Cyrus,* the *Walton* belonging to Captain W. H. Owen, Rhuddgaer, the *Mornington,* second mate of the St. John barque *The Queen,* and, after taking his first mate's ticket in November 1875, he passed as master in June 1877[103] After serving as mate of the Bangor owned barque *Alice Platt,* he joined the *Malleny,* whose captain, W. Curwen, had seen service in a number of Davies ships, including the *Caspian,* in the 1870s when Robert Thomas obtained his first command in the *Glentilt.* Richards had had to wait longer for his promotion, but when Curwen left the *Malleny* after their voyage to Rangoon in 1885 Hugh Richards took command. He was 41 when he lost his life, with all his crew, when the *Malleny* went to pieces on the Tuskar Rock during the fearful gale of October 1886. Each year there were gaps in the ranks of Thomas's contemporaries who had risen to command the ships of the Davies family, and those of William Thomas, Liverpool, and the comparatively newly formed but struggling North Wales Shipping Companies. Reading through the Crew Agreement Lists and tracing the careers of the masters of these North Wales ships through their applications to take their various examinations, from Second Mate to Master, one is constantly reminded how very similar were the backgrounds of the officers, and 'afterguard', and how many of them came from the same close-knit communities. Inevitably in such communities there was much grief when one of the vessels was lost and, much more rarely, joy when there was news of some success.

Thus it was that in 1887/1888 Captain Robert Thomas of Llandwrog gained a very special place in the conversations of the maritime community of North Wales, and not only there but in seaports throughout the world. The voyage which started from Cardiff in October 1888 must have seemed to Thomas himself and to the crew of the *Merioneth* just another routine

---

[103] Details relating to masters' careers have been taken either from their records in P.R.O. BT 122-127 or from the applications which they themselves made when requesting examination for master, the Board of Trade records now housed in the National Maritime Museum.

passage to San Francisco – the *Dunnerdale, Caernarvonshire* and *Flintshire* had already sailed, the *Dunnerdale* on 26 July from Cardiff, the *Caernarvonshire* and *Flintshire* from Liverpool on 25 August and 22 September respectively, all bound for 'Frisco.

The *Merioneth* left Cardiff on Saturday, 15 October, 1888, and on the following morning cast off the tug towing her, off Lundy Island and began to run under light variable winds which off Madeira turned into a strong South West breeze, changing to North West, and North and settling finally into a moderate East North East trade wind. The N.E. trade wind was lost in 7°N but next day there followed light South East trade winds which took the *Merioneth* towards the Equator. Good trade winds carried the *Merioneth* to 20°S where they lost them, but there then followed moderate winds to Staten Island which they sighted on 29 November. Cape Horn was sighted on 2 December and the *Merioneth* passed Diego Ramirez Island on the following day. By now the barometer was very low, there were strong westerly winds with snow, but Captain Thomas carried as much canvas as he dared in view of the good time which it was now apparent they were making. By 10 December the *Merioneth* had reached 50° lat. in the Pacific, having only been thirteen days from the corresponding parallel in the South Atlantic. From 50° to 40° they had 'very hard westerly winds, including a very moderate gale from the westward with a very high crossed sea'. There followed some days of fair weather, then very squally with S.E. trades from 20°S 90°W; on 2 January the Equator was crossed in 107°W, and the S.E. trades were lost in 5°N. Between the trade winds they had a couple of days of westerly wind and then on 5 January they took in the N.E. trades. With the winds ever freshening the *Merioneth* moved from 8°N to 27°N in good time, but there followed a frustrating period when they lost the N.E. trades and had very bad weather and rain on 19 January. The passage was completed by 20 January, 1888. This is the account of the voyage, told briefly and baldly, based upon Captain Thomas's report, but it was soon obvious that in making the passage in 96 days the *Merioneth* had broken all records, and the *Daily Journal of Commerce,* San Francisco, 2 March, 1888, carried the account which is reproduced opposite. The exuberance and enthusiasm of the report suggest that the journalist responsible was himself a Welshman or of Welsh descent, but it has to be said that the Press generally seized upon the story and Captain Thomas and his crew became the toast of San Francisco.

Before going ashore, and despite all the excitement, Robert Thomas made time to write a letter home. Naturally enough it is a very happy letter, which conveys not only Thomas's feelings but also indicates, as indeed do some of the other letters, the almost family attitude towards the other vessels and their officers. The *Flintshire* did not arrive until 23 January; her master, Captain Owen Pierce, seven years younger than Robert Thomas, was already a good friend, whose home was at Glanalaw, Llanddeusant, near Holyhead. He had begun his seafaring career as a boy in the *Etta,* one of the Davies ships, in 1864, the same year as Robert Thomas had joined the Company, and had subsequently seen service in the *Cilminar, Glentilt* and *Conway Castle,* all of them Davies ships. Mr Stewart, Captain Thomas's mate on the *Merioneth* for the record passage, had previously served as mate to Captain Pierce aboard the *Flintshire,* so he too had reason to look forward to the arrival of his old shipmates. Another old friend, Captain William Roberts, master of the *Caernarvonshire,* was already there to greet them, and he is included in the photograph of the record-breaking crew, together with Mr Thorndyke, the *Merioneth*'s Second Mate, and Mr Cooper, Third Mate, who was later to serve as mate to Captain Richard Edwards, another of Robert Thomas's friends, aboard the *Montgomeryshire,* before taking command of one of the Davies ships himself. The *Dunnerdale* had had a very long passage out, as Thomas indicates in his letter – Mrs. Thomas would have known Captain John Williamson well as he came from her native Shetland, where he was born, near Lerwick, in 1833. He had sailed in Liverpool ships since 1854 and had qualified as master in 1869. Captain Williamson commanded several of the Davies ships, and it may be that Robert Thomas had served under him when he was a second mate in the *Northumberland* or the *Superior.* Captain Williamson took over command of the

OUR MERCANTILE MARINE.

One of the Swiftest Sailers of the Seas,

ill. THE GOOD SHIP MERIONETH.

Amongst the 127,000 tons of shipping now in our port are some very fine specimens of naval architecture, but none finer than the noble ship Merioneth, now lying at Port Costa. The Merioneth is especially famous as having made the quickest passage ever known between Great Britain and San Francisco. She left Cardiff on October 16th, arriving here January 20th, only taking ninety-six days between the two ports. The best previous passage was that of the Young America—99 days from Liverpool—but now, at least, Uncle Sam must confess that his best effort has been outstripped by Britain, or at least by old Gwallia, for the Merioneth, as her name would indicate, is a Welsh ship, with a Welsh commander and owned by Welshmen. This memorable voyage was not marked by any casualty worth mention, only indeed the loss of the main topgallant yard. There was but very little bad weather the whole way out. Her top sails were never reefed from Cardiff here. The foresail was never in but twice during the voyage. After being twenty-three days out the equator was crossed November 7th, in longitude 21 west. This was a very good run, and Captain Thomas began to feel that he was about to beat the record of previous quick passages. Cape Horn, the westerly cape of storms, was rounded December 2d. Strong west winds and squalls here, only sped her on her way, and again she crossed the equator soon after the New Year, on January 2d, in longitude 107 west. A run of eighteen days brought her safely to the Golden Gate. Her cargo of coal, consigned to J. D. Spreckels &

Bros., who have always several ships in port, was soon delivered, and she was ready for another voyage.

The Merioneth is of iron, 1366 tons burthen, and was

BUILT

At Liverpool in 1875 by the celebrated builders, Roydon & Sons, her owners being Messrs. Hughes & Co., Menai Bridge, North Wales. She is built on the lines of a yacht, formerly the property of Richard Davies, Esq., Lord-Lieutenant of Anglesea, and the principal mem-

ber of the firm that owns her. As may be seen from the accompanying sketch by our special artist, she is a model, of symmetry and peculiarly well adapted for speed. Her graceful outlines, as she lies like a bird on the waters, easily carry this conviction to every mind. Her length is 231 feet, her breadth 38 feet 9 inches, depth of hold 23 feet 6 inches. She has a gross tonnage of 1408 and a registered one of

Flintshire from Captain Pierce in 1891 and remained her master till 1895 when he was over sixty years of age.

Frisco 21st Jan. 1888

My own darling,

This is a great pleasure to me to inform you of this fine passage, the best for 10 years of any ship to Frisco. The *Flintshire* has not arrived although he sailed nearly a month ahead of me. *Carnarvonshire* is here and we have beat him [by] three weeks. There, what do you think of your old man now? (God be praised for it and may our hearts give Him the glory). I am writing this early as I will have no time on shore to write. I have not got your letters yet, but I hope there are some for me on shore. I don't know what I can tell you more just now. I am well in health and in spirits.

I will perhaps wire to you when I go on shore if not too dear.

Kiss my darlings for me and double kisses to my precious baby. I have such longing for my sweet angel that sometimes I am afraid of something being the matter with her.

Williamson also is here, 153 day passage poor fellow. Ours as you know is 96 days. With love & kiss,

Your loving husband,

R. Thomas

The next few weeks were full of excitement and also frustration for Robert Thomas. There were the presentations: from J. D. Spreckels, the famous flag, flown proudly by the *Merioneth* in many ports during the next years; the set of charts to Mr Stewart from the United States Hydrographic Office; the quartz gold-headed cane presented by the Welsh community of San Francisco at the assay office of Thomas Price at the corner of Sacramento and Leidesdorff streets.[104] The American press seem to have been defeated on this occasion in their effort to master the Welsh language! 'A number of the Captain's countrymen were present and the Welsh bard Abedoy O. Fon [*sic*] delivered a eulogistic poem in the Welsh language. The usual good cheer

---

[104] The cane is still in the possession of Captain Thomas's grandson, Mr. R. Froom of Childwall, Liverpool.

followed the presentation'. But Thomas, like so many ship masters at San Francisco at the time, was being held up by slowness in loading a return cargo for Europe and the near impossibility of getting a full crew. Desertions were so commonplace in San Francisco as in all the West Coast ports of America and also in Australia that even the best run ships rarely managed to retain more than the 'afterguard' – in Robert Thomas's case men like Tom Paton the sailmaker, a Milford man who had previously served in the *Anglesey,* but was now to remain with him until his death in 1903, going with him from the *Merioneth* to the *Afon Alaw.*

An interesting feature of the letter which follows is the list of people back home in Caernarfon to whom Captain Thomas sent newspapers bearing the account of the *Merioneth's* record passage. The De Winton firm contributed much to the development of steam engines for the slate quarries and for small steamers in Gwynedd; Mrs Edwards was the indomitable lady who had taught the rudiments of navigation to the seamen of Caernarfon and the neighbouring villages for close on half a century,[105] Captain Owen was probably Robert Thomas's friend who was master of the Caernarfon owned barque *Mona,* and the Captain Evans referred to may have been his long standing friend Captain Andreas Evans who later became master of the *Cambrian Hills.* Andreas Evans was born in the same village as Robert Thomas, Llandwrog, in 1850 and actually served as an ordinary seaman in the *John Davies* in the period during which Robert Thomas was also aboard her in the mid-sixties. Although Andreas Evans was almost seven years younger than Captain Thomas, the two remained lifelong friends and Captain Andreas Evans eventually commanded the *Afon Alaw* after Thomas's death.

[105] *Ships and Seamen of Anglesey,* 373; *Meistri'r Moroedd,* 11.

My own darling Wife,

No letters from you last week so I suppose you are not
going to write again. I am sorry that I stopped you so soon
but of course I never expected to be here so long. I have
not had one man yet but shall go at it tomorrow hammer
& tongs.

I am sending several papers by same mail as this next
Wednesday. You better keep those addressed to you and
the children. I am myself sending one to Barrack, Mr.
William Williams & H. Jones of the Golden Goat, and I
am sending some to your care. I am also sending them
all one apiece in Glasgow.

I will now say nothing about the Welsh present here.
I will wait till I get it. I greatly wish I had one more letter
from you to hear how the children were, but I sincerely
hope they are all right by this time. You had better write
bye & bye to Scott, Falmouth asking him to wire my
arrival off the Lizard and if my orders are there or likely
to be (in case I go to Falmouth).

Pierce & also Roberts strongly advise me not to go to
Cork, but all depends on the wind. I leave to you entirely
about the children if you possibly can bring them do so,
as I am longing very much for their company and may
God grant that we may all meet well & comfortable. You
must keep quite jolly till I get home. You have the whole
summer before you.

I wish very much we were sent to Dublin again, I think
I would prefer it to Liverpool. We would have more time
together and I hope no overlooker to attend to. I have
sent a paper to Mr. Griffith, 5 North Church St. They
will be pleased to see it. Also to Capt. Evans. I wonder
if I could get a fine ship to take you with me. It just
sickens me to be in this old cabin all by myself like this
fine Sunday. No one to speak to or to care for me, all
wishing to see Monday morning to get me away on shore
out of the way. I am flying my fine flag every day now;
it's greatly admired and envied by a great many. I wonder
if Brucey could work it with wool to put in a frame.

I expect to see these notices of the paper nicely pasted
together and framed by the time I get home. I send
every notice &c. to the clever ones, and copies of the
Journal of Commerce.

Wednesday

Not a Sailor shipped yet, it is too bad after my fine passage to be kept here all this time. I have no heart to write to the children now but you must make Brucey understand how I am situated. I am sending a great lot of papers to Carnarvon by this mail, so you will hear much about it when you go down town. T. Thomas, Capt. Parray, Capt. Owen, Mrs. Edwards, R. Jones, Editor, Observer &., Lewis Lewis — and Mr. De Winton, and also one to T. O. Jones so there will be quite a talk about it. I really do not know what to write to you this time. I have made Tom a Boatswain; he won't get any more wages but it will be a lesson for him how to command sailors when he gets to be 2nd mate.

Mr. Stewart has sent your address to his cousin in Queenstown who will wire to you when we are off the port.

Pierce is being loaded very fast now so I expect he will be away nearly same time as we. I will most likely send you some Photos of the ship ere I leave. They cost me nothing. I think you will admire them, especially the group. Tell my pets to be very good till I get home and we shall have the greatest gossiping that ever we had. It would be fine outing to hire a Bus for the day and get a picnic at Dinas Dinlle. I suppose Berta will be quite a talker by the time I get home. I am almost sure that she will remember me.

I am making a fine hencoop for the fowls and I am going to keep some of them till I get home so as to have nice fresh eggs, and the children will like to play with them. They lay such splendid eggs, but I am as you know not much of a hand for eggs, although they would do me much good, but I am quite fat enough now, fatter indeed than ever I was before since a boy.

Well my own cariad I know this will vex you but I greatly hope that the next letter will inform you that I am ready to sail.

Kiss my pets for me and many kisses to & love to yourself.

I remain

Your loving husband

R. Thomas

160

The crew of the *Merioneth* at San Francisco after the record passage from Cardiff in 1887/8. Captain Thomas is standing back row, extreme left. Next to him stands Captain W. Roberts, master of another Davies ship, the *Carnarvonshire*, then (left to right in back row), Mr. G. E. Stewart, Mate; Mr. A. G. Thorndike, Second Mate; Mr. Cooper, Third Mate. Others identified in the photograph include Thomas Paton, the sailmaker, on extreme right of second row (bearded, with hat on knee), and immediately behind him, Howells, cook, and Jules, steward. Thomas Wood Roberts is seated in the centre of second row, and on his right is John Roberts. Tom Jones is the second from left in the front row. (Details given to Mr. R. Froom many years ago by his aunt, the late Miss C. B. Thomas.)

The *Merioneth* at San Francisco (undated). The coal cargo has been discharged and the crew are on the foc'sle head, possibly about to weigh anchor preparatory to shifting berth for loading the return cargo for Europe.

The Steel 4-Masted Barque *Afon Alaw,* in the Elbe, *c.* 1900.

San Francisco
Sat. 31 March/88

My own darling wife,

I really don't know what to tell you. I have so far only two men but I have strong hope to get some more today. This is very annoying. I have to be here on a corner all day watching old sailors and got to listen to all kinds of impudence from scamps, but I am not alone for there are several others like me.

The *Dolbadarn Castle* arrived yesterday 144 days. You will remember that young man with me last voyage was at school in Dublin and used to give the children money and sweets, well he did pass and at my recommendation (as you know from Cardiff) he got 3rd Mate of *Dolbadarn Castle*. I am very sorry to hear that on the passage he fell off the crosstree to the deck and was killed on the spot. The children will be sorry to hear it and so will you.

At last I got the stick and it's quite beautiful, gold & gold quartz handle. I am very proud of it and you must be very smartly dressed to be able to accompany me out with this stick. You will I am sure be very proud of it and if I am spared it will be hung up in the parlour for it is much too precious to carry about.

Thomas Wood is *very ill,* but is I believe on the turn. You best not mention it till you hear from me again, but the Doctor says he will be alright in a few days; he is now living in the halfdeck and gets all attendance. I will keep this letter open till mail time so as to tell you how many men I got. I sent the children a lot of papers by last mail; my poor pets it's all I can do for them. There is no need to tell you not to let them forget me, they love me too much for that.

I sincerely hope we shall have a nice discharging port, and all live on board, it has its failings, but on the whole it's far more comfortable than lodgings.

Well my own precious old cariad this is a very mean letter, but I feel mean & miserable now.

Kiss pets for me.

Your ever loving husband,
R. Thomas

2 p.m. Sat.

have got five men today & require only one more. shall sail Tuesday morning one more letter from me RT

It must have been galling to Captain Robert Thomas to see the *Caernarvonshire* leaving for Europe on 14 February, the *Dunnerdale* on 20 March, and it was doubtful even if he would get away before the *Flintshire*. The *Merioneth* eventually sailed on 4 April and the *Flintshire* on 21 April, 1888, but as if to confound everyone there was no doubt as to which ship made the speediest passage homeward. There were in fact several smart passages that year but again it was the *Merioneth* which surprised everyone (including one suspects Captain Thomas and his crew), by arriving off Queenstown on 8 July, a homeward passage of just 95 days. The unfortunate Captain Williamson in the *Dunnerdale*, although he had left a fortnight before the *Merioneth*, did not arrive at Queenstown until early November, having had to put in to Callao to repair rigging damaged in a storm on 27 April – there is a brief account of this passage, based on the notebook kept by a member of the *Dunnerdale*'s crew, R. E. Parry (father of Sir Thomas Parry, sometime Librarian of the National Library of Wales, and Vice-Chancellor of the University of Wales) in *Meistri'r Moroedd*.[106] If everything seemed to be going badly for Captain Williamson and the *Dunnerdale*, the *Merioneth* and Captain Robert Thomas were given considerable publicity regarding their quite remarkable achievement.

Captain George E. Stewart, who was mate aboard the *Merioneth* for these record passages and had served in the Menai Bridge Company's ships from boy to master, contributed to a discussion about the *Merioneth* in *Sea Breezes*[107] many years later and gave the following record of both her outward and homeward passages :

---

[106] *Meistri'r Moroedd*, 148-9.
[107] *Sea Breezes* (1st series) 12, 152; 9, 108.

Ship *Merioneth*
Sailed Cardiff for 'Frisco
Sailed Oct. 1887

Passed	Position	Days Out
Equator	Atlantic	23
50° South	Atlantic	43
Staten Is	East Side	45
Diego Ramirez	East Side	50
50° South	Pacific	54
Equator	Pacific	74
Arrived	'Frisco Harbour	96

Sailed April 1888 'Frisco for Cardiff.

HOMEWARD PASSAGE

Passed	Position	Days Out
Equator	Pacific	14
50°S	Pacific	37
Diego Ramirez	–	43
50°S	Atlantic	48
Equator	Atlantic	65
Arrived	Queenstown	95

Total days at sea taken on 2 passages 191 days.

In his letter to *Sea Breezes,* Captain Stewart explained: 'We were delayed in 'Frisco for over two and a half months, leaving for home on April 4, 1888, and anchored in our port of call on 95th day . . . total sea sailing time out and home 191 days, voyage ending in Dublin where we were paid off with nine months and one day's pay. I doubt if this was ever beaten'. In the light of endless discussions regarding the distance sailed in one day claimed for the clipper ships Captain Stewart's next sentence is interesting: 'May I say that the *Merioneth* was not a fast ship; I do not think she ever made one day's run of over 250 knots during the voyage, but a large credit is due for these records to the old Liverpool firm of paint manufacturers, Messers. J. & W. Wilson & Company, who painted the ship's bottom with their patent white enamel paint, which after the voyage was just like china.' Both George Stewart and Robert Thomas would undoubtedly have admitted to having good fortune with the weather, but modestly Stewart did not add what seamen everywhere recognized, the hard driving sail-carrying and expert ship-handling and precise, accurate and skilful navigation of which Captain Robert Thomas and his experienced mate, George E. Stewart, had good reason to be proud.

Maritime historians have confirmed Stewart's prediction that the *Merioneth*'s voyage to San Francisco would stand as a remarkable record. Basil Lubbock, who spent a life-time studying the achievements of the great sailing ships of the world, wrote many years ago in his classic *The Last of the Windjammers*, recalling outstanding voyages, that

'The little *Merioneth* of Davies's Windmill Line will always be remembered by sailormen for her wonderful voyage from Cardiff to San Francisco and back in 1887-1888.'[108]

More recent writers like A. A. Hurst in his *Square Riggers, The Final Epoch,* discussing the scrapping of vessels in Italy in 1922, reminded readers of the history of the *Merioneth*'s 'really splendid feat' which 'had set the shipping world talking when she passed through the Golden Gate with coal only 96 days out from Cardiff, and then capped it by coming home in 95 days.[109] That most authorative of our modern British writers on fast sailing ships, David MacGregor, in his recent *The Clipper Ships,* has an appendix in which he lists the 'Principal Record Passages made by Clippers' and among the records of famous vessels such as the *James Baines,* the *Red Jacket* and *Flying Cloud* for voyages to Australia and elsewhere, there is

---

[108] B. Lubbock, *The Last of the Windjammers* (1927), Vol. 1, 203. The Davies family ships were known as the *Windmill Line* because of the Windmill pump which was put aboard all their ships, having been invented by one of their overlookers, John Griffiths. According to the late Captain Hugh Roberts, marine superintendent to William Thomas, Liverpool, who had commanded the *County of Flint, Crocodile* and *Kate Thomas,* Griffiths did not receive adequate recompense from the Davieses for his patent.

[109] A. A. Hurst, *Square Riggers, the Final Epoch* (1972), 85.

one heading for the record passage from Europe to California. Only one vessel is named, '*Merioneth,* Cardiff to San Francisco, 96 days'.

The acclaim of merchants and Welsh residents in San Francisco was obviously welcome, but what probably gave Robert Thomas the greatest satisfaction was the recognition by his fellow master-mariners wherever he went that the *Merioneth*'s voyage was outstanding in every respect. And it was not only the master-mariners – old seamen talked of Captain Thomas and his ships for many years afterwards. Two examples must suffice. In 1938 N. Kiernander wrote to *Sea Breezes*[110] recalling seeing the *Merioneth* over forty years previously : 'I saw her in Falmouth many years ago flying the Champion Flag. I had just finished my time in sail. We arrived in Falmouth from 'Frisco for orders. One evening a ship passed in, let go the anchor a couple of lengths ahead. The next day being Sunday morning, the usual routine was observed of hoisting the "house Flag" and "red duster" at eight bells. It was a surprise to most sailing ships in the harbour to see a white silk flag from the mizzen truck, as large as a main royal, fluttering in the breeze, with red lettering a foot high . . . I wonder how many old salts are alive who saw that flag in 1892 ?' Commodore Gerald N. Jones, C.B.E., D.S.O., distinguished master of Cunard liners, recalled, after the Second World War, his early days in full-rigged sailing ships, and the occasion when a ship-mate, a fine seaman from Amlwch, Harry Hughes, was lost overboard from the *Ladye Doris* on passage home from San Francisco in 1904/1905.[111] Running with the wind aft, and yawing badly, with mountainous following seas breaking over her as she yawed, the master bitterly regretted he had not hove to before nightfall. It was Harry Hughes's watch below, but he was called to take the wheel because of his outstanding ability as helmsman, and all aboard the ship recognized the difference whilst the Amlwch

[110] *Sea Breezes,* 23, 112.
[111] *Sea Breezes* 22, 23-31; cf. *Ships and Seamen of Anglesey,* 259-260, 467-471.

man was at the wheel throughout the worst hours of that stormy night. Tragically, no doubt as a result of tiredness, Hughes fell from the footrope at the lee yardarm when the hands were aloft next day. Commodore Jones wrote movingly of the scene aboard the ship when, as was the custom, Hughes's effects were auctioned on the following Sunday morning, but his evocative words are quoted here as they reflect indirectly, but most accurately, the reputation Captain Robert Thomas and the *Merioneth* had earned, not only in the minds of Harry Hughes and Gerald Jones, but seamen everywhere:

'First there was Harry's wooden sea-chest, its lid open allowing us to see the painting of a ship under full sail on its inside. We had watched Harry painting that ship; he had taken off the lid for the purpose and lovingly had made the picture, using ship's paint and a few small brushes which he had bought in San Francisco. It was a picture of a ship in which Harry had served – the *Merioneth,* built by T. Royden in 1875 and owned by Hughes and Company of Liverpool . . . in January 1888 [she] arrived at San Francisco with a cargo of coal from Cardiff, making the passage in 96 days. She then made the homeward passage to Queenstown in 95 days. This was a superb round voyage, and rarely if ever equalled. Harry Hughes was very proud of the fact that he had been an able seaman in this well known ship.'

Robert Thomas would have appreciated that tribute.

MASTER OF THE *AFON ALAW*

The weeks which followed the *Merioneth*'s arrival in Dublin on 1 September, 1888 passed swiftly. Captain Thomas had had his wish, expressed in his letter from San Francisco, regarding the port of discharge, and no doubt Mrs Thomas and the children soon made the trip from Holyhead to Dublin to join him. As it has not been possible to trace any letters belonging to the Davies family relating to the event, one cannot but hazard a guess that the owners too would have made the short sea voyage from their native Anglesey to visit the ship which had brought them such favourable publicity. Appointed Lord Lieutenant of Anglesey in 1884 by Gladstone, the first Welsh Nonconformist to be so honoured, Richard Davies had held his seat in 1885, but he had had a rough time in the election, pelted with stones and eggs, and it was accepted by even his supporters that he was more unpopular than ever, whilst his political opponents mocked him for his 'Seventeen Years Barren Service' as a 'thorough bred silent member', as the *North Wales Chronicle* of 31 October had put it.[112] At odds with his local Liberal Association over Gladstone's Home Rule Bill – it was alleged by some that he and his brother Robert Davies had acquired too much land in Ireland – Richard Davies had resigned from politics in 1886, and the triumphant return of the *Merioneth* in 1888 would certainly have been a matter of great interest to him and his family, and to his brother Robert Davies. Charles Pierce, their nephew, now living at Bryn Dinas, in Upper Bangor, and a very prominent citizen, Mayor and Alderman, who still managed the ships, would certainly have been delighted at the *Merioneth*'s triumph. But there was little respite for

[112] For the most recent assessment of Richard Davies's career, see David A. Pretty, 'The Political Career of Richard Davies, Treborth, 1868-1892', in *Transactions, Anglesey Antiquarian Society and Field Club*, 1979, 39-40.

Captain Robert Thomas. The *Merioneth*'s cargo had been discharged by 3 August and by 8 September she was sailing again from Cardiff for Bombay, arriving there on 11 January, 1889.

Two days after his arrival Captain Thomas wrote to his daughter 'Brussey' to say how much he appreciated her 'kind and intelligent letters, also Xmas cards from you all for which diolch yn fawr iawn i chwi a blwyddyn newydd dda a llawer iawn ohonynt i chwi oll. A bendith Duw ar eich pennau oll yn awr ac yn y dyfodol'.[113] This New Year greeting is one of the few sentences which Captain Thomas wrote in Welsh to his daughters, for although Welsh was obviously his own first language, their mother was Scottish and English was the language of the home in Caernarfon, although they must have spoken some Welsh with their neighbours and their father's family. Captain Thomas in these letters from Bombay chose to take up a point made in his eldest daughter's letter about William of Orange and proceeded to give her his view of history, which, not surprisingly for the nineteenth century, was the typical Whig interpretation of history, with phrases like 'Elizabeth was a good just woman and the only thing her enemies had against her was because she beheaded that wicked Murderess and unprincipled Mary Stuart. James I was a simple fool'. More interestingly he records that he is writing the letter on a Sunday 'and it has been such a noisy one, the deck full of natives, barbers with their razors, shoemakers repairing shoes on deck, tailors mending clothes, jugglers with charmed snakes, crepe Shawls vendors and ostrich feather sellers etc.' And it is evident that the master mariner had been tempted, as had his crew, by the lively scene he describes, for he adds wryly that his wife may not approve of his purchases: 'I am afraid Kate Thomas will grumble at Bob for spending on things which she could get at Caernarvon for half the money.' Finally, in this group of letters

[113] 'Thank you very much and a very Happy New Year to you all. And may God bless you, now and in the future'. Captain Thomas's eldest daughter, Catherine Bruce, had been born in Glasgow in 1878, his second daughter, Cecilia Ruth, at Caernarfon in 1882, and the youngest daughter, Roberta Isabel, also at Caernarfon in 1888.

one gets the impression of the oppressive heat of Bombay and Robert Thomas's longing to be back on the San Francisco run: 'I don't know what more I can tell you except that I am getting very very thin; this hot weather kills me. I wish I was on the other trade, far healthier.'

The *Merioneth* was in fact to remain in the Indian Ocean for yet another voyage, for from Bombay they proceeded to Akyab and Bassein before returning to Bremerhaven in July 1889, and sailing again from Cardiff in September for Rio, Akyab, Rangoon, Rio, San Francisco and home to South Shields in July 1891. This voyage of almost two years was to be Captain Thomas's last in the *Merioneth*. She had left San Francisco in March 1891 and arrived at South Shields on 27 July. Here Captain Thomas received what must have been to him a most welcome letter from Henry Rees Davies, Richard Davies's son, a graduate of Trinity College, Cambridge, who had now taken over the management of the Company.[114]

Menai Bridge
31st July 1891

Private

Capt. Thomas
Merioneth
Dear Sir,

As you have very possibly heard, we are now building a new ship of about 2000 tons register, which will be completed in all probability in six or seven months time. We have decided to offer you the command of her, but in case you accept, we would not require your services until she begins to rig out, say in 4 or 5 months time. Will you kindly inform us upon what terms you would be prepared to stop at home for these 4 or 5 months. Please regard the contents of this letter as strictly private and confidential.

Yours truly,
Hughes & Co.
H. R. Davies.

[114] Henry Rees Davies became a leading figure in the public life of Anglesey as County Councillor, J.P., High Sheriff and as Vice-President and Chairman of the Council of the University College of North Wales donated many valuable books to the University Library. He was also a very active secretary of the Anglesey branch of the R.N.L.I., *Ships and Seamen of Anglesey*, 269.

As Basil Lubbock, and those historians who have followed him, have pointed out, the 1890s saw the building of some of of the finest of all the large sailing ships and it was natural that H. R. Davies wished to replace the older vessels owned by the company with the type of ships being built for, among others, many of the Liverpool Welsh shipowners. William Thomas, Liverpool, had the fine steel four-masted barques *Republic, Dominion* and *Nation* built for him at Sunderland by Doxfords, in 1891, and the *Annie Thomas,* a steel full-rigged ship, in 1896 by Mackie and Thomson on the Clyde. Thomas Williams and Company had the *Cambrian Hills,* another steel full-rigged ship built in 1892 by A. Rodger and Company at Port Glasgow. It was to the Clyde that H. R. Davies too went, to the yards of Alex. Stephen and Company, who deservedly had a fine reputation for building ships. Two ships were ordered by Davies, both to be named after rivers in Anglesey, the *Afon Cefni* and the *Afon Alaw.* By September 1891 Davies was obviously pleased to inform Captain Robert Thomas that his new ship, the *Afon Alaw,* would soon be ready for him :

Menai Bridge,
Sept. 28 1891

Capt. Thomas

Dear Sir,

According to a report just received from Messrs. Stephens the Builders, the *Afon Alaw* is likely to be completed & delivered in 2½ months from date, therefore it is likely that we shall require you at Glasgow in less than the two months previously indicated to look after sundry matters, chiefly the setting up of the Rigging about which you have knowledge & experience. In the meantime you better look around to see how various things in other ships are fitted up so that you may be the better posted up when you get to Glasgow how best to fit odds & ends on board our vessel.

Yours truly
Hughes & Co.
H. R. Davies.

Unfortunately none of the letters written by Captain Thomas during this period of his life have survived, but he must have found his new ship a source of great pride, for contemporary accounts and photographs indicate that both the *Afon Alaw* and the *Afon Cefni* were beautiful examples of Clyde ship-building in the 1890s. The *Afon Alaw* was a very different ship from those wooden North American built ships in which he had first served the Davies family. In addition to being much larger – she was over a hundred feet longer than the *Minnehaha,* for example – the *Afon Alaw*'s masts and yards were steel, not wood, and most of her rigging made of wire rope, with steam powered winches for her heavy gear, 284.4′ long, with a beam of 41′ and a depth in hold of 23.7′. She was not much broader than the iron-built *Merioneth,* but she was fifty or more feet longer and with a tonnage of 2,052 tons, a much heavier vessel, with her tall masts dwarfing the crews who manned her decks.

By December 1891 the *Afon Alaw* was ready to sail and left Glasgow on 14 December, arriving at Cardiff on 17 December to take on a cargo for Colombo and Rangoon. Captain Thomas had several of his old hands from the *Merioneth* with him when he sailed on 27 January, arriving Colombo 15 May and Rangoon 10 June, whence they sailed on 1 July, to discharge their return cargo at Bremerhaven in November 1892. The *Afon Cefni,* her sister ship, on a similar maiden voyage, took much longer, although it has to be said that she had also called at Rio. Whilst the *Afon Alaw* made a voyage to San Francisco in 1893, return-ing by April 1894, the *Afon Cefni* did not arrive in Hamburg from her maiden voyage until September 1893. A worse fate awaited her. On 5 January, 1894, the *Afon Cefni* sailed from Swansea. There the entries in the Davies's Sailings Book end, with the note, 'Lost, Ship never heard of again'.

The *Afon Cefni* had been reported off Lundy Island at noon on the day she sailed, but on 31 January, 1894, came a worrying report from the Scilly Isles: 'Picked up today at St. Agnes lifebuoy with *"Afon Cefni,* Liverpool" and signal flags painted on it, also piece wood, three feet long, painted white having *Afon Cefni* burnt into one side, and "X" on other'. The Menai Bridge office were quick to send a confidential reassuring letter on behalf of the owners to Lloyd's, received on 2 February: 'The latest intelligence we have of the vessel is contained in a communication from the Captain, and sent ashore in the tug boat, the ship being at the time off Lundy Island at Noon on 5th ult. "The wind is now strong, gale from the E, with heavy snow showers; everything is working well, crew well behaved." We find the weather record at Scilly for the first few days of her being at sea is as follows:

				Bar.	Wind direction	Force
Scilly	8 a.m.	Jan.	6	29.40	SS W	4
		„	8	29.68	S E	7
		„	9	29.55	SS E	3
		„	10	29.60	SS W	5

As the wind was favourable for sending her into sea room, we are of opinion that ship is alright but that encountering heavy seas she may have washed the lifebuoy and piece of wood mentioned overboard.'[115] There are two points of interest regarding this letter. In the first place, it does not mention the possibility of the vessel being lost through fire, although the *Afon Cefni* was carrying a cargo of South Wales anthracite, and coal in iron and steel hulls was a cargo which called for careful ventilation. In 1894, at least six other coal laden vessels were lost and a further eight in 1895. Secondly, such a careful letter would have hardly been written so soon in the days of the eccentric Robert Davies, but H. R. Davies was a very keen yachtsman with a lively interest in the lifeboat service, and years later was to make a valuable study of the wrecks and rescue services of Anglesey.

Despite the owners' optimism, a fortnight later came more disturbing news; additional wreckage marked *Afon Cefni* had been picked up not far from Penzance, 'two pieces of teak board marked *Afon Cefni* in gilt letters' on 7 February, and on 11 February another piece of wood marked *Afon Cefni*, 'apparently from a boat', at the Lizard where six days later 'a mahogany

[115] *L.W.S.I.*, 9 February, 1894; also 2 & 16 February, 1894.

boat's nameboard with cut letters marked *Afon Cefni*" was picked up and placed in the custody of the coastguards. In March two lifebuoys which had obviously been in the water some time were washed ashore near Shoreham. Both were marked *Afon Cefni*.[116] On 17 August, 1894, the *Afon Cefni* was posted missing at Lloyd's.[117] Whether Captain J. Hughes and his crew were lost because of the vessel going on fire or because she foundered in bad weather was not established. To have lost such a fine new ship was a severe setback, and the many North Wales seamen who had just recently been discharged from her after her maiden voyage and were now serving in other Davies ships, men like H. O. Jones, aged 36, of Caernarfon, who had been moved just before she sailed to be mate of the *Flintshire* (he later became her master), must have speculated endlessly regarding the mysterious fate of the *Afon Cefni*. The news must have also come as a shock to Captain Robert Thomas and his crew aboard the *Afon Alaw* on their return from San Francisco.

The *Afon Alaw* sailed from Limerick in April 1894 for Swansea, and for the next six voyages, in fact, Swansea was to be Captain Thomas's port of departure. Amongst his papers is an undated cutting from one of the South Wales newspapers which he must have put aside after one of his visits to Swansea. Bearing the caption 'A fine vessel at Swansea, The *Afon Alaw* in the Central Dry Dock', an unnamed reporter describes his visit to the *Afon Alaw* accompanied by Captain Jermain, the Company's marine overlooker.

> 'This magnificent sailing vessel which for a few days has been lying at the North Dock Basin still forms a feature of admiration at the Central Graving Dock where she is undergoing slight repairs . . . The captain who takes pride in the fact of being a Welsh speaking Welshman genially explained the use and convenience of each modern appliance on the vessel. It should be prefatorily

---

[116] *L.W.S.I.*, 9 March, 1894.
[117] *L.W.S.I.* 17 August, 1894, '*Afon Cefni*, Hughes, of Liverpool, official number 99,932, sailed from Swansea for San Francisco with a cargo of anthracite coal on 5 January, 1894, was off Lundy Island same day, and has not since been heard of'.

remarked however that the Ship is a picture of cleanliness in every part. Her shining white masts and sails and varnished deck houses and brasses gleam radiantly as a tribute to the skipper – Captain Thomas of Liverpool – and his merry men . . . The main cabins amidships are really beautiful in design and appearance, the men's quarters being kept in a highly creditable state, affording a complete refutation to the suggestions of cramped space and unhealthy surroundings so often urged in these days against owners of vessels in the treatment of their men. Everything — fore and aft – is in tip top order, and the privilege of boarding and viewing the vessel is an estimable one that will not soon be forgotten. It might be mentioned that Captain Thomas – who takes such jealous pride in the appearance of the vessel – was commander of the sailing ship *Merioneth* owned by the same company, when that ship made a record voyage from San Francisco.'

Clearly the journalist had enjoyed his visit aboard the *Afon Alaw*! As he read the newspaper, however, Captain Thomas, now fêted wherever he went, must have thought how different this all was to those early agonising days towing the old *Pioneer* with a warp to the muddy shore against the stream of the Danube. Ashore in Swansea or San Francisco he had many companions among the master mariners – by the turn of the century several of the young men who had sailed with him, some on their first voyages, were now masters themselves – George E. Stewart, his mate on the record passage, and Cooper, the third mate; D. R. Stephens, ordinary seaman aged 17 on board the *Merioneth* on the famous voyage, was master of the sister ship *Cardiganshire* in 1899-1902.[118] There were also, of course, his own contemporaries whom he had known as masters of Welsh ships for a quarter of a century whether at anchorages off the West Coast of South America or in the ports of Australia

---

[118] N.M.M. Crew Agreement Lists, *Lloyd's Register*. Captain G. E. Stewart became master of steamers, H. Cooper was master of the *Flintshire* in 1901.

or India.[119] But once at sea, Captain Thomas must have been only too conscious of that loneliness of which he had written so tellingly in 1883 aboard the *Merioneth*. He had obtained command of the fine ship he had longed for, but his owners' policy precluded any possibility of having his family with him, although other Welsh shipowners had long agreed to allow men like his boyhood friend Captain Andreas Evans to have his wife and child aboard the *Cambrian Hills*.[120]

The Crew Agreement List of the *Afon Alaw* for the voyage from Swansea to San Francisco which commenced on 25 May, 1894, and ended 7 August, 1895, indicates that some of his old crew from *Merioneth* days remained with him, men like Tom Paton, the sailmaker, from Milford, and Evan Jones, the cook, from Cardigan, who was 54, four years older than his captain. The mate for this voyage was Thomas Owen, aged 30, a native of Caernarfon, with Rees Jones Williams, aged 27, from Port Dinorwic, as second mate, and William Jones, aged 38, a native of Llanelli, as Steward. Thomas Williams, aged 44, from Anglesey, the carpenter, and William Williams, aged 20, also from Anglesey, the bosun, had already sailed with Captain Thomas on the previous voyages of the *Afon Alaw,* but Robert Williams, of Caernarfon, the bosun's mate, was new to the ship. Among the sixteen ABs were four more Welshmen, David Hughes, 23, and Hugh Owen, 19, both from Amlwch, David George, 20, from Dinas Cross, and John Jones, 21, from Caernarfon. There were four Swedes, one Dane, one German, a Spaniard, one Italian, one Irishman and three Englishmen among the remaining ABs.

[119] In 1896, for example, Captain Robert Hughes of Trefdraeth in Anglesey was master of the *Carnarvonshire*; his old friend Captain Richard Edwards, a Caernarfon man whose home was in Bangor, was in command of the *Montgomeryshire,* having taken over from Captain J. Hughes who was subsequently lost in the *Afon Cefni*; Captain John Davies, a Newport man, was master of the *Lord Cairns,* which he had commanded since 1882, and with other companies there were men like his great friend from Llandwrog, Captain Andreas Evans, master of the *Cambrian Hills*.

[120] The Davies family rule against masters' wives sailing with their husbands had lost them several fine seamen, including probably the ablest of them all, Captain William Williams of Rhiw, in South Caernarvonshire. *Ships and Seamen of Anglesey,* 256-258; *Meistri'r Moroedd,* 55-65.

Captain Thomas's last six voyages to San Francisco in the *Afon Alaw* are recorded starkly, as are all the voyages of their ships from the 1840s to 1905, in the Sailings Book of the Davies family, a simple notebook without any title or means of identification except for the names of the ships. Apart from the record of the voyages, there is little other information available regarding Captain Thomas's life during these years – there are no letters between 1890 and 1902, and although the *Afon Alaw*'s location is regularly noted in *Lloyd's Weekly Shipping Index* there is little else – it was only when a vessel became a casualty, was wrecked or missing that she received more than routine attention in such a publication. One can assume that Captain Thomas in the *Afon Alaw* went quietly about his business, making steady if unspectacular passages, facing the routine hazards of the Cape Horn trade and the frustrations of desertions in San Francisco, discharging and loading problems – and in between, the all too brief leave at home with his family who moved during this period to live at 27 Berkley Street, Princes Park, in Liverpool, where so many many Welsh sea captains had settled.

The pattern of trade for the remaining ships of the Davies fleet (the *Dolbadarn Castle* was sold in 1893, the *Bacchus* in 1896, whilst the *Denbighshire* had been lost after a collision off Dover in 1889 and the *Caernarvonshire* wrecked on the West Coast of Ireland in 1896) was now very much centred on San Francisco. In 1896 and 1897 the *Lord Cairns, Flintshire, Anglesey, Merioneth, Cardiganshire* all sailed with South Wales coal cargoes for San Francisco and although occasional voyages were made to Yokohama, Nagasaki, Sydney and, during the Boer War, to South Africa, the San Francisco grain trade remained the most important.

Looking at the one line entries in the Sailings Book one tends to take these voyages for granted, but the circumstances of the losses of the *Merioneth*'s sister ships, the *Denbighshire* and *Caernarvonshire,* both well found vessels, indicate some of the hazards which also faced Captain Robert Thomas throughout this period. The *Denbighshire* was being towed by the tug *Racer* of Cork from Dunkirk in ballast to Cardiff to take on another

Members of the crew of the *Afon Alaw*, photographed by H. H. Wilson, San Francisco, sometime between October 1894 and March 1895. There is a note on the back of the original, 'Cecilia R. Thomas, ship *Afon Alaw*, Queenstown, July 26, 1895, off Isle of Man, from Mr. Owen'.

Members of the crew of the *Afon Alaw* at San Francisco, 1897. On the back of the photograph is a note, 'Ship *Afon Alaw*, Frisco to Queenstown, 163 days, 16 September 1897. 27 February, 1898. Howell mate, Roberts, 2nd mate, orders Hull-Swansea'. Captain Thomas is standing third from right. Next to him, on his right, is probably the mate, Howell, and on the extreme right is John Roberts, who had served with Captain Thomas in the *Merioneth*. The man standing on the extreme left is probably Tom Paton, the sailmaker.

AFON ALAW VOYAGES

Discharged	Sailed from	Arrived	Sailed	Arrived	Sailed	Arrived	Sailed	Arrived
1891	14 Dec. Glasgow	17 Dec. Cardiff	27 Jan.	15 May Colombo	29 May	10 June Rangoon	1 July	Nov. 26 Bremerhaven
1892	10 Dec. Geestamunde	28 Dec. Penarth	4 March	8 August Frisco	21 Oct.	20 March Off Kinsale		April 28, 1894 Limerick
1894	28 April Limerick	4 May Swansea	26 May	15 Oct. Frisco	8 March	22 July Queenstown		7 August Fleetwood
1895	27 Oct. Hamburg	10 Nov. Swansea	19 Dec.	2 May, Frisco	16 Sept.	25 Feb. Queenstown		7 March Hull
1898	March Hull	2 April Swansea	4 July	30 Nov. Frisco	12 July	26 Nov. Queenstown		5 Dec. Fleetwood
1899	21 Dec. Fleetwood	3 Jan. Swansea	24 Feb.	12 July Frisco	6 Sept.	25 Feb. Queenstown		18 March. Fleetwood
1901	March Fleetwood	29 March Swansea	11 May	21 Oct. Frisco	21 Dec.	5 May Queenstown		10 May Fleetwood
1902	May Fleetwood	25 May Swansea	25 June	30 Nov. Frisco	—	Sold at San Francisco 1 Nov., 1903		

cargo of coal when the steamer *Duke of Buckingham* collided with her on a dark night in January 1889. The bows of the steamer were stove in but the *Denbighshire* sank almost immediately, 'Sailmaker, name unknown, and Steward, William Green drowned, Captain Atkinson and remainder of crew landed here [Dover] this morning from tug *Racer*.'[121] *Lloyd's Weekly Shipping Index* for 17 April, 1896, gives the news of the loss of the *Caernarvonshire* : 'Castletownshend, April 11, 11.15 a.m. Ship *Caernarvonshire*, official number 76380 of Liverpool, 1227 tons reg., from San Francisco, wheat laden, went ashore 12.30 a.m. today, thick weather, Yokane Point, Castletownshend, Crew saved own boat. Vessel probably became total loss.' By the time the Lloyd's surveyor arrived at the wreck 'found master and crew landed in their boats and gone away.' He eventually traced them but reported that the master 'will do nothing until over-looker comes from Cardiff.' Within a couple of days the owners' representative and an officer of the Liverpool Salvage Association were on the spot but they could do little. '*Caernarvonshire* to be sold on Friday next as she lies on rocks. Cargo washing out. Deck bursting up. Cargo will also be sold.'[122]

So much for the official account. Captain D. T. Williams, later of the Blue Funnel Line, was a young seaman aboard the *Caernarvonshire* and years later recalled the circumstances.[123] Apparently they had not sighted land since leaving San Francisco and there had been no opportunity to check the chronometers. Earlier on the fateful day the *Caernarvonshire* had been carrying full sail, 'our vessel was under such pressure of canvas that she was heeling over and scooping seas on board over the lee rail.' Sail was shortened during the dog watches, but she was still proceeding at a good rate of knots when she struck the rocks shortly after midnight. Those on watch between eight and midnight had seen several fishing boats' lights, but they had not been able to pick up the Fastnet Light, and as Captain Williams recalled 'what had happened was that we

---

[121] *L.W.S.I.*, 25 January, 1889.
[122] *L.W.S.I.*, 17 April, 1896.
[123] *Sea Breezes* (new series), I, 419.

had over-run our distance. Not seeing the Fastnet the master knew that by this time he must have passed it, and decided to haul off the land until daybreak. However, it was lucky that we went ashore where we did; if we had gone a little further we would have run on the cliffs.'

There were others who were not as fortunate as the crews of the *Caernarvonshire* and the *Denbighshire*. In 1899 two of the best known Welsh shipmasters were lost without trace, both of them Nefyn men, and in command of vessels managed by William Thomas, Liverpool. Captain Thomas Jones, master of the *Dominion*, was not heard of since sailing 19 January, 1899, from Honolulu for Royal Road, British Columbia, and Captain William Meredith, known even among a generation of hard driving sail-carrying masters as an exceptionally hard driver, master of the *Annie Thomas,* was not heard of since spoken to in the vicinity of Cape Horn, 19 October, 1899, Cardiff to Acapulco with coal.[124]

Robert Thomas would have known all about these disasters for he had been around the sailing ship world of Liverpool and North Wales for close on forty years, and nearly a quarter of a century as a shipmaster himself. This then is the background to that fateful voyage when he left Swansea for the last time on 25 June, 1902. As they sailed past Lundy on that summer's day and noted the familiar landmarks as the *Afon Alaw* moved steadily towards the Atlantic, whilst the mate and second mate chose the men for their respective watches, Captain Thomas no doubt reflected upon the number of times he had sailed out of these very waters after an all too brief spell ashore, and wondered how they would fare this voyage, for a winter passage round Cape Horn was a daunting prospect, however often one had sailed that way before. The *Afon Cefni* and the *Annie Thomas,* fine vessels like his beloved *Afon Alaw,* had sailed this way and had simply gone 'missing'; would his good fortune, which had

---

[124] *Ships and Seamen of Anglesey,* 458; Lubbock, *The Last of the Wind-jammers,* II, 173-4 (but note the confusion between the two masters — it was Meredith who was in command of *Annie Thomas*); *Parl. Papers,* LXXXVII, & LXVIII, Appendix C.

been with him since that wretched voyage in the *Glentilt,* desert him now? Anyone who has read Dana or Conrad, or more recent seamen – writers like Alan Villiers or Sir Francis Chichester[125] – will know what lay ahead, and certainly Captain Thomas, who had a lifetime of actual experience of the *'War with Cape Horn',* as Villiers calls it, could have had no illusions as to what might lie ahead. But even he was to be surprised in the event, for this turned out to be the worst passage for weather he had ever experienced.

The *Anglesey* (which had sailed from South Shields six days before the *Afon Alaw* left Swansea) and the *Afon Alaw* both arrived in San Francisco on 30 November, 1902, passages of over five months. In a shaky hand, very different from that of the 'diary' and his other letters, Robert Thomas wrote home to 27 Berkley Street, Liverpool, soon after the *Afon Alaw* had sailed into San Francisco, a letter which he had originally intended to send to the Menai Bridge office of the owners, but in view of his state of health had decided to send home, with probably one of his officers sending a fair copy to the owners. The letter speaks for itself. It is difficult for those of us who have never experienced such a passage to gauge the strain on, and the toll taken of, the master of a large sailing ship in such circumstances. Some time ago I showed the letter to Captain W. H. Hughes, D.S.C., of Holyhead, himself a Cape Horner in sail, and his first reaction and comment was simply : 'Only a fine seaman could have written that letter.' The faulty trimming of coal at Swansea – Alan Villiers has written how the coal-trimmers of Newcastle, New South Wales, killed many ships – the fearful gale off the River Plate, the bitter cold, snowstorms, icebergs, the difficulties of getting accurate observations of the sun and so ascertaining their correct position, the technical complexity and dangerous manoeuvre of wearing ship in such weather, keeping clear of icebergs during the daylight hours, wearing ship at night to N.E. under small sail, again hopefully

---

[125] Francis Chichester, *Along the Clipper Way* (1966), has some good extracts from the writings of men who sailed the Cape Horn route, including of course Dana and Conrad.

Captain Robert Thomas (standing) and his lifelong friend, Captain Andreas Evans, both of Llandwrog, photographed at the studio of T. H. Wilton, San Francisco. This was probably taken sometime between October and December 1901 on Captain Thomas's penultimate voyage in the *Afon Alaw;* Captain Andreas Evans, who was seven years younger than Captain Thomas, was master of the *Cambrian Hills* at the time of this photograph, but later commanded the *Afon Alaw* before she was sold by William Thomas to Norwegian owners.

The photograph (again by T. H. Wilton, Elite Studio) of Captain Thomas's grave at Cypress Lawns, San Francisco, sent by Miss C. B. Thomas to her mother, 3 May, 1903.

Miss C. B. Thomas aboard the *Afon Alaw* after her father's
death. In the photograph are: Watkins, a Bristol man,
Richard Lloyd Hughes (who later married Miss Thomas's
sister), Miss Thomas, Mrs. Mason and Hugh Williams, the
bosun, from Holyhead. Standing behind Miss Thomas is the
mate, Mr. Hewitt. The boy seated on the deck is Mrs.
Mason's son.

The same group: Watkins holding chain, R. Lloyd Hughes, Miss
Thomas, Mr. Hewitt, the Mate, Mrs. Mason (with one of her
sons behind her, holding chain), Hugh Williams, Holyhead, the
Bosun, about to look at his watch, having had more than enough
of such frivolity!

Miss C. B. Thomas aboard the *Afon Alaw*.

Group aboard *Afon Alaw*.

to be able to take immediate action to avoid icebergs – all these were problems faced by the Cape Horn sailing ships, and it is little wonder that so many of them were lost without trace between 1895 and 1905.[126] In this last letter which he struggled to write, painstakingly and obviously feeling far from well, Robert Thomas has stated the case of the 'Cape Horn breed', those thousands of men who braved such conditions for a mere pittance, whilst at home owners such as the Davies family lived in luxury, the wealthy patrons of Welsh and English chapels, schools and the new University College at Bangor. The stately homes at Treborth, Bodlondeb and others belonging to the family on the banks of the Menai Straits, the English Methodist Chapel at Menai Bridge and Robert Davies's astonishing philanthropy to the missionary movements have to be seen in the light of a letter like this from one of their most faithful servants, a master mariner who had not only to contend with the ferocity of the natural elements but had also had to leave on such a voyage 'without a cook or a steward'. It was this 'miserable monotonous' diet and the 'cooking . . . wholly uncharacterized by skill' which David Lloyd George described in discussing conditions aboard Sailing Ships in introducing the Bill to amend the Merchant Shipping Acts in 1906.[127] This was possibly Captain Robert Thomas's last letter :

San Francisco
December 1902

Messrs. Hughes & Co.
Gentlemen,
I have [arrived] here all safe after a terrible long passage. We had a good passage from Swansea to the River Plate, passing Rio in 38 days and about 50 days to the Plate where we met with fearful gale which threw the ship on her beam end by the shifting of the cargo altho we had the same shifting boards as we had with wheat except for the hatchways [?] the [coal] as usual from Swansea was not half trimmed. A lot of holes in the lower hold. Indeed I don't think that there is today not 200 tons on

[126] Alan Villiers, *The War with Cape Horn*, xii-xiv.
[127] *Parl. Debates*, Fourth Series, 154, March, 1906, 238-94.

again. and got through the

four days after in a heavy gale and a
fearfull blizzard two men on the look
out and all the watch with me on the
Poop. the men on the lookout reported
an Iceberg right a head. which owing to
thick blizzard must have been very close
we put the helm hard up and providentially
she went off on her heal. if she had ever
touched it with such a sea on she must
have gone down at once.
The Braces were frozen as thick as my arm
and it was impossible to work the yards

   I have come round C. Horn to the westward
28 times and its no exaggeration to state
that I never had such weather as this
We never had any snow blizzard last voyage
nor did we a single Iceberg. Whereas
this time we had hard blizzard some part of
every day. While the Ropes were hardly ever
clear of Ice.

   Gentlemen you know I came away without
neither cook or steward. Its seldom that I find
a crew without two or three men able to cook
a little. The one that took the berth is a norwegian
a thorough scoundrel will steal and wast all
he possibly can — now Robert. from Holyhead
is steward. he is a very faithfull young man

Extract from Capt. Thomas's letter describing his last voyage round
Cape Horn, 1902.

the tween decks and the ship in consequence has been rolling & making terrible weather of it. We could not trim it for 2 days nor did we dare to wear her round. The upper tarpaulin torn to ribbons by the was[h] of the sea. On the 2nd day we got her trimmed enough to wear round and new tarpaulins put on. The wearing of the ship got some of the coal to trim itself. From here to 50°S in the Atlantic we had very bad weather almost constant gales from the Southward. This gale off the River Plate commenced with a fearful thunder storm and lightning struck the fore Royal truck and carried away two long splinters but did not other damage. The eyes of the back stay kept it from splitting more. We put a lashing on it and when we got to finer weather put an iron band on it with screw nuts quite tight. We passed Staten Island with fair wind and clear and we had a splendid breeze to within 30 mile of C. Horn when the wind came from the Westward and so we stood to the S.W. The 2nd day we got amongst the Ice, small Ber[g]s about 30 to 50 feet high, but there were dozens of them. I expected to get clear of them before dark. But from the masthead there was Ice everywhere as far as the eyes could reach. So we wore round to the N.E. before dark and stood that way under easy sail till daylight. We passed several in the night, and at daylight wore round again and got through them. Four days after in a heavy gale and a fearful blizzard, two men on the look out and all the watch with me on the poop, the men on the lookout reported an Iceberg right ahead which owing to thick blizzard must have been very close. We put the helm hard up and providentially she went off on her head. If she had ever touched it with such a sea on she must have gone down at once. The Braces were frozen as thick as my arm and it was impossible to work the Yards. I have come round C. Horn to the westwards 28 times and it's no exaggeration to state that I never had such weather as this. We never had any snow blizzard last voyage nor did we [see] a single Iceberg, whereas this time we had a hard blizzard some part of every day, while the ropes were hardly ever clear of Ice.

Gentlemen you know I came away without either cook or steward. It's seldom that I find a crew without two or three men able to cook a little. The one that took the berth was a Norwegian, a thorough scoundrel who steals and wastes all he possibly can. Owen Roberts from Holyhead is steward. He is a faithful young man. He was with me as A.B. three years ago. There has been no end of growling about the food. I would never come away again without a Cook & Steward.

This I intended for the owners so I send it to you instead and sending them a better one.

Lloyd's Weekly Shipping Index for the closing months of 1902 and the beginning of 1903 contained many reports of vessels experiencing very severe conditions both in the vicinity of Cape Horn and the South Atlantic and nearer home. The *Cardiganshire,* commanded by a former member of Robert Thomas's crew, Captain D. R. Stephens, which had left San Francisco on 26 July, 1902, homeward bound reported freak conditions in the Pacific and 'from 40°S. in Pacific to about 20°S. in the Atlantic the weather was more than usually severe, hard squalls from S.W. with hail and snow. Off the Plate again had one hail squall in which the hail stones measured two inches in circumference and lasted ten minutes.' The *Blythswood,* commanded by Captain Owen Barlow Pritchard, one of the two Caernarfon brothers well known as masters of large sailing ships, had left Liverpool in May 1902 and arrived in San Francisco on 18 October reporting that on 4 August, in 56°47'S, 64°31'W, 'had a very heavy gale from SSW with high confused sea, seas going completely over vessel, stove in the forward boat on the Starboard side and carried away the skids.' Others reporting hurricane force winds and abnormal conditions included the *Earl Dunraven,* off Acapulco, the *Balclutha* (now part of the San Francisco Maritime Museum) which arrived in San Francisco a couple of weeks before the *Afon Alaw* and the *Anglesey,* the *Indrapura,* 'experienced fearful weather' and the *Tacoma* 'had a terrible voyage'. As the weeks passed, Captain Robert Thomas's health deteriorated, so much so that his eldest daughter, Miss Catherine Bruce Thomas, the 'Brussy' of the 'Diary', now aged 24, went from Liverpool to be at her father's bedside. It is not possible to reproduce all the letters she wrote home to her family, but those that follow give some indication of Captain Thomas's last days and his death on 28 April, 1903.

184

When Miss Thomas arrived in San Francisco she received much help and sympathy from her father's friends, not only among the crews of the *Afon Alaw* and the *Merioneth,* but also other ships' masters and crews who obviously held Robert Thomas in high esteem. It is possible to identify some of those mentioned in Miss Thomas's letters through reference to *Lloyd's Registers,* the *Weekly Shipping Index,* Crew Agreement Lists and the Board of Trade papers relating to Masters. Captain John T. Rowlands, who appears to have taken charge of affairs and helped Miss Thomas with all the arrangements for her father's funeral, had succeeded Robert Thomas as master of the *Merioneth* in 1891. The *Merioneth* had arrived in San Francisco in August 1902 from Nagasaki, and according to *L.W.S.I.* had been in port since November, a little earlier in fact than the *Afon Alaw* and the *Anglesey.* John Timothy Rowlands, her master, born February 1849 at Walton East, Pembroke, was a very experienced seaman, having served for years in coasters, American ships and, of course, the vessels of Davies, Menai Bridge. He had been mate of the barque *Lady Louisa* of Cardiff when she was wrecked off the French coast in November 1875 and had passed master in January 1882. In 1885 he was mate to Captain J. Davies, in the *Lord Cairns,* one of the Davieses' large iron full-rigged ships, and had obviously pleased the Company as master in other Davies ships before he was appointed to succeed Captain Thomas in the *Merioneth.*

The other friends mentioned in the letters were probably masters who had known Captain Thomas for many years. Captain A. Longmuir, master of the *Achnashie,* the large steel 4-masted barque which had arrived at San Francisco from Newcastle, N.S.W., on 27 December, 1902, had probably met Thomas when both their vessels were being built in the Clyde – the *Achnashie* was owned by Thom and Cameron Ltd., 93, Cheapside Street, Glasgow, and had been completed at the yards of R. Duncan and Company, Port Glasgow, in 1892, not long after the *Afon Alaw* left the yards of Alex. Stephen. The *Lady Wentworth,* another steel 4-masted barque built by Scott and Company at Greenock in 1896, had arrived at San Francisco a day before the *Afon Alaw,* having left the Tyne

185

on 9 July; her master was Captain A. Murchie and it was he and Captain Thompson, master of the *Anglesey,* who headed the funeral procession with a certain Captain Macmillan whose ship is not named. Other vessels mentioned in some of Miss Thomas's letters as being anchored near the *Afon Alaw* were the *Mayfield* and the *Port Crawford,* both built by Russell and Company on the Clyde. The masters of these vessels were Welshmen, Captain T. Roberts in command of the *Mayfield* and Captain O. Williams, master of the *Port Crawford.* This was the time when a large number of sailing ships found themselves at San Francisco for months on end waiting for freights, which were getting fewer and fewer.[128] Of the others mentioned in Miss Thomas's letters, Thomas Rowlands, the blacksmith, was probably a prominent member of the Welsh community in San Francisco; Hewitt, mate of the *Afon Alaw,* had sailed with Captain Thomas for some time, and 'Dick' was Richard Lloyd Hughes of the *Afon Alaw* who later became a master mariner himself and married the youngest of Robert Thomas's daughters, Roberta Isabel Thomas. Captain Richard Lloyd Hughes, M.B.E., was an apprentice aboard the *Afon Alaw* and came from a Gwynedd seafaring family, for his father, Captain Richard Hughes, was at one time master of the Caernarfon emigrant ship, *Hindoo,* owned by the Owen family of Rhuddgaer, Anglesey. In later years, when he was master of James Chambers & Company's ships, the Liverpool 'Lancashire Shipping Line', Captain Richard Lloyd Hughes had an oil-painting of the *Afon Alaw* in his quarters and this is still in the family's possession.[129]

Catherine Bruce Thomas inherited her father's love of writing. She had travelled across America to be with him; in the follow-

---

[128] In *Sea Breezes,* 23, 227, an 'old salt' wrote 'We were laid up at Martinez 1903 in company with the *Loudon Hill, Lady Wentworth, Anglesey, Mayfield, General Gordon, Afon Alaw, Red Rock, Black Braes* and many other old timers whose names I can't remember. I wonder if any of the names I have mentioned recall to any of your readers those times when 'Frisco and Martinez were full of fine ships, laid up and waiting for a charter while the French ships ran at a loss, but were subsidised by their Government?'

[129] Information from Mr. R. Froom, Liverpool.

ing letters selected out of the many she wrote home she not only indicated her private grief and sought to console her family at home, but she also presents an evocative portrait of life aboard and around the large sailing ships in San Francisco Bay at the turn of the century. Let her describe in her own words that sad and moving final chapter in San Francisco.

Br. Ship *Achnashie*
Martinez Bay,
California

May 14 1903*

My Own dear Mama,

We received yours & Cecilia's dear letters yesterday, when Hewitt, Dick & I were on shore & read them together. I had been waiting anxiously for them as I was wondering all the time how you had taken the news & was so afraid of your *taking seriously ill.* We are glad that *Cecilia & Robert* were *with you* as I knew you would be alright with them. Mrs. Longman & the Captain were reading your letters last night & were so sorry you received the cable at night as it would make you feel *much worse we know and especially with the storm and rain.* Surely we will never forget it, and I can just see you all in the front attic before my eyes.

The letters from me will be just about reaching you now I know & you will be thankful that dear Papa *did not suffer & was unconscious* most of the time from the Wednesday until the following Tuesday morning & you would be so glad that I held him those long four days & nights, & that his hand never left mine, as I held it firmly for hours & hours & as long as I held it he was quite content & went into that sleepy stupor like a child. Auntie Ann & Auntie Ellen would I know be glad that he understood my repeating Mae Iesu Grist and that his mind was clear & intelligent for a few minutes at 2.30 a.m. on the last night & he looked into my face so intensely when I kissed him & *told him not to be afraid with Brucey bach,* & with all the words I could summon

---

* In order to preserve a logical sequence the letter written on 14 May has been printed before that written on 6 May.

in those precious three or 4 minutes I gave him all the strength of my mind & soul, which all in the room were certain he understood. After putting his fingers into mine once more while once more I spoke right close to his ear repeating that last line 'I'r ochor draw pen-gronin bach' he slowly seemed to drop back into the heavy stupor, though he must have known he was going as his eyes wandered for a few seconds round us all and he must have seen us all crying round the bed, but after those few minutes he never regained consciousness until he passed away at 11 o'clock next morning –

The first week at the hospital he was improving and quite sensible, taking his food, that is his liquid food, well & used to glance over the paper every morning. It was only on the Wednesday afternoon of 2nd week that the cloud or stroke seemed to come upon his brain. He got quite cured of the vomiting the first week at the hospital and had it not been for the stroke on his brain like poor Aunt Lizzie, he had every chance of getting better inside, with both stomach and liver. His right side entirely was paralysed two days before death and it was the left poor hand I always used to hold. Before I used to wash his hands & scrub his nails and pare them often on the ship. On the Sunday before he died, the special nurse Miss Heyes sponged him all over from the waist down with warm water, making him as comfortable as possible. In fact there was not an hour at the hospital that he had not something to refresh him* & I used to be in & out of the hospital kitchen every minute in search of new drinks & foods, and the nurses were continually shifting him and giving him stuff & twice a day as I told you he had a bath or rather sponge & rub over with alcohol or brandy. I am glad I always gave him sips of good brandy in milk but the whole cause was the Paralysis on the brain which had been coming on him for months. I hope by now that you have received the pictures of the cemetery. How thankful you would be to see what a beautiful place he was put to rest in, and sailors from here & there will I know go to see him often & perhaps some of us will come out here yet. – I am longing very much to see you & I know you are for me. I left San F. on Monday after-

---

* [inserted above the line]:   *Afon Alaw cabin*
I am reigning mistress here of all the ship & how I wish you were here & more still how I miss *him.*

188

noon and of course Capt. Rowlands came to fetch me down, also Mrs. Mason came to see me off, while at the Ferry was dear Dick to take me to Martinez. After bidding the others goodbye we went on the Ferry boat & sailed across the Bay (one of the most beautiful in the world). All during the train Journey places & people brought before me all the scenes of our last Journey up to town together & both Dick & I dreaded seeing the *Afon Alaw*. We at last came in sight of Martinez laying beautiful in the setting sun, with the mountains & bay further than ever & the 12 great ships laying peacefully at anchor in the smooth shining water. It almost broke my heart to see the 'Afon Aloo' as he used to call it & think he would never walk on the poop again or look up with pride to her tall white masts. At the station was a crowd assembled to meet me, Capt. Longmuir, his 2nd mate, Mr. Hewitt, Prossers, Wilcox & Watkins, Capt. Murchie & a lot of apprentices & all the dogs from Prossers, marshalled by General Thompson. We all went down the wharf among the marsh fields & over the wooden bridges. It brought everything fresh to my mind again and the Italians just bringing in the fish all looked pleased and sorry to see me & some spoke very kindly. The boat of the *Achnashie* with my old friends the apprentices were ready & after bidding a hearty good-night to my own boat crew & the other boats of the different ships, and I may say I noticed Wilcox had taken the trouble to put on some black clothes & and even a black & white shirt & a new cheap black cap to come to meet me. It was strange going off in another boat but Capt. & Mrs. Longmuir are the kindest people you could imagine, and arriving on the *Achnashie* which is a bigger ship than the *Afon Alaw* & a first class ship where everything is in grand style we were met by Mrs. L. & the mate while all the officers expressed their sympathy with us & I was introduced all round. I had never been on such a ship. The Cabins are twice the size of the Vildandens & magnificent, filled with beautiful flower palms, while canaries & pet animals are all over the place while luxury of all sorts appears in every way. We had a beautiful tea & found my room like a yacht's cabin upholstered in old gold & painted white & gold while the bed is a little nest & my washhand stand is most convenient. I had all my best linen clean & plenty of good clothes so I am alright. I have lived on board the *Achnashie* now for 4 days but must keep all further

189

descriptions till I see you. I have been most happy. Nobody I ever knew has had such a good time and ridiculous kindness like I have had here. I firmly believe God is giving me all this just to make me happy before I go back to my old life. The weather here is tropical; I wear my white blouses with black skirt & bow and my sailor hat. It is too hot for anything else. Every day Mr. Hewitt comes with Dick to fetch me in the boat which has now been converted into a sailing yacht, as all the boats here sail & the Captains race every afternoon. Hewitt is a splendid yachtsman and you may imagine how pleasant our mornings are spent. We go on shore & return laden with roses & other flowers, and mornings & evenings there are all the ships' boats at the Jetty, so imagine the meetings and the life there is here. We are now the three of us just going up the roads to the country for an evening walk in the cool. Never were three greater friends, and as the boat is waiting I must now close. I have a long letter to send you later about my arrival in the dear old cabin here & my arrangements for coming home. With best & fondest love & let me know, if there is time, how dear mouse is. I dreamt of her last night, so good bye my dear faithful mama now.

592 San José Avenue,
San Francisco
May 6, 1903

My Own dear Mama & Auntie Ann,

In my last letter I told you that dear Papa's remains were brought over by these kind friends headed by Capt. Colville to my apartments, just through the hospital garden & over the sandy road here. The room where he lay was beautfiully prepared, the walls & ceiling were all pale yellow, and the sitting room furniture was all taken out, merely the picture of Mrs. Mason's little dead girl hung on one side of the room. There was a rich Turkish carpet covering the floor and the window & curtains handsome so that with the room and the handsome coffin and beautiful flowers, while the sun streaming in all day long, made it a room that one could always have in one's memory as being beautiful & clean & sunny. The Undertakers do everything so well in America, and they made up a large bier in the centre of the room on which the oak coffin lay covered with flowers & all round the room were these great anchors of flowers & the fire place & mantelpiece were hidden by flowers, while in the fireside corner of the room was a small oak table with a lovely large shaded lamp of pink china, which at night made the whole room look so beautiful that everyone remarked on it and in the mornings in the sunlight and with the pale grey blinds that were all over the house drawn down you can just think how it looked. Everything was peaceful & still & the boys here, Charlie & Wallace, were so good & never made a noise once, the only sound to be heard being the canary birds singing all day & the pigeons at the back of the house. I wish you could have seen the place. It was an *English* funeral, altogether no one *ever* has a departed person *in a house* in America. It is *all done* at the Undertakers & I know Papa had a horror of such a thing & I would not have had him lay in an American parlour for *any money*. I intend to pay Mrs. Mason well for her goodness, and you might send her a pair of *good gloves* from Hendersons, 6¾ for one thing. This house has been a perfect Godsend to us, as by having the funeral from here *everything looked so well especially as it was such a magnificent funeral all round*. In the afternoon Capt. & Mrs. Colville, Mr. Thomas Rowlands (Blacksmith),Capt. Rowlands & myself went 11 miles from here to Cypress Lawn Cemetery and there chose a single grave. Cost with perpetual care was £6. ($30) and it lays just beside a grove of tall shady gum trees in the midst of other beautfiul graves in the soft green grass and close to the hedge which divides Cypress Lawn from the Jewish cemetery. Close by Mr. Thomas Rowlands's wife was buried three weeks ago, so that every Sunday when he comes out there he will go & visit our grave & promises to do so always. This man is much respected here as is his partner the young Orkneyman & Papa relied on them always. To describe the beauty of the cemetery, the marble amongst the green grass & the dark trees, together with the masses of glorious flowers & tropical plants, is beyond me but you can imagine it for yourselves and I know it will comfort you to know where he is laid. On the road there we passed through a beautiful fertile country, farmhouses & ranches were to be seen here and there among the hills and great green fields of peaceful beauty, while here and there were yellow cornfields filled with brilliant blue cornflowers and the glaring California poppies. All along the route were gardens & grazing grounds while flowers of all hues were to be seen on every hand. On the right hand side the hills slope down to the seashore so that here & there one can see the green fields stretching almost to the water's edge & beyond that the great blue Pacific ocean lays, on summer days peaceful and sparkling in the sunlight while on stormy days the roar of the breakers on the beach can be heard for miles. I am so glad he is close to the sea, and surely you will be pleased that he is far away from the city and in a place where he would love to see. So countrified is the district that on our way we passed little children with sabots on and several cowboys driving cattle along the road – mounted on sprightly little horses & using great long lassoo whips. After doing all business at the undertakers, where I chose a handsome *light oak* coffin lined with cream satin, Mrs. Colville broke down entirely at this point (With all her faults she has plenty of feeling). They never have but ugly black caskets in this country and dress their dead up like figures for a ball (ask Uncle Jameson). I *would not* have any suit or gaudy attire near him, but after Mrs. Prosser & I ransacking all the big shops for *English* garments, I was obliged to fall back on a fine *cream serge shroud* with quilted satin *sleeve cuffs & front* & the collar & tie arrangement made as English as possible. Mrs. Prosser being Swedish holds the same ideas as we do. So does Mrs. Mason and everyone agreed all round that the garment was handsome & *suitable* for dear *Papa's age* and *position*.

This sorrowful business being over, the Colvilles (who are the most curious couple I ever met & who I will describe later) took Capt. Rowlands & myself to the first French Restaurant in town. We did not feel like it, as you can think, but Capt. Rowlands looked so ill & I had not had food for days, as you know, that we went. The courses seemed ghastly in a way but after the fatigue the splendid food & wine did us all good. Capt. Colville then went home to look after the live-stock and Mrs. C we took to Mrs. Jordan's house while we went home. Here at the teatable I found dear little Mrs. Prosser, who had been sent up by Frank & the old man to stay the night with me as they were afraid I should not like sleeping alone, so she had come all the way from Martinez. (Don't miss writing to Prossers *whatever you do*). She helped Mrs. Mason & I to entertain or rather interview the continual stream of visitors who came to see us. All next day Capt. Rowlands & Hewitt went round doing the business & Mrs. Prosser, Mrs. Jordan, Mrs. Colville & I started out to buy mourning. They dress here quite different to us. You would think a labourer's wife a society lady here and the style beats everything you ever saw, tho' the women really themselves are nothing extra. We soon got a becoming little hat for me, the crown of fancy chip straw with a trim of pleated tulle. Mrs. Jordan did everything & got it trimmed with sprays of small maidenhair in black velvet, round & a large black velvet bow at the back, & I never had a prettier hat. Mrs. Colville then treated us to a dinner at another great gorgeous café. We had a private room & as expensive a meal as you could think of, all sorts to eat & drink. Mrs. *Colville is rolling in money, so is he, the whole crew of them live as if it was the last day,* but I like Mrs. Jordan. However they were my kind friends & I noticed all the *good* people kept aloof when the real action came in. All the times I have been with them I only drink wine and you can steer clear of all the other stuff if you are careful.

During the next few days we all had a great deal of business to do, the last night especially many people called until I was nearly dead. After all was over the last night Mrs. Mason and I went about midnight to take a last farewell of dear Papa. We wished so fervently you had all been there. The room shall always live in my memory, heavy with the perfume of so many flowers and the soft lamp light falling on the silver handles & ornaments on the coffin & altogether the beautiful peaceful room was more like a picture than anything else. It is the custom to embalm the departed here and this we had done (as it was *necessary* & did not cost much extra). If I could picture to you how *peaceful* he loked & the *steadfast expression* of his face you would be thankful, I know, but I must leave it to you. He looked better in death than in life and there was no trace of suffering or uncertainty near. How pleased you, Aunty Ann, Auntie Jane & all would have been had you seen him, & I am sure proud of the handsome appointments & the great funeral. Mrs. Mason prayed beside the coffin & we then took a last goodnight after so many nights together of waiting & watching.

Next morning Mr. Prosser attended to refreshment for the Captains & others coming a distance. Crowds of

193

sailors were arriving by about ten. Capt. Rowlands was here hours before of course. Mr. Rainey & Mr. Warren took all the men to view the coffin and all the Captains were taken by Capt. Rowlands. There was a long long line of seafaring men coming & going into the room. Every ship in the place was well represented. Billy Williams & our own men & boys were very much affected and we all cried together while Capt. Jones of the *Bukeley* here who had only heard the news that morning after being a friend of his here for 25 years stood behind my bedroom door & cried like a child. It was a beautiful morning; the sun was streaming in and every thing look so beautiful. The rooms all over the house were filled with ladies & friends, while *every Captain in the place* formed one of the *finest sets of men* I have ever seen, & what a comfort it was to see all the rugged brown faces of the men, most all in shabby blue suits but each with a black tie & steady & respectful. Poor faithful Paton stood near holding a large new *Union Jack flag* belonging to the *Anglesea*. The Undertaker had a list of everything & mustered the men. After a short tho' beautifully read service by the Seaman's pastor Mr. Rainey (who I told you during our days of watching with Papa at the hospital prayed so kindly with us twice) the flag was placed over the coffin & the flowers which were many & very large & bulky were given to the men of the *Merioneth* from the half deck & our own, together with several apprentices from *Achnesie* & *Lady Wentworth* &c. These young fellows took charge of them altogether. You would have cried to see them in their sailor clothes holding the beautiful things.

In a moment the coffin was borne by the special pall bearers, who each had gloves & heavy bands of crape, headed by Hewitt & Paton & were as follows.

(1) Hewitt	(2) Paton
(3) Mate of *Merioneth*	(4) Mate of *Anglesea*
(5) 2nd mate *Afon Alaw*	(6) Steward *A. Alaw*

These men carefully carried the flag covered coffin with the *Afon Alaw* wreath laying on it down the steps & into the waiting hearse. A great crowd was round & every head uncovered. I had invited the Captain here to the funeral & he was so pleased, poor old gentleman. Next came Capt. Rowlands, myself and Capt. Thompson and

behind us the Colvilles & Prossers, Mrs. Mason & Mrs.
Capt. Longman *being chief Mourners.* There was only
one carriage as we only had a few yards to go. Into this
*Mrs. Capt. Longman, Mrs. Prosser, Mrs. Colville & Mrs.
Mason* with Capt. Rowlands & myself took our seats &
then the procession started. Behind the hearse walked the
Pastor & pall bearers & the sailor boys with the flowers,
next came the Carriage with us & behind us came all the
women & shore friends, a great long line stretching down
the street & after these came all the Captains, headed by
Capt. Murchie, Capt. Thompson & Capt. MacMillan.
All were walking three abreast and when I tell you there
were 178 people present you will imagine what a beautiful
funeral we had & what respect & kindness was shown.
Arriving at the station the Electric Cars were waiting and
the coffin was placed in the first, while the men placed
the flowers round. No one was allowed in the compartment
but the pastor & his assistant Mr. Warren, who watched
with him then for the last time. Capt. Rowlands, myself
& the chief mourners among the ladies were given the
best seats in the next car & the rest of the car was entirely
taken up by ladies & even Mrs. Warren & the dear baby
boy (I told you I used to have on board to tea) were
there. After that came a car filled every inch by the
Captains, sailors & other men friends. The road was
smooth & the route as pretty & country like as before
described to you. Everyone was most affected & never had
seen such an impressive funeral before. Arriving at the
Cemetery the coffin was borne by the cemetery bearers
& just as they halted first up the beautiful avenue (which
you will see in the picture sent you) one of the bearers
turning round and seeing all the long straggling line of
sailors behind asked most excitedly 'My God, who am I
carrying?' and on being informed that it was Capt.
Thomas of the *Afon Alaw* seemed quite upset, & afterwards it turned out that he was a Norwegian sailor who
after making two voyages in the ship had run away last
time and taken to working on shore. The procession which
went up those beautiful walks of the cemetery was such
as you would have wished to follow him to the grave,
and everything was well ordered and attended to while
round the grave I shall never forget the scene, such a
great crowd of Captains and sailors & so many friends.
They do things so well in this country & you will be
surprised to hear that the grave was *entirely* lined with

195

cypress branches & white Marguerites & Ivy, *like Miss Catherine's*. The flag was taken off & I don't think there was a dry eye in the place as the coffin was lowered into the wooden box inside the grave. All the chief mourners had chairs; I don't think we could have held up without them. The burial service for the dead was read by the Pastor in his white robe, & the grave surrounded by kind rough faces as you can think. We all waited & the boys placed the wreaths & anchors as you see them in the picture. Then we all turned back in a great long line. I shook hands with all the Captains & thanked them all, also everyone thanked Capt. Rowlands & Tom Rowlands (Blacksmith) for their splendid efforts throughout. We came home & the chief Mourners had tea here along with our own officers & the household here. You can think throughout of the efforts put forth by Mrs. Mason & I trust you will write letters to the people I enclose a list of without delay. I can only now send you all my best love & trust you are feeling better able to go on.

Your loving daughter

Brucey.

ACCOUNT OF DISPOSAL OF EFFECTS BY MATE:

Martinez   May 15 1903

The Chronometer is at Opticians in the city & Capt. Rowlands will endeavour to sell it at a good price.

The Sextant has been sold to Hugh Williams 2nd mate *Afon Alaw* £3.10.

Top-Coats Mr. Hewitt is endeavouring to dispose of the three (including the black Freege Irish Coat) to some well off Fishermen, who can pay ready money and has offered them to several officers in the Bay.

Best Suit & Grey Pants I shall have to bring home or leave in mate's care for passage home.

Compass Am bringing home to keep.

Large Field glass am also bringing home to keep for ever.

Large new Chest am bringing home for Cecilia.

All underclothing Has been very well disposed of to steward, Dick, Jack, Chibby & Wilcox.

Tinned meats (Private) am bringing all home in Cecilia's chest.

Books – Mate has found a letter giving promise to credit
amount of £3.15.0 paid at building of ship with allowance for wear & tear. Have found & checked all Books.
Charts Have checked all & found all belong to owners.
Sea boots have put into slop chest, *much worn.*
Private Books Have given Dick several nautical books and
Hewitt some, with ones I don't want, & bringing home
all his favourite old ones in chest.
Gloves & mits Have given them to Paton & 2nd mate,
also disposed of collars & oddments to members of crew
in *return for them all buying.* Am bringing home
handkerchiefs (Napkins &c &c McIntosh & caps to
Paton, also braces etc. & one pair braces to Hewitt with
other oddments.)
White Jackets Have given one each to mate, 2nd mate,
Steward & Cook & sold the rest for good price.
Opera glasses Am bringing home.
Boots sold yellow ones to mate & black ones to Wilcox.
Bringing home shoes last worn and cloggs.

When they paid their last respects to Captain Robert Thomas
some among that 'great long line' of seamen gathered in Cypress
Lawn Cemetery may have forseen that the end of the Windmill
Line was also very close at hand. The *Afon Alaw* was sold at
San Francisco seven months later on 1 November, 1903,[130] but
the *Montgomeryshire* had already been sold on 3 April, 1903,
the *Flintshire,* on her return from San Francisco to Fleetwood,

---

[130] The appointment of Captain John Davies of Newport, former master
of the *Lord Cairns,* to replace Robert Thomas was not greeted by Hewitt
and the crew of the *Afon Alaw* with enthusiasm, according to Miss
Thomas's letters. The *Afon Alaw* was bought by William Thomas, the
Liverpool ship-broker, under the name of the *Cambrian Warrior Ship
Co. Ltd.* — this was common practice when a ship replaced a vessel
which had been lost. Captain J. Davies remained in command of the
Afon Alaw for some years, and was followed by Captain Evan Jones,
who made many smart passages in her, according to Lubbock. On
William Thomas's death in 1915 most of his vessels were sold; the *Afon
Alaw* was sold to Norway for £8,000 and renamed *Storebror.* It was
appropriate that when she was delivered to her Norwegian owners, her
master for that voyage was one of Thomas's most experienced masters,
Captain Andreas Evans, Robert Thomas's old friend from Llandwrog.
In January, 1918, the *Afon Alaw* was sunk in the South Atlantic by the
German raider *Wolf* when on passage to Montevideo in ballast.

had been towed to Barrow and sold there on 18 May, 1903, the *Cardiganshire,* and *Lord Cairns,* both at Swansea, sold on 22 May and 25 June, 1903, respectively. Only the *Anglesey* and *Merioneth,* both at San Francisco forlornly awaiting freight, like so many fine sailing ships, remained. Eventually, on 12 May, 1904, after over an year's idleness, the *Anglesey* sailed for home, arriving in Liverpool 16 September where she finished discharging her cargo on 17 October, 1904. She was sold in May 1905 to Norwegian owners. The *Merioneth* also had a long spell at San Francisco; it was 24 June, 1904, when she eventually sailed, arriving Queenstown 16 October and proceeded to Dublin to discharge her cargo. She was then towed to Liverpool and sold to Italian owners in May, 1905, the last of the Windmill Line.[131] Richard Davies, the politician, had died in 1896, Charles Pierce in 1901 and in December, 1905, Robert Davies, Bodlondeb, died, a wealthy but lonely man.

The 'diary', letters, and career of Robert Thomas of Llandwrog span most of the age of Victoria and in many ways he was a true Victorian, a man of his times. He had come up the hard way. No life could have been harder, even in those days of appalling slums and wretched poverty, than that of a boy aboard Thomas Hobley's ships. He was a self-made man in the widest sense for he had educated himself and had provided his daughter with a much better education than he himself had had, but he was a man whose eagerness for education was probably unusual among his fellow-mariners. He was a generous man, tolerant, with a great love for children and humane consideration for his crews whose affection for, and loyalty to, him are particularly clear in Miss C. B. Thomas's letters from San Francisco. The evidence suggests that his were 'happy' ships, with few incidents reported, and his record passages merely underline his abilities in handling and navigating his ships in all kinds of weather. Moreover, in the letter which he

---

[131] According to the Davies Sailings Book the sales of the *Anglesey* and *Merioneth* were not completed until Oct. 1905, but it is clear from *L.W.S.I.* that both vessels were sailing under the Norwegian and Italian flags in the late spring and early summer of 1905.

wrote to his young daughter from the *Merioneth* on that weary passage home from San Francisco on Sunday, 4 November, 1888, he expressed what commanders of ships have felt throughout the ages.

'How miserable these long passages makes a man and we can do nothing only wait & depend on the wind. How wicked also it makes one's heart always grumbling and growling at the wind and I often find myself blaspheming. May God forgive me and not take me at my word for I often say & call for such winds that I would be sorry to see coming. How much harder it is for people in trouble to live a good & godly life to what it is to persons who are strangers to trouble & suspense. A Sailor's cup of grace must be very full when he is able to live a godly life but there are some people of such a nature that nothing can trouble them, and are always happy and contented. I often look with wonder at my own sailors, so happy & jolly together, playing & skylarking together like children while I am sad and almost weary of life, and what a contrast there is in our position in every respect.

I often wonder whether this is nature or wickedness. I can remember when no one could be more jolly than me but somehow higher I get in the world the less comfort I feel. I never knew what real anxiety of mind was till I got command of a ship and indeed there is much responsibility on a ship master, more I think than any other class of servants in the world. They have a vast amount of property under their care and a very slight deviation or mistake may cause the loss of his ship, lives & cargo, or on the other hand the loss of his certificate & situation. He may act faithfully & honest & do everything well in his own mind which may after all turn out a failure & loss &c. He has to act by himself so much. He is not like a shore servant, always able to ask his master's advice &c. But a ship-master has no one only himself and must act according to his good Judgement, whether right or wrong it will turn out. An owner of the ship also always expect good passages and do not always take into consideration that the man has to depend on wind and weather. A ship well fitted out does not always secure a good passage as now in my case.'

Robert Thomas, Llandwrog, was a true ship-master, a man apart.